PAUL ^{AND}_{THE} ROMAN
IMPERIAL ORDER

PAUL AND THE ROMAN IMPERIAL ORDER

EDITED BY RICHARD A. HORSLEY

TRINITY PRESS INTERNATIONAL
A Continuum imprint
HARRISBURG • LONDON • NEW YORK

Trinity Press International, P.O. Box 1321, Harrisburg, PA 17105
Trinity Press International is a member of the Continuum International Publishing Group.

Cover art: Lesueur, Eustache. The Sermon of Saint Paul at Ephesus, 1649. Erich Lessing/Art Resource, NY. Louvre, Paris, France.

Cover design: Wesley Hoke

Library of Congress Cataloging-in-Publication Data

Paul and the Roman imperial order / edited by Richard A. Horsley.
     p. cm.
  Includes bibliographical references and index.
  ISBN 1-56338-421-3 (pbk.)
   1. Paul, the Apostle, Saint—Political and social views. 2. Bible.
N.T. Epistles of Paul—Criticism, interpretation, etc. 3. Christianity and politics—
History of doctrines—Early church, ca. 30-600. I. Horsley, Richard A.

BS2655.P64 P38 2004
227'.067—dc22

                       2003016692

Printed in the United States of America

03 04 05 06 07 08   10 9 8 7 6 5 4 3 2 1

CONTENTS

———◄○►———

Abbreviations

————◄○►————

AB	Anchor Bible
ABD	*Anchor Bible Dictionary.* Edited by D. N. Freedman. 6 vols. New York, 1992
AGJU	Arbeiten zur Geschichte des antiken Judentums und des Urchristentums
AJP	*American Journal of Philology*
AnBib	Analecta biblica
ANRW	*Aufstieg und Niedergang der römischen Welt.* Edited by H. Temporini and W. Haase. Berlin/New York, 1972–
ANTC	Abingdon New Testament Commentaries
BAGD	Bauer, W., W. F. Arndt, F. W. Gingrich, and F. W. Danker. *Greek-English Lexicon of the New Testament and Other Early Christian Literature.* 2d ed. Chicago, 1979
BASOR	*Bulletin of the American Schools of Oriental Research*
BBR	*Bulletin for Biblical Research*
Bijdr	*Bijdragen: Tijdschrift voor filosofie en theologie*
BR	*Biblical Research*
CAH	Cambridge Ancient History
CBQ	*Catholic Biblical Quarterly*
ConBNT	Coniectanea biblica: New Testament Series
EDNT	*Exegetical Dictionary of the New Testament.* Edited by H. Balz, G. Schneider. 3 vols. ET. Grand Rapids, 1990–1993.
EKKNT	Evangelisch-katholischer Kommentar zum Neuen Testament

ExpT	*Expository Times*
FRLANT	Forschungen zur Religion und Literatur des Alten und Neuen Testaments
GLQ	*GLQ: A Journal of Lesbian and Gay Studies*
HBT	Horizons in Biblical Theology
HNT	Handbuch zum Neuen Testament
HNTC	Harper's New Testament Commentaries
HTKNT	Herders theologischer Kommentar zum Neuen Testament
HTR	*Harvard Theological Review*
ICC	International Critical Commentary
Int	*Interpretation*
JB	The Jerusalem Bible
JBL	*Journal of Biblical Literature*
JJS	*Journal of Jewish Studies*
JRS	*Journal of Roman Studies*
JSNT	*Journal for the Study of the New Testament*
JSNTSup	Journal for the Study of the New Testament: Supplement Series
JSOT Press	Journal for the Study of the Old Testament Press
JSOTSup	Journal for the Study of the Old Testament: Supplement Series
JTS	*Journal of Theological Studies*
KEK	Kritisch-exegetischer Kommentar über das Neue Testament (Meyer-Kommentar)
LCL	Loeb Classical Library
LXX	Septuagint
NASB	New American Standard Bible
NewDocs	*New Documents Illustrating Early Christianity.* Edited by G. H. R. Horsley and S. Llewelyn. North Ryde, N.S.W., 1981–
NICNT	New International Commentary on the New Testament
NovT	*Novem Testamentum*

NovTSup	Novum Testamentum Supplements
NRSV	New Revised Standard Version
NT	New Testament
NTS	*New Testament Studies*
OBT	Overtures to Biblical Theology
RAC	*Reallexikon für Antike und Christentum.* Edited by T. Kluser et al. Stuttgart, 1950–
RB	Revue biblique
RGG	*Religion in Geschichte und Gegenwart.* Edited by H. D. Betz et al. 4th ed. Tübingen, 1998–
RSPT	*Revue des sciences philosophiques et théologiques*
RSV	Revised Standard Version
SBL	Society of Biblical Literature
SBLDS	Society of Biblical Literature Dissertation Series
SBLSP	*Society of Biblical Literature Seminar Papers*
SMTSMS	Society for New Testament Studies Monograph Series
TDNT	*Theological Dictionary of the New Testament.* Edited by G. Kittel and G. Friedrich. Trans. G. W. Bromiley. 10 vols. Grand Rapids, 1964–76
ThWAT	*Theologisches Wörterbuch zum Alten Testament.* Edited by G. J. Botterweck and H. Ringgren. Stuttgart, 1970–
TPINTC	TPI [Trinity Press International] New Testament Commentaries
UBS	United Bible Societies
WBC	Word Biblical Commentary
WMANT	Wissenschaftliche Monographien zum Alten und Neuen Testament
WUNT	Wissenschaftliche Untersuchungen zum Neuen Testament
YCS	*Yale Classical Studies*
ZNW	*Zeitschrift für die neutestamentliche Wissenschaft und die Kunde der älteren Kirche*
ZPE	*Zeitschrift für Papyrologie und Epigraphik*

INTRODUCTION

Richard A. Horsley

Protestant interpreters have traditionally understood Paul in opposition to Judaism. Luther's discovery of "justification by faith" in Paul's Letter to the Romans, the solution to his frustrating quest for a sense of righteousness, became the formative religious experience through which Paul's letters have been read. Paul became the paradigmatic *homo religiosus* whose quest for salvation by a compulsive keeping of the Law in his native Judaism drove him to his dramatic conversion to God's grace manifested in Christ. As the great apostle of Christ, Paul then created a new, universal, and spiritual religion, Christianity, which transcended the parochial and particularistic bounds of Judaism. Protestant theology has thus determined both the overall framework in which Paul has been understood, that of Christian theology, and the other against which Paul was always juxtaposed, Judaism.[1]

This approach to Paul that has dominated NT studies for generations is based on the unquestioned and distinctively modern Western assumptions that Paul is concerned with religion and that religion is not only separate from political-economic life, but also primarily a matter of individual faith. The temporal kingdom and spiritual kingdom have little to do with each other, except insofar as the former maintains a civil order in which the latter can be cultivated. And, of course, Paul himself supposedly insisted on

---

1. Wayne A. Meeks, "Judaism, Hellenism, and the Birth of Christianity," and Dale Martin, "Paul and the Judaism/Hellenism Dichotomy: Toward a Social History of the Question," both in Troels Engberg-Pedersen, *Paul beyond the Judaism/Hellenism Divide* (Louisville, Ky.: Westminster John Knox, 2001), provide an excellent recent overview of the issue since the dominant influence of Ferdinand Christian Baur.

unquestioning obedience to the civil magistrates, even imperial or monarchic rulers, as God's instruments of civil order.

When NT scholars struggled to rethink their theology and exegesis in the aftermath of the Holocaust, they made two dramatic shifts. In one, the great hero of faith who articulated foundational Christian theology was discovered to share the same fundamental "covenantal nomism" of Judaism, from which he originated. Paul's new religion of personal faith was no longer seen as sharply opposed to Judaism. "In short, this is what Paul finds wrong with Judaism: it is not Christianity."[2] The issue, however, remained strictly one of religion, and in effect, Paul was still understood as involved in, and indeed the creator of, a new religion different from his old one.

In the other and more significant shift, Krister Stendahl changed the focus from Paul's theology to the people with whom Paul was dealing in his mission, as indicated in the title of his influential book *Paul among Jews and Gentiles*.[3] This was a far more serious challenge to standard NT scholarship and its theological basis. Paul was not intending to found a new religion, argued Stendahl. Paul as *homo religiosus* obsessed with an introspective conscience is a Western Christian projection. His *apokalypsis* of Christ was not a conversion to a new religion but a commissioning for mission. Paul himself never left Judaism, or more accurately, Israel. He merely brought the gospel of Christ to the Gentiles. And their positive response to that good news created a crisis in which he struggled to understand the relations between the Jews and the Gentiles in God's overall plan of salvation (Rom 1–11).

Neither of these post-Holocaust shifts in Pauline scholarship sufficed to change the fundamental framework within which Paul is understood. The fundamental problem for Paul-interpreters was still Paul and Judaism. Stendahl's shift of focus from theology to people, however, and his insistence that Paul did not leave Israel, prepared the way for an eventual change in framework. It was still necessary to question the assumption of the separation of religion and political-economic life. Once that peculiar modern Western assumption was questioned, it was then possible to *contextualize historically* Paul's work among Jews and Gentiles. The context was the Roman Empire. Both the Jews among whom Paul originated and

---

2. E. P. Sanders, *Paul and Palestinian Judaism* (Philadelphia: Fortress, 1977), 552–53. Critical discussion of these shifts in understanding of Paul is in Neil Elliott, *Liberating Paul: The Justice of God and the Politics of the Apostle* (Maryknoll, N.Y.: Orbis Books, 1994), esp. ch. 3; and John G. Gager, *Reinventing Paul* (Oxford: Oxford University Press, 2000), ch. 2.

3. Krister Stendahl, *Paul among Jews and Gentiles* (Philadelphia: Fortress, 1977), reprints his highly influential essay "The Apostle Paul and the Introspective Conscience of the West."

the Gentiles among whom he carried out his mission were subjects of the Roman Empire. The Roman imperial order, in all its facets, constituted the context in which the movement that Paul joined and helped to lead took its origins in the province of Judea. And it was the context into which he took his gospel of Jesus Christ, who had been crucified by the Romans but had been vindicated by God in resurrection as Lord and Savior—imperial titles ordinarily used only for Caesar.

Focus on the Roman imperial order as the context of Paul's mission, however, is leading to another recognition. Instead of being opposed to Judaism, Paul's gospel of Christ was opposed to the Roman Empire. Paul, of course, was hardly a rabble-rousing revolutionary, fomenting provincial rebellion against Roman rule; Rom 13:1–7 is the virtual opposite of active revolution. He did not preach about how Rome oppressed subject peoples. So far as we know, he did not pronounce prophetic oracles of divine judgment against the emperor in Rome. Nor did he actively oppose or agitate against local representatives of Roman rule in the cities where he organized new communities. Indeed, he insisted that the Thessalonians "live quietly" and "mind [their] own affairs" (1 Thess 4:11). Nor did he even proclaim his gospel in public space, so far as we know, but in the less conspicuous space of households. Instead, Paul set his gospel of Christ and the new communities he catalyzed in opposition to the Roman imperial order: the whole system of hierarchical values, power relations, and ideology of "peace and security" generated by the "wealthy, powerful, and nobly born" and dominated by "the rulers of this age," at the apex of which stood the imperial savior. Imperial power relations operated in complex ways through cultural-religious forms integrally related to social-economic forms of domination, and not simply by the sword; likewise, Paul pursued his mission in complex cultural modes integrally related to the social formation that he and others were catalyzing.

That Paul's gospel opposed the Roman imperial order, not Judaism, becomes increasingly evident the more we reexamine principal facets and key terms of his gospel, as evident in virtually all his letters.[4] In 1 Thessalonians, from beginning to end, God's kingdom and the true Lord, Jesus Christ, are opposed to the Roman Empire and its ideology of "peace and security," which stand under the imminent destruction of God's judgment (1:10; 2:12, 19; 3:13; 4:14–18; 5:1–11, 23). In 1 Corinthians, from Paul's first long argument to his ecstatic "explanation" of the resurrection,

---

4. Neil Elliott, *Liberating Paul*; Dieter Georgi, *Theocracy in Paul's Praxis and Theology* (Minneapolis: Fortress, 1991); Richard A. Horsley, ed., *Paul and Empire: Religion and Power in Roman Imperial Society* (Harrisburg, Pa.: Trinity Press International, 1997).

Paul opposes his gospel to the Roman rulers and the imperial order. "The rulers of this age" have been outsmarted in God's *mysterion,* the apocalyptic plan for the fulfillment of history; having "crucified the Lord of glory," they are "doomed to perish" (2:6–8). God has chosen the foolish and weak of the world, the very opposite of the powerful, nobly born, wealthy, and wise elite, who dominate the imperial order (1:26–27; 4:8–10). Those chosen ones, the saints, will soon participate in God's judgment of the (Roman) world order, whose form is passing away (6:1–4; 7:31). Meanwhile, the resurrected Christ is enthroned in heaven, preparing to destroy "every ruler and every authority and power" (15:24). In Philippians, Christ Jesus appears to have displaced Caesar as emperor, having been "highly exalted" and given a name "above every name" (2:9). Indeed, Christ has become the true (counter-imperial) Savior who will imminently bring into effect God's "political order" or "commonwealth" for his assemblies (3:19–21, RSV).

In the Letters to the Romans and Galatians as well, where this message is less explicitly stated and more implied in the key arguments, Paul opposes Christ and the gospel to Caesar and the Roman imperial order, not to the Law and Judaism. At the outset of his long main argument in Rom 1–11, Paul states that Christ has displaced Caesar, has been "declared to be Son of God with power" (1:4). His main point, when he reaches the climax of the argument in Rom 9–11, is that according to God's mystery/plan, Israel is to be included in the fulfillment of history along with the other peoples (see esp. 11:25–36). In that argument "Christ is *the goal* [not the terminus] of the Law" (10:4, author). Throughout the whole argument, implied if not expressed is the belief that history, as God is bringing it to fulfillment, is not running through Rome—contrary to all assumptions and propaganda in the imperial metropolis. Similarly in Galatians 3, where Paul argues that Christ instead of the Mosaic covenant has become the means through which other peoples can become adopted as children and heirs of the promise to Abraham, Paul's argument takes the broad perspective of universal international history. Christ has become the means by which fulfillment has come in history, which has been running through Israel, not through Rome, contrary to all appearances under the Roman imperial order. In contrast to the standard Protestant theological assumptions of previous Pauline studies, therefore, Paul does not oppose Christ and the Gospel events of fulfillment to the Law and Judaism. In Paul's Letters, Christ and Gospel events stand opposed to Caesar and the Roman imperial order.

Moreover, just as Paul's gospel of Christ as Lord evidently stood opposed to the Roman imperial order, so the local representatives of that imperial order evidently opposed Paul and his assemblies. The opposition was reciprocal. Paul says he was "shamefully mistreated at Philippi" (1 Thess 2:2), apparently for "advocating customs that are not lawful for . . . Romans to adopt or observe" (Acts 16:21). Then in Thessalonica his recruits and apparently Paul himself suffered "persecution" (1 Thess 1:6; 2:14–16; see Smith's article below), apparently for "acting contrary to the decrees of the emperor, saying that there is another king [or emperor] named Jesus" (Acts 17:7). After working in Corinth for a year and a half, Paul was evidently compelled to leave the city by the Roman proconsul of Achaia, Gallio (cf. Acts 18:12). And while working in Ephesus he was imprisoned, perhaps so seriously that he was anticipating his martyrdom (Phil 1:7, 14; 2:17; cf. 1 Cor 15:32; 2 Cor 1:8).

These many indications in Paul's Letters show that his gospel and mission stood sharply opposed to Caesar and the Roman imperial order, and not to the Jewish Law. Hence, Pauline scholarship needs to take a keen interest in understanding why and in what ways Roman power and the Roman imperial order impinged upon, and were objectionable to, Paul and the people among whom he worked. Because of the separation of religion and politics in modern Western NT scholarship, however, it has generally been assumed that such questions were irrelevant to our understanding of Paul and his Letters. Thus, the field is only beginning to investigate the conflictual relationship of Paul and the Roman imperial order.

This has been one of several interrelated areas of focus for the "Paul and Politics Group" of the Society of Biblical Literature, as exemplified in a number of contributions to a previous collection of articles.[5] Accordingly, that group sponsored a session at the 2000 Annual Meeting on "Paul and the Roman Imperial Order," for which the papers by Efrain Agosto, Erik Heen, Jennifer Knust, and Abraham Smith were originally written. Simon Price was invited to respond to those papers because of the importance of his book *Rituals and Power* in helping NT interpreters toward a more adequate understanding of the integral relationship of the imperial cult and both imperial and local power relations.[6] Those four articles are now supplemented by the explorations of other key aspects of Paul and the Roman imperial order, by Neil Elliott, Robert Jewett, and Rollin Ramsaran. Most of these articles deal with the ideological, rhetorical, and other cultural aspects of Paul's and his assemblies' conflict with the Roman imperial order, while several focus on political-economic aspects. It may be helpful

---

5. The essays by Briggs, Callahan, Elliott, Horsley, Wan, and Wright in Richard A. Horsley, ed., *Paul and Politics: Ekklesia, Israel, Imperium, Interpretation* (Harrisburg, Pa.: Trinity Press International, 2000).

6. Simon R. F. Price, *Rituals and Power: The Roman Imperial Cult in Asia Minor* (Cambridge: Cambridge University Press, 1984).

at the outset, as a general background to all of these articles, to envisage how the Roman imperial order determined the conditions of and for Paul's mission and letters.

The New World (Dis)Order as the
General Conditions of Paul's Mission

Recent constructions of "the social world of the apostle Paul" have perpetuated the standard view that the *pax Romana* provided a benign context for the Pauline mission and rise of "Christianity." The Roman imperial order established after the great victory of Octavian at Actium created a "general climate of stability and security . . . for urban people in the provinces."[7] That was surely true for the tiny minority of power and privilege who headed the Roman imperial order in the cities of Greece and Asia Minor. And such a picture is precisely what is portrayed in most literary and epigraphic sources, which were the products of privilege.[8]

Paul's letters and the later book of Acts, as well as the writings of the Judean historian Josephus and the Alexandrian Jewish philosopher Philo, however, all indicate just the opposite. Judging from these sources, it appears that the "new world order" established by the Romans under Augustus and his successors was experienced as disorder by many urban as well as rural subject peoples in the provinces. The Romans and the wealthy aristocracies of the peoples and cities they conquered, whose dominance they confirmed and strengthened, strove to establish and perpetuate a political-economic order that underwrote their power and privilege. Yet subject peoples did not simply acquiesce in the new imperial order, and some of the arrangements imposed did more to exacerbate local conflicts than to pacify the subject populace. This is often not discerned and discussed, perhaps largely because the literary and epigraphic sources express the viewpoint of the elite, who had a considerable stake in the Roman imperial order.[9]

----

7. Wayne A. Meeks, *The First Urban Christians: The Social World of the Apostle Paul* (New Haven, Conn.: Yale University Press, 1983), 11–12.

8. Extensive survey and illuminating discussion of such material is in Clifford Ando, *Imperial Ideology and Provincial Loyalty in the Roman Empire* (Berkeley: University of California Press, 2000). Cf. the unevenness of acquiescence in the Roman imperial order evident in D. J. Mattingly, ed., *Dialogues in Roman Imperialism: Power, Discourse, and Discrepant Experience in the Roman Empire* (*Journal of Roman Archaeology*, Suppl. 23; Portsmouth, R.I.: JRA, 1997).

9. See now the "Introduction" and articles in Mattingly, *Dialogues in Roman Imperialism*. Ando, *Imperial Ideology and Provincial Loyalty*, asserts repeatedly (e.g., xii, 5, 6) that "the populations" of the provinces around the Empire found Roman power attractive, appreciated the political and economic stability, and even accepted Roman coercion as legitimate. It is questionable, however, whether the extensive source material he cites gives evidence for any but the elites.

We are best informed about the area and people of Palestine by "Christian" sources such as Paul and the Gospels as well as the histories of Josephus. There the movement(s) of Jesus-believers took its origins among Galileans and Judeans after the Roman execution of Jesus of Nazareth by crucifixion, apparently for serious disruption of the *pax Romana*. Josephus, like other provincial aristocrats, may himself have believed that Roman conquest and Roman rule worked by the grace of (his own) God. But his histories provide extensive accounts of how in Judea and Galilee resistance persisted against Roman rule for centuries after the initial conquest by Pompey in 63 B.C.E.[10] At the death of the Rome-imposed king Herod, around the time Jesus was born, widespread revolts erupted in every major district, led by popular messiahs, evoking a brutally punitive Roman reconquest. Ten years later, at the imposition of direct Roman rule in Judea, activist Pharisees and other scribal intellectuals led an organized resistance to the Roman tribute. In the Jerusalem temple that Herod had rebuilt in grand Roman-Hellenistic style as one of the wonders of the Roman imperial world, Roman troops had to stand guard against popular agitation at the annual celebration of the festival of Passover that commemorated the people's original liberation from foreign rule. In mid-first century, peasant prophets led numbers of followers in anticipating new divine acts of liberation, such as an exodus-like crossing into the promised land, a Jericho-like collapse of the walls of Jerusalem, and disappearance of the occupying Romans and their client rulers, the priestly aristocracy.

Diaspora Jews, descendants of earlier generations of Judeans resettled in various cities of the eastern Empire, such as Saul of Tarsus, came on pilgrimage to the temple and Jerusalem. Some of them became zealous defenders of the Judean way of life against the encroachments of the dominant Hellenistic-Roman culture (what Paul calls *ioudaismos,* Gal 1:11–17). Such fanatical attempts to preserve the traditional ways and official attempts to clamp down on resistance both led to internecine conflict. Resistance movements were repressed by the rulers for threatening the imperial order and/or persecuted by self-appointed leaders of long-range resistance because their agitation might bring down the massive destructive violence of the Empire.

---

10. In the following paragraphs I am drawing on my examination of the many facets of Roman rule and Judean and Galilean resistance in several books and articles, including Richard A. Horsley, *Jesus and the Spiral of Violence: Popular Jewish Resistance in Roman Palestine* (San Francisco: Harper & Row, 1987), chs. 1–5. For resistance in other areas, see Stephen L Dyson, "Native Revolts in the Roman Empire," *Historia* 20 (1971): 239–74; and "Native Revolt Patterns in the Roman Empire," *ANRW* 2.3 (1975): 138–75. For more general resistance to the Roman imperial order, see Ramsay MacMullen, *Enemies of the Roman Order* (Cambridge, Mass.: Harvard University Press, 1966), the perspective of which is indicated by the title.

Such are precisely the circumstances of turmoil and agitation, repression and persecution, that both Paul (Gal 1:13; Phil 3:4–6) and the book of Acts (4–5; 7:54–8:3) describe in portraying the movement of Jesus' followers in Jerusalem and beyond, at the time Paul received his call to join rather than continue his attacks against that movement. Such conditions continued in Jerusalem and Judea during the formative period of his mission activity, as the movement spread rapidly outward from Jerusalem and then from other centers such as Antioch in Syria. For example, the emperor Gaius's brazen order to install his statue in the Jerusalem temple, by military force if necessary, evoked massive resistance throughout Galilee and Judea and would have led to revolt if Gaius had not suddenly died. The Romans then installed the Herodian king Agrippa I in Jerusalem (41–44 C.E.) as well as Galilee, who actively attacked the leaders of the Jesus movement (Acts 12:1–5).

The turmoil only escalated further in the next two decades, as Paul extended his mission to Asia Minor and Greece. A group of scribal intellectuals known as the *Sicarioi* (dagger men), utterly frustrated at the collaboration between the predatory high priestly families and the repressive Roman governors, even launched terrorist attacks on key priestly aristocrats at festival times. The continuing Judean resistance and Roman repression that escalated until full-scale insurrection erupted in 66 is significant for Paul's mission and other branches of the new movement because that movement and its leaders would have been identified with/as Judeans elsewhere in the Roman Empire. And, of course, Paul himself understood his mission and movement as an extension of the promises to Israel.

The general climate of instability and insecurity, while less extreme than in Jerusalem, also prevailed for urban people in other provinces. Communities of Jews resident in several cities of the eastern Roman Empire sought to maintain their identity and way of life, resisting assimilation into the dominant political and cultural order.[11] Apparently through influence on Romans in high places, they managed to obtain special permission from the Romans to conduct their own community affairs according to their own cultural traditions. In Alexandria and in other cities as well, this evoked the hostility of other subject peoples, either at the exemptions the Jews enjoyed or in jealousy of their rights to pursue indigenous traditions.

In Alexandria, for example, anti-Jewish riots broke out under the emperor Gaius, which led to an imperial crackdown on Jewish rights in other cities and his brazen move against the Jerusalem temple. From Philo's "defense" written to the emperor Gaius, we can recognize just how

---

11. See, e.g., Paul Trebilco, *Jewish Communities in Asia Minor* (Cambridge: Cambridge University Press, 1991).

serious an issue it was, even for Jewish elites who were culturally heavily assimilated into Hellenistic-Roman culture, to continue to be subjected to imperial rule; we see how important it was to them to resist further assimilation and subjection to the Roman imperial order. But what could be done about the Roman rulers, who could become ferocious and brutal, other than to try to tame and soothe them (*Legatio ad Gaium; De somniis* 2.89)? As Philo, who was realistically aware of "how mightily the winds of necessity, . . . force, violence, and princedom" could blow, advised his fellow Jews, "When the times are right, it is good to set ourselves against the violence of our enemies and subdue it; but when the circumstances do not present themselves, the safe course is to stay quiet." He did not want to put the whole community in danger of riot or repression (*Somn.* 2.89, 92; cf. 2.83–84).[12]

A similar climate of instability and insecurity characterized urban life in Antioch, the large city on the Empire's eastern frontier, where Paul was based during an intermediate phase of his mission. Antioch already hosted a large community of Jews, which helps explain Herod's lavish beneficence to the city (paving the main street with marble; Josephus, *Jewish Antiquities* 16.148; *Jewish War* 1.425). Contemporary with Paul's mission based there, it was from Antioch that Gaius launched his invasion of Judea, which almost resulted in massive insurrection. This conflict was somehow the trigger for a circus riot between "the Blues" and "the Greens," which in turn led to attacks against Jews and Jewish synagogues in the city (Malalas *Chronographia* 244.15–245.1). Simmering hostilities against the Jews erupted again in the 60s (Josephus, *Jewish War* 7.46–62).

Political stability may have prevailed in the cities where Paul carried out his own distinctive mission, but that stability imposed by the Roman imperial order surely meant insecurity for many if not most urban people. Most of the cities and peoples among which Paul carried out his mission were sites and subjects of Roman imperial conquest and/or colonization. The most dramatic case would have been Corinth.[13] In one of the key steps by which the Roman warlords established themselves as the sole superpower in the Mediterranean basin, they utterly destroyed the ancient city of Corinth in 146 B.C.E. and left the area desolate. A century later, in 44 B.C.E., Julius Caesar established a colony there, peopled by the surplus

---

12. See further Neil Elliott, "Romans 13:1–7 in the Context of Royal Propaganda," in Horsley, ed., *Paul and Empire*, 197–202; and E. R. Goodenough, *Introduction to Philo Judaeus* (2d ed.; Oxford: Blackwell, 1962), 55–62.

13. Short sketch of the historical background to Paul's mission in Corinth, in Richard A. Horsley, *1 Corinthians* (ANTC; Nashville: Abingdon, 1998), 22–30; lengthy historical survey with extensive documentation, in James Wiseman, "Corinth and Rome I: 228 B.C.–A.D. 267," in *ANRW* 2.7.1 (1979): 438–584.

populace of freed slaves and other undesirables from Rome itself as well as veterans of Caesar's Gallic wars. Corinth became the center of *Romanitas* in Greece, as well as the eastern hub of the Empire's commerce. In the period before Paul's mission, therefore, Corinth would have been filled with people displaced from their places and cultures of origin, including slaves and descendants of slaves, and various people following the routes of commerce.

The Romans had taken control of Macedonia early in the second century B.C.E. The building of the great military road, the Egnatian Way, greatly strengthened their control and enabled them to use Macedonia as a base for extension of their power into Asia Minor.[14] The town of Philippi was colonized twice by the great Roman warlords. Antony refounded the town with a colony of his veterans in 42/41 B.C.E., followed by a second imposition of Roman army veterans after the battle of Actium (31 B.C.E.). At the time of Paul's mission, the descendants of the Roman veterans dominated the city in a typically Roman administration, with the descendants of the earlier Hellenistic towns in the area, other migrant Greeks, and native Thracians forming the bulk of the populace, many in surrounding villages. The Romanitas and Roman orientation of the dominant elite is clear. There was considerable potential for inherent tensions between the elite and the populace and among factions of the populace. The key battle in which Antony and Octavian defeated Brutus and Cassius, thus "saving" the Roman people, was celebrated by two famous altars constructed on the battlefield near the town. Philippi thus played a special symbolic role in Roman imperial history. Thessalonica, although not colonized by Roman veterans, displayed a relatively intense cultivation of Roman and particularly imperial favor in its coins and temple to Caesar. The city's emphasis on the imperial cult was an expression of its sense of political insecurity since it had backed the losing side at two critical points during the Roman civil wars. This strong orientation toward Rome was reinforced by the Roman garrison in its citadel and a significant but semi-separate group of Roman businessmen in the city.

Rome itself, finally, was hardly an imperial metropolis that provided security for its residents. Bread and circuses did not extend far into the vast majority of the teeming population who were economically marginal. Foreign immigrants and newly formed groups could easily become suspect. The Jewish couple Prisca and Aquila, who worked shoulder to shoulder

---

14. Recent surveys of the historical context of the Pauline mission in Philippi and Thessalonica, in Craig de Vos, *Church and Community Conflicts* (SBLDS 168; Atlanta: Scholars, 1999), chs. 4 and 6; Peter Oakes, *Philippians: From People to Letter* (Cambridge: Cambridge University Press, 2001).

with Paul and others in Corinth and Ephesus, had been among the Jews whom Claudius expelled from Rome in 49 (Acts 18:2), because of controversy over a certain Chrestus (Suetonius, *Claudius* 25.4). And fifteen years later, in 64, Nero blamed the great fire in Rome on "Christians," who were crucified and burned as living torches to illuminate the emperor's races in the Vatican Circus (Tacitus, *Annales* 15.44; Suetonius, *Nero* 16.2).

Impact of Roman Imperial Order on the Peoples of Paul's Mission

Amid the general context of instability and insecurity for many of the city inhabitants of the eastern Roman Empire, there were particular ways in which the Roman imperial order affected their lives.[15] Among these were some of the fundamental political-religious and economic forms that virtually constituted power relations in the imperial order.

Disruption and Displacement of Subject Peoples

A major factor in the insecurity and instability of local life under the Roman imperial order was the violent disruption and displacement of indigenous peoples by Roman conquest, enslavement, and colonization. The effects would have been considerable, deep-running, and long-lasting, as the parallel experiences of imperial conquests and disruptions of peoples in the nineteenth and twentieth centuries might suggest. Not only Judeans and Galileans in Palestine but also even relatively assimilated elite Jews such as Philo of Alexandria realized that they were subject people. Other peoples shared the experience of subjugation to Rome. Galatia, the first stop in Paul's own separate mission, had only recently been taken over by the Romans, and acquiescence and adjustment to Roman rule was only in the beginning stages there, as in Palestine. In the small city of Philippi, two successive sets of Roman military veterans had been imposed as the dominant political-economic class, and indigenous farmers had been dispossessed by the Roman colonists. It is difficult to imagine that the Macedonian and Thracian people and more recent Greek immigrants would have lacked a sense of being a subject people.[16] Among the Thessalonians the memory of rebellion put down by a Roman commander was kept fresh by officially honoring the Roman commanders as the "savior" of the city.

---

15. The impact of the Roman imperial order is not the same as what is called "Romanization." Ramsay MacMullen, *Romanization in the Time of Augustus* (New Haven, Conn.: Yale University Press, 2000), provides a recent discussion of the limited degree of Romanization in various areas of the Empire. Cultural influences, moreover, were multilateral and multidirectional.

16. De Vos, *Church and Community Conflicts*, 238–47; Oakes, *Philippians*, 19–35.

Although each of the cities in which Paul helped catalyze an "assembly" was different from the others, Corinth surely constituted the most diverse and fragmented social atmosphere. There was no continuity of stabilizing tradition from ancient times, since the Romans had destroyed the city in 146 B.C.E. By Paul's time a new clique of wealthy and powerful magnates, lacking even the minimal prestige of "noble birth" and long-standing leadership, would have emerged from the Roman colony of army veterans, free slaves, and undesirables sent there in 44 B.C.E. And as Corinth emerged as the central city of Roman Greece and the principal center of trade between Rome and the East, a great diversity of other root-less people gradually gathered there. It is not clear what if any principles of social cohesion would have existed below the level of the newly constructed civic culture in this multicultural, multilingual, and multiethnic metropolis. While most of the people Paul interacted with in Galatia, Philippi, and Thessalonica would likely have experienced local disruption, those he worked with in Corinth may well have been the products of more extensive and pervasive disruption and displacement.

Slavery

The most extreme form of displacement, of course, was slavery. It had been basic to the political economy of ancient Greece, and it became increasingly fundamental to the Roman political economy as well during the period of expansive imperial conquests in the late Republic.[17] In a remarkable coincidence of forces, during their conquests of new territories the Roman warlords seized tens of thousands of new slaves. These slaves were then bought by Roman patricians, including the warlords, to work lands that they seized from the peasants because of debts acquired while the men were serving in the legions that the warlords used in their conquests. Roman soldiers were replaced on the land by the slaves they helped to capture while serving in the legions. The resulting dependence on slave labor

---

17. Recent studies of Roman slavery include Keith Hopkins, *Conquerors and Slaves* (New York: Cambridge University Press, 1978); Orlando Patterson, *Slavery and Social Death: A Comparative Study* (Cambridge, Mass.: Harvard University Press, 1982; and Keith R. Bradley, *Slaves and Masters in the Roman Empire* (Brussels: Latomus 1984); *Slavery and Society in Rome* (Cambridge: Cambridge University Press, 1994). Survey of recent scholarship appears in Richard A. Horsley, "The Slave Systems of Classical Antiquity and Their Reluctant Recognition by Modern Scholars," *Semeia* 83/84 (1998): 19–66. Further discussion and documentation of the points and issues in the following paragraphs can be found in the above studies. The implications of these more critical analyses of ancient slavery for Paul's mission and letters are explored in Horsley, "Paul and Slavery: A Critical Alternative to Recent Readings," *Semeia* 83/84 (1998): 153–200.

in the Roman economy thus powerfully reinforced slavery as a standard feature of life in the Greek cities and other areas of the Empire. Even though most families, being extremely poor, could not afford slaves, the slaveholding patriarchal family was understood as the fundamental building block of society and civilization in Greek and Roman antiquity. Slaveholding was thus not only the economic basis of the elite who dominated the Roman imperial order but also both the political-economic basis of the social order and the normative ideal of imperial culture.

New Testament scholarship, heavily dependent on a traditional western European classics scholarship that idealized Greek and Roman civilization, has generally underestimated the severity of slavery and its basic importance in the ancient Greek and Roman political economy.[18] Only a generation ago, slavery was being portrayed as relatively benign, on the false and misleading assumptions that in the early Empire slaves could reasonably expect emancipation after age thirty (life expectancy for most slaves was probably less) and that slaves must have been relatively happy since the incidence of slave revolts is low. Those assumptions, however, were based on a misreading of Augustan directives and on a lack of attention to a whole system of social and political constraints, repressive measures, and physical and psychological intimidation and degradation that left little or no room for slaves to communicate and organize across households. Recent discussions of slavery as a means of "upward mobility" have been based on a limited and unrepresentative sample of epigraphs and an overestimate of the "influence" that "managerial slaves" such as those high in the *familia Caesaris* would have wielded. Precisely because the NT field has downplayed slavery and its effects in the Roman Empire, it is necessary to consider the various and wide-ranging ways that it affected subject peoples.

We can focus on a few of the obvious connections in which Roman practices of slavery may have affected the people Paul worked with, since a more extensive survey is impossible in this context. Some of the thousands of Galileans enslaved in the areas of Magdala and Nazareth in 52 and 4 B.C.E., respectively, or their descendants, likely ended up in cities such as Rome or Corinth. Whether of Galilean or Syrian or Galatian extraction, a certain number of slaves in cities such as Corinth and Ephesus became participants in the assemblies Paul helped catalyze. Others who joined Paul's

---

18. Reviewed in Horsley, "The Slave Systems of Classical Antiquity." On the other hand, some previous discussions of Paul and slavery have proceeded on the assumption that it would have been an option in the Roman Empire to advocate the abolition of slavery (and that Paul must have been conservative for not advocating its abolition). But slavery was integral to the Roman imperial order in much the same way as capitalism is to "the American way of life."

assembly in a city such as Corinth were probably descendants of freed slaves. Those slaves and freedmen/women, along with others in Paul's assemblies, knew well the circumstances in which people became slaves and what those meant in terms of "natal alienation" as well as in terms of human degradation. More generally, the very presence of slaves in the society undermined any economic leverage that free laborers, the vast majority of whom were poor or marginal anyhow, might have had with the wealthy and powerful who controlled each city. And of course, in the context of the obvious "pecking order" and shame and degradation that slavery entailed, the poor and marginal were always faced with the threat of sinking into slavery.

Patronage

One of the principal reasons that little attention has been given to power relations in that part of the Roman Empire where Paul pursued his mission is the ostensibly "kinder-gentler" face that the Roman imperial order presented to its subjects in such already "civilized" areas. Following its military conquest of the cities of Greece and Asia Minor, Rome did not maintain large armies of occupation there, as it did in "uncivilized" frontier areas. Nor did Augustus and his successors develop an elaborate imperial bureaucracy to "administer" the Empire. Rather, what held the Empire together as much as anything was the elaborate network of personal relations between the imperial family and the provincial elite and the elaborate "honors" sponsored by the latter for the former. City and provincial elites cultivated the personal patronage of the emperor, and in turn patronized public life in the cities.[19] The Roman imperial order thus presented a public face of

---

19. See esp. the works by Price, Zanker, and Gordon, reprinted in Horsley, *Paul and Empire.* Basic treatments of the patronage system include Richard Saller, *Personal Patronage under the Early Empire* (New York: Cambridge University Press, 1982); Saller, "Status and Patronage," ch. 28 in *The High Empire,* A.D. *70–192* (ed. Alan K. Bowman, Peter Garnsey, et al.; CAH 11; 2d ed.; Cambridge: Cambridge University Press, 2000), esp. 838–51; Andrew Wallace-Hadrill, ed., *Patronage in Ancient Society* (London: Routledge, 1989), esp. the reflective theoretical article by Wallace-Hadrill; and Wallace-Hadrill, "The Imperial Court," ch. 7 in *The Augustan Empire, 43* B.C.–A.D. *69* (ed. Alan K. Bowman, Peter Garnsey, et al.; CAH 10; 2d ed.; Cambridge: Cambridge University Press, 1996), 296–306. Summary of the implications of these studies and analyses appears in Horsley, *Paul and Empire,* 88–95, "Introduction" to part 2. The closely related development of an imperial patronage network and the sponsorship of the imperial cult by local elites belong to the general maneuvering of provincial aristocracies to situate themselves favorably in the new imperial order; see, e.g., Price, *Rituals and Power;* Susan Alcock, ed., *The Early Roman Empire in the East* (Oxbow Monograph 95; Oxford: Oxbow, 1995); and Greg Woolf, *Becoming Roman: The Origins of Provincial Civilization in Gaul* (Cambridge: Cambridge University Press, 1998).

beneficence to its subject peoples, at least in the cities. New Testament scholars have previously explored how patron-client relations provided a pattern that may have influenced relationships in Pauline communities and conceptions of the people's relationship with God. Patronage relations among the imperial elite, however, are also one of the principal ways by which the local elite maintained public order and exerted control over the people. It is difficult, moreover, to imagine that subject peoples were totally unaware of this. The cohesion of the imperial order at the top and its control of the people was structured in a variety of interconnected personal and public relationships.

The Roman emperor and/or Senate did, of course, send out governors to the various provinces. But besides cultivating such Roman officials, wealthy and powerful city and provincial figures also cultivated personal relations with the emperor and/or imperial family members. They made lavish gifts to the imperial family and endowed public honors in various forms, in gratitude for the award of imperial favors they sought and received. They also developed reciprocal relations with other figures in Rome close to the center of power (see Plutarch, *Moralia* 814C). Because the city and provincial magnates involved in these relationships were also the highest-ranking officials of their local city governments, such personal patronage relations overlapped with the official patronal relations of emperor and city or province. Yet the personal patronage relations between the emperor and the local elite constituted the more important and effective lines by which power flowed between imperial center and local and regional wielders of power. Pliny portrays the good emperor as more of a paternal protector and benefactor than an efficient administrator (*Panegyricus* 2.21).[20] The Empire was held together at the top by a vast network of patronage. And patronage was the means by which prominent figures enhanced and maintained their wealth and prominence in cities such as Corinth or Ephesus.

With their positions of wealth, power, and privilege thus secured by their personal relations with the imperial court, local elites continued to generate the wealth and power to dominate affairs in given cities. There, in return for their beneficence to the city, by the funding of a public building or festival, they were elected to high office and honored with public inscriptions and monuments. On a more limited scale, as well, wealthy men became patrons of local *thiasoi* or *collegia* of artisans or burial clubs, funding their banquets and in return having their names honored and birthdays celebrated. The flow of power at the top for the mutual benefit of the imperial and provincial elite was thus made to appear to work for

---

20. Peter Garnsey and Richard Saller, *The Roman Empire: Economy, Society, and Culture* (Berkeley: University of California Press, 1987), 149.

the benefit of the subject peoples. And there was no separation of religion and politics, "church and state," since the public beneficence of the local magnates often consisted of building a temple to the gods or the emperor, in reward for which they attained public religious as well as civic office. Hence, their patronage of their cities manifested the necessity of the political-economic gulf between the elite and the people. It was grounded in, and expressed in, the divine world on which the public order was founded. And under the Roman Empire, that divine world became imperial as well.

Imperial Cult

The most important and effective way that urban and provincial oligarchies constructed and maintained the Roman imperial order was their sponsorship of the imperial cult.[21] To cultivate imperial favor and open access to imperial power and favors, local elites honored the emperor or imperial family members by setting up shrines and building temples in redesigned city centers *(agorai)* and by funding festivals and imperial games. The imperial cult was not imposed from the imperial center, where Roman reserve required that living emperors decline to be worshiped as a god. The celebration and honoring of Augustus and his successors as divine figures, Lords and Saviors of the world, was developed by the elite in the Greek cities themselves, on the basis of the already-existing civil religion, in cities such as Ephesus, Corinth, and Thessalonica.

New Testament interpreters had tended to underestimate the importance of the imperial cult, dismissing it as more of a set of empty political gestures than a serious religious expression. Classical historians, on the other hand, had tended to dismiss the emperor cult as having little serious political role in the imperial order. One of the significant contributions of Simon Price to the new appreciation of the importance of the Roman imperial order for understanding Paul's gospel and mission is his theoretical critique of modern Western Christian assumptions about religion. Not only is religion not separate from politics, but religious expressions include far more than personal faith, and can even include the architectural construction of the urban environment. Indeed, religious expressions can participate in the construction of political power relations.

The inscriptional, numismatic, and other archaeological evidence that Price and others have investigated and interpreted indicate that in the early Roman Empire, the imperial cult went far toward constituting Roman imperial power relations in the Greek cities. In the prominent placement of temples, statues, and shrines dedicated to the emperor, the presence of

---

21. See esp. the important work of Simon R. F. Price, *Rituals and Power;* excerpted in Horsley, ed., *Paul and Empire*, 47–71.

the emperor came to "pervade public space." Insofar as the emperor's birth was celebrated not only as the beginning of the year but the beginning of a new era, the imperial cult came to structure urban time. Insofar as major regional festivals such as intercity games were now dedicated to the emperor or founded in his honor, the imperial cult became the most important expression and guarantor of social cohesion. And insofar as the emperor was now the principal divine force in each city's pantheon, the emperor stood at the center of the divine powers in which societal life was grounded. The locally developed and sponsored imperial cult thus came not only to embody a public cognitive system of imperial power relations, but also to construct the order of the imperial world.

The impact of the imperial cult on people in the Greek cities would have been persistent and unavoidable. Emperor and Empire were structured and literally inscribed into their very urban environment. In order to imagine how the presence of the emperor pervaded public space, Americans could think of how the visual displays, music, aromas, and advertising of the five-week festival of Christmas pervade public and private life from Thanksgiving to New Year's Day. Although the imperial cult and its festivals did not invade private life, they did last not simply for five weeks, but all year round.

Rhetoric

Yet another form by which imperial power relations were constituted was public rhetoric.[22] New Testament scholars have investigated Greek and Roman rhetoric in order to appreciate better the form taken by Paul's arguments. Again, the modern Western assumption of the separation of cultural and religious forms from political life and power relations blocked recognition of rhetoric as a major means by which the Roman imperial order was maintained. Roman officials and writers such as Cicero had long since theorized explicitly that the two basic motives leading to conformity to the established order were fear of the sword and consent, which was generated by persuasion. Under the Roman Empire, however, rhetoric functioned quite differently from the way it had under the earlier Greek city-state.

Rhetoric developed as an instrument of participatory politics in which rival politicians would attempt to persuade the city assembly to take a particular course of action or reach a particular verdict in a judicial case. In a society composed of slaveholding patriarchal families, of course, rhetoric also assumed and articulated particular relations of domination,

---

22. The following paragraphs draw upon Richard Horsley, "Rhetoric and Empire—and 1 Corinthians," in *Paul and Politics*, 72–82, and sources listed there.

legitimating slavery and the erosion of women's rights. It seems a bit of an overstatement to imagine that "rhetoric provided the rules for making critical judgments in the course of all forms of social intercourse,"[23] even in a democratic classical Athens. Under the Roman Empire, however, the decisions about all important matters of city affairs had already been made, either in Rome or by the oligarchies whose power Rome strengthened. Indeed, the Roman patricians who created the Empire had always opposed democracy. To guarantee elite control of the Greek cities, the Romans simply abolished city assemblies, gradually destroyed the lawcourts, and established a property requirement for holding public office.[24] Correspondingly, the Roman and Greek aristocracies further developed rhetoric as a key instrument of imperial order. As lawcourts became more and more the instruments of the aristocracies, judicial rhetoric served to legitimate their decisions. Stripped of their power, *ekklēsiai* deliberated about inconsequential issues, mainly in the service of established power relations, such as additional honors to the emperor or the election of oligarchs to office in return for their magnanimous public beneficence, such as building a temple.

Civic festivals, of course, required public eloquence. And the agora or theater was a good place to hear a good speech. Indeed, public declamation became a principal form of public entertainment in lecture halls as well as temples and theaters. But those public speeches were delivered by figures of power, influence, and/or wealth who belonged to the oligarchic circle.[25] And the most prominent theme in oratory of the early Empire "is that of peace, established and maintained by the emperor throughout the whole world, ... an end to stasis," ... and a "recognition that the Empire provides its inhabitants with *asphaleia,* security against external attack."[26] Greek intellectuals such as Plutarch expounded for all to hear how beneficial Roman rule was for subject peoples. For in contrast to other empires, under Roman power they were "free," not "enslaved." Indeed, Roman

---

23. Burton L. Mack, *Rhetoric and the New Testament* (Minneapolis: Fortress, 1990), 29, 31.

24. G. E. M. de Ste. Croix, *Class Struggle in the Ancient World* (Ithaca, N.Y.: Cornell University Press, 1981), 300–26; confirmed for Achaia and Corinth, by Susan Alcock, *Graecia Capta: The Landscapes of Roman Greece* (Cambridge: Cambridge University Press, 1993).

25. See, more broadly, Simon Swain, *Hellenism and Empire: Language, Classicism, and Power in the Greek World,* A.D. *50–250* (Oxford: Oxford University Press, 1996); and Ewen Bowie, "Literature and Sophistic," ch. 7 in *The High Empire,* esp. 900–3.

26. V. Nutton, "The Beneficial Ideology," in Peter Garnsey and C. R. Whittaker, eds., *Imperialism in the Ancient World* (Cambridge: Cambridge University Press, 1978), 210–11, with references.

dominion was truly the work of the gods (*Mor.* 814F; *The Fortune of the Romans* 316, 323).[27] That theme of an end to strife in the imperial "peace," however, also betrays an uneasiness among the oligarchs about the "exploitation and inequality" in the Roman imperial order of which they were the beneficiaries.[28] As Aristotle had observed centuries before, "Party strife is everywhere due to inequality" (*Pol.* 5.1.6 1301b27).

Oratory, however, provided more than entertainment. It constituted a principal source of culture. Along with the imperial temples, shrines, and festivals and the other constructions of the very environment of civic life, rhetoric produced the dominant cultural content of civic life. The impact on the life and consciousness of the residents of cities such as Corinth or Thessalonica would have been ubiquitous, steady, and pervasive. The combined impact of the imperial cult and public oratory on ordinary people subject to the Roman imperial order would have been analogous to that of television programming and advertising in late-twentieth-century urban life. With all important political-economic-religious matters already dictated by imperial power and nothing significant to be decided any longer by ostensibly democratic civic institutions, the dominant forms of culture encourage tacit acceptance of, and consensus about, the order of things.

Paul and the Roman Imperial Order

The essays in this volume provide explorations of particular aspects of Paul's opposition to the Roman imperial order. Because of the standard orientation of NT studies, little has been done previously in this connection. Only recently has it been suggested that Paul couched his gospel in pointedly anti-imperial terms and that he understood his assemblies as communities of an alternative society.[29] So the essays below are all somewhat exploratory ventures into uncharted territory. These investigations lead to the conclusion that Paul was "in but not of" the Roman imperial order. He shared the language of the Empire and even some of the particular forms of persuasion, he borrowed the themes and terms of the Empire, and he established communities that remained resident in the dominant culture. Yet he

---

27. As Edward Said comments about modern Western imperial culture, "The rhetoric of power all too easily produces an illusion of benevolence when deployed in an imperial setting." *Culture and Imperialism* (New York: Random House, 1993), xvii.

28. Fuller discussion is in Lawrence L. Wellborn, "On the Discord in Corinth: 1 Corinthians 1–4 and Ancient Politics," *JBL* 106 (1987): 94–96.

29. For example, Dieter Georgi, *Theocracy in Paul's Praxis and Theology*; Elliott, *Liberating Paul*; the essays or chapters reprinted in Horsley, *Paul and Empire*, parts 3–4; and the essays by Neil Elliott, N. T. Wright, and Allen Callahan, in Horsley, *Paul and Politics*.

used those themes and terms to articulate the gospel of, and build assemblies loyal to, a Lord and a God who not only offered an alternative to, but stood in judgment over, the imperial Savior and the ostensible "peace and security" he offered.

The investigation by Robert Jewett demonstrates that the opposition between Paul and the Roman imperial order extends even to their respective understandings of the natural order. Jewett closely examines how differently Rom 8:18–23 reads when set against the background of the Roman imperial ideology of the renewal of nature. Central to the propaganda of Augustus, and his successors, were massive monuments, such as the Ara Pacis, and celebrative festivals in Rome and throughout the Empire that claimed that his imperial peace had restored Mother Earth to a veritable supernatural fertility and productivity, bringing about a golden age of prosperity. In the diverse membership of the Roman assembly, Paul was addressing an audience that knew quite well that Roman imperial conquests and economic exploitation had in fact devastated villages and fields, deforested mountains, and eroded the natural environment in general. And to them he portrayed the world as "groaning and travailing" as it awaited its liberation, along with that of "the sons of God," from the futility to which it had been subjected—by implication, by arrogant and sinful imperial practices.

Abraham Smith finds that Paul's mission and community formation was enmeshed in the continuing political conflict between pro-Roman elites and more popular resistance among various subject peoples. The personal turmoil out of which Paul came to join the movement of Jesus-followers, of course, was fully embedded in, and inseparable from, just such a struggle among Diaspora and Judean Jews over Roman imperial rule. And Smith observes that much of the conflict in Judea itself during late-Second Temple times was between the pro-Roman aristocracy and their retainers, on one hand, and on the other hand Judean groups that came together in resistance to Roman rule. Convinced by those who view 1 Thess 2:14–16 as original to Paul's letter, Smith argues that a parallel conflict in Thessalonica accounts for Paul's reference to events in Judea and is the context in which to understand Paul's exhortation to the Thessalonians. He urges them to stand fast in their community solidarity against their attackers, who defend and boast in the "peace and security" supposedly guaranteed by the Roman imperial order.

Neil Elliott explains how Paul borrowed key symbolism from Roman imperial ideology to oppose the Empire, focusing primarily on imagery of the imperial triumph in 2 Corinthians. In pointed contrast to the imperial triumphal procession that acclaims the irresistible power of the conquering military hero, Paul portrays himself as the defeated and despised victim of imperial violence. In his reversal of the public performance of the imperial triumph, God's power is manifest in Paul's humiliation and Christ's crucifixion, because Christ's crucifixion by "the rulers of this age" is the inaugural event by which God is now subjecting the imperial rulers. Elliott also provides a vivid recent example of how contemporary Christians draw upon Paul's anti-imperial performance of embodied divine power to counter the torture of personal bodies and the body politic by the Pinochet national-security state sponsored by the United States.

Rollin Ramsaran provides a timely and provocative reminder that rhetoric is political and that Paul's rhetoric must be heard in the Roman imperial context. Whether or not he had been formally educated in the forms of Greco-Roman rhetoric, he clearly used standard types of argument in his Letters. The overall agenda and perspective of his arguments, however, can only be understood in the context of resistance to the Roman imperial order in the Judean apocalyptic tradition. In 1 Corinthians in particular, Paul appears to deploy Greco-Roman forms in the broader pattern and perspective of a Judean apocalyptic rhetorical register. Ramsaran thus provides an important corrective and antidote to recent presentations of Paul's arguments as if they simply replicated the forms in Greco-Roman rhetorical handbooks.

Efrain Agosto examines Greco-Roman letters of recommendation to the emperor or high-ranking persons by patrons such as Cicero and Pliny for their protégés, communications instrumental to the patronage system that held the Empire together at the top, and how the commendation passages in Paul's Letters compare. He finds that Paul's commendations differ significantly from letters of recommendation seeking positions of power and status for the advancement of personal careers of members of the Roman or provincial elite. Despite some similarities in motif, such as close personal relations, Paul rather emphasizes sacrificial service to the movement he and others are building. Paul's commendations do apparently aim at strengthening his own network of friends and trusted associates in the leadership of the movement he is building. That movement itself, however, stands in opposition to the imperial system that the elite are administering.

Drawing on the research of classical historians such as Price, Erik Heen shows how Paul used a key image from the imperial ideology to oppose it. Heen highlights the aristocratic passion for honors as perhaps a key factor driving their sponsorship of honors to the emperor and their beneficent funding of construction of public spaces and buildings *(euergetism)*, which effectively secured their positions of power, privilege, and local dominance in the imperial order. He is thus able to provide an illuminating new context for, and a compelling new perspective on, the "Christ-hymn" in Phil 2:6–11. Instead of being a "christological" expression of Christ's preexistence, this hymn uses a key phrase from the imperial cult to portray Jesus Christ as the very opposite of the emperor: far from valuing and seeking honors equal to god, he was martyred by the Roman rulers (on a cross)—after which he was elevated into the highest position as the counter-emperor. Drawing on James C. Scott's work on disguised modes of resistance, Heen enables us to see how Paul's communities carved out a breathing space for an alternative community living out an alternative set of values by imaging Christ, not Caesar, as the true ruler of their lives, precisely because he had become a paradigm of mutual service.

Jennifer Wright Knust finds that Paul's critique of the dominant society as hopelessly caught up in sexual lust and promiscuity is largely an adaptation of standard criticism in Greek and Roman cultural discourse. Early Roman imperial ideology, however, claimed that Augustus and his successors had restored public morality. Indeed, the emperor himself, fully in control of his own passions, had tamed vice and immorality in the public order by the preservation of law and custom. In this imperial context, Paul's claim that society at large is full of fornication would have been understood as a critique of both emperor and Empire. To argue that the emperor in fact has failed and that Christ is the true answer to sin suggests an anti-imperial stance. In thus adapting a standard critique of sexual immorality to oppose the imperial order, however, Paul in effect reinscribed into his own anti-imperial discourse the hierarchical assumptions of sex, gender, and slavery implicit in that critique.

While these essays are all focused primarily on Paul and the politics of the Empire, many of them inevitably deal with other aspects of the overall agenda of the Paul and Politics Group. Nearly all of them discuss "Paul and the politics of interpretation" in some way. Those by Agosto, Elliott, Martin, Ramsaran, and Smith deal with "Paul and the politics of his assemblies" to a lesser or greater extent. And those by Ramsaran and Smith also touch on "Paul and the politics of Israel." In that same connection, the essays by Elliott and Jewett, like those of Ramsaran and Smith, make clear that Paul's opposition to the Roman imperial order draws heavily on the Israelite/Judean cultural tradition in which he was deeply grounded and to which he remained thoroughly committed.

Keying from what was construed as his acceptance of slavery, and working on conservative or reformist assumptions that the established order is acceptable or inevitable, standard NT scholarship has consistently read Paul as a social conservative.[30] The only question is whether he was trying to challenge or change certain aspects of the social order, such as

---

30. Elliott, *Liberating Paul*, 31–52.

gender or ethnic relations. The explorations of various issues, themes, and passages in Paul's letters in this volume indicate that in many interrelated respects, the Roman imperial order is the context in which Paul's gospel and mission must be understood. They also indicate that Paul presented his gospel and organized his assemblies in opposition to that order, and even in effective resistance to it.

Nevertheless, although Paul was primarily "in but not of" the Roman imperial order, insofar as he borrowed key terms and standard discourse from the dominant culture, he perpetuates certain imperial images and patterns of social relations. Inasmuch as we are also concerned with the subsequent "politics of interpretation," we must take into account the influence and impact of Pauline imagery, language, and Letters on the Christian church and culture that read them as sacred Scripture. However much Paul may have been using imperial terms for Jesus Christ in opposition to the imperial Roman lord and savior, he bequeathed imperial images of Christ to the church that became the established imperial religion under Constantine and remained so in western Europe. But Christ thus became the imperial Lord, and no longer the anti-imperial imperial Lord. It seems a great irony, then, that such imperial images of Christ were used by Western Christianity in its collaboration with the powerful Western nation-states in their imperial conquests and domination of other peoples. A related aspect of that irony, moreover, is that "critical" NT studies developed not only during the heyday of western European imperialism but as one of many academic disciplines in complicity with it.

– 1 –

THE CORRUPTION AND REDEMPTION OF CREATION

Reading Rom 8:18–23 within the Imperial Context

Robert Jewett

Introduction

In the immense literature about Paul's letter to the Romans, including the extensive debate over the interpretation of chapter 8, I have not encountered an effort to relate the details of Paul's argument to Greco-Roman ideas about the corruption and redemption of nature. For example, in his influential studies of Romans in the context of imperial propaganda, Neil Elliott points to thematic parallels between chapters 8 and 13 and observes that the references to suffering "would have evoked sharp echoes" of imperial violence; but rather than dealing with the issue of creation itself, Elliott follows the traditional track in concluding that Paul "requires subordination rather than defiant opposition to the authorities."[1] Although Jacob Taubes interpreted Paul's "political theology" as "a political polemic against the Caesars," he made no effort to address the issue of creation.[2] Bruno Blumenfeld's recent discussion of this passage makes no reference to Roman attitudes toward nature.[3] Dieter Georgi states in passing that Romans 8 differs

---

1. Neil Elliott, "Romans 13:1–7 in the Context of Imperial Propaganda," in *Paul and Empire: Religion and Power in Roman Imperial Society* (ed. R. A. Horsley; Harrisburg, Pa.: Trinity Press International, 1997), 194, 196. While Neil Elliott, in *Liberating Paul: The Justice of God and the Politics of the Apostle* (Maryknoll, N.Y.: Orbis, 1994), 173, does refer to Paul's yearning for the "redemption of the whole creation (Rom. 8:22–23)," that evokes his "personal agony for his people, the Jews," he does not suggest that Paul has Roman imperial views of creation in view.

2. Jacob Taubes, *Die Politische Theologie des Paulus: Vorträge gehalten an der Forschungsstätte der evangelischen Studiengemeinschaft in Heidelberg, 23–27 Februar 1987*, ed. A. Assmann et al. (Munich: Wilhelm Fink Verlag, 1995), 27.

3. Bruno Blumenfeld, *The Political Paul: Justice, Democracy and Kingship in a Hellenistic Framework* (JSNTSup 210; Sheffield: Sheffield Academic, 2001), 360–64.

from Roman views of the "idyllic" quality of nature.[4] He cites the *Carmen Saeculare* that Horace wrote in connection with the imperial games organized by Augustus, although he concentrates on the glorification of the emperor rather than on the restoration of nature.[5] Following Georgi's lead I would like to bring imperial views into more direct correlation with Paul's argument. Since understanding Paul's argument depends on knowledge of Greco-Roman views, I begin with the imperial ideology of nature.

The Corruption and Redemption of Nature in Greco-Roman Culture

Hesiod's influential view of nature envisioned an original, golden age as a time of happiness when "the earth produced spontaneously," when there was no violence, while the entire human race lived with luxurious happiness.[6] In *Works and Days* (109–201) Hesiod articulates a theory of decline from this idyllic beginning, in which human failure is linked with nature's corruption. The later ages of silver, bronze, and iron are marked by increasing levels of violence and impiety, when humans lose their superior mental and moral qualities. "The Golden Race disappears for no assigned cause; the Silver because of *hybris* and impiety; the Bronze by internecine war; the Heroes by external war; the Iron by exhaustion, or perhaps because of their evil-doing."[7] In Aratus's *Phaenomena* (100–135) and Ovid's *Metamorphoses* (1.89–112) are similar descriptions of the ages of Gold, Silver, and Bronze.

In 44 B.C.E. the young Augustus used the appearance of a comet and the prophecy of Vulcanius concerning the end of one age and the beginning of another to justify the apotheosis of the assassinated Julius Caesar.[8]

---

4. Dieter Georgi, "God Turned Upside Down," in *Paul and Empire* (ed. R. A. Horsley), 155.

5. Dieter Georgi, "Who Is the True Prophet?" in *Paul and Empire* (ed. R. A. Horsley), 36–46.

6. Arthur O. Lovejoy et al., *Primitivism and Related Ideas in Antiquity* (Baltimore: Johns Hopkins, 1935; repr. New York: Octagon, 1965), 28. See also Lutz Käppel, "Hesiod," *RGG* 3 (2000): 1703–04; A. Kurress, "Aetas, Aurea," *RAC* 1 (1950): 144–50; K. Kubusch, *Aurea saecula, Mythos und Geschichte: Untersuchung eines Motives in der antiken Literatur bis Ovid* (Frankfurt am Main/New York: P. Lang, 1986).

7. Lovejoy et al., *Primitivism*, 31.

8. See John T. Ramsey and A. Lewis Licht, *The Comet of 44 B.C. and Caesar's Funeral Games* (American Philological Association American Classical Studies 39; Atlanta: Scholars, 1997) 140–45. They note (145) that when Augustus later wrote his *Memoires*, Vulcanius's prophecy about the end of the ninth age and the beginning of the tenth was "made to concern the return of a Golden Age."

Virgil provided a "messianic"[9] development in this line of thought during the period of upheaval after the assassination. In his *Fourth Eclogue* a regent is prophesied who would restore the golden age of paradise, when the earth would again produce its bounty without any human work, and when the blight of human impiety would no longer pollute the earth.[10] In the light of Virgil's later support of Augustus,[11] this prophecy was thought to have been fulfilled when he established the *pax Romana*:

> And in your counselship . . . shall this glorious age begin. . . . Under your sway, any lingering traces of our guilt shall become void, and release the earth from its continual dread. . . . But for you, child, shall the earth untilled pour forth. . . . Uncalled, the goats shall bring home their udders swollen with milk, and the herds shall fear not huge lions. . . . The serpent, too, shall perish, and the false poison-plant shall perish; Assyrian spice shall spring up on every soil. . . . The earth shall not feel the harrow, nor the vine the pruning-hook; the sturdy ploughman, too, shall now loose his oxen from the yoke. (Virgil, *Ecl.* 4.11–41)

In Virgil's *Aeneid* (6.789–794), the link with the reigning Augustus becomes explicit: "Here is Caesar and all of Iulius's progeny, coming beneath the revolving heaven. This man, this is he, whom you often hear promised to you, Augustus Caesar, son of a god, who will establish once more . . . the Golden Age in the fields once ruled by Saturn." This tradition provides the background for proclaiming Augustus and his successors as inaugurators of a new, golden age, the "Age of Saturn," in which paradisial conditions on the earth would be restored.

The Saecular Games were organized by Augustus in 17 B.C.E. to mark "the birth of a new age" in which the "fertility of Mother Earth" was seen

---

9. Hildebrecht Hommel, "Vergils 'messianisches' Gedicht," in vol. 1 of H. Hommel, *Sebasmata: Studien zur antiken relilgionsgeschicte und zum frühen Christentum* (Tübingen: Mohr [Siebeck], 1983), 267–72, shows that the poem was written in 41 B.C.E., during the period of uncertainty and revolution.

10. Andreas Alföldi, "Der neue Weltherrscher der vierten Ekloge Vergils," *Hermes* 65 (1930): 369–85, esp. 369, analyzed the propaganda of the divine ruler who would emerge to redeem Rome from its decline and restore paradisial conditions of plenty on the earth.

11. Hommel, "Vergils 'messianisches' Gedicht," 303, notes that the predicted redemptive king in the poem was the son of the consul Asenius Pollio, Virgil's patron. Apparently it was only later that this prediction was applied to Augustus.

to be restored and "guarded by the Fates and the Goddesses of Childbirth."[12] While there had been earlier plans to inaugurate this celebration, which had been postponed for political reasons,[13] Augustus used the appearance of another comet to justify this celebration that announced the beginning of the new age.[14] Horace was commissioned to write the official poem for the celebration, the *Carmen Saeculare,* which featured the renewal of nature:

> May the earth be fertile for harvests and herds
> and give to Ceres her garland of wheat ears;
> may the crops be nourished
> by Jupiter's good breezes and showers.

A later stanza of Horace's poem celebrates the fusion of morality, peace, and prosperity:

> Now Faith and Peace and Honor and ancestral Decency
> and slighted Virtue venture to return,
> and blessed Plenty appears once more
> with her brimming horn.[15]

In the ensuing years one monument after another was erected to celebrate this restoration of the "fruitfulness of nature,"[16] a sequence that reached its high point in the Ara Pacis Augustae. The imagery on the Altar of the Augustan Peace symbolizes "the return of this lost age of bounty and goodness."[17] Allusions to the promised regeneration of the earth are visible in every aspect of this magnificent altar. The motifs of the ivy and grapevine that appeared in Virgil's *Fourth Eclogue* as signs of the new age

---

12. Mary Beard, John North, and Simon Rice, *Religions of Rome,* vol. 1: *A History* (Cambridge: Cambridge University Press, 1998), 203.

13. Beard et al., *Religions of Rome,* 1:205 n.126; see also Georgi, "True Prophet?" 37.

14. Paul Zanker, *The Power of Images in the Age of Augustus* (Ann Arbor: University of Michigan Press, 1988, 1990), ch. 5; trans. of *Die Bildnisse des Augustus: Herrscherbild und Politik im kaiserlichen Rom* (Sonderausstellung der Glyptothek und des Museums für Abgüsse klassischer Bildwerke; hrsg. von Klaus Vierneisel und Paul Zanker; München, 1979), 171. See also Ramsey and Licht, *The Comet of 44 B.C.,* 140–45.

15. Joseph Clancy, trans., *The Odes and Epodes of Horace* (Chicago: University of Chicago Press, 1960), 189–90.

16. Zanker, *Die Bildnisse des Augustus,* 177.

17. David Castriota, *The Ara Pacis Augustus and the Imagery of Abundance in Later Greek and Early Roman Imperial Art* (Princeton, N.J.: Princeton University Press, 1995), 125.

are prominently displayed.[18] New plants are invented to depict the paradisial conditions of a world made truly new, while the organization of plants and animals in rows and ranks conveys the new, hierarchical order.[19] The floral displays and allusions to Apollo and Bacchus convey the message "If the Golden Age was to return, this would surely depend in good measure upon the renewal of the pristine Roman values and religious tradition" brought by Augustus.[20] These scenes are coordinated with scenes of victory over the Parthians, which serve to confirm the divine blessing on the new regime.[21] The twin pillars on the altar symbolize piety and conquest, both of which were allegedly blessed by the gods. The altar gives expression to Virgil's idea that "those who adhere to divinely appointed law and justice may in a way sustain or capture the blessing formerly enjoyed by the Golden Race."[22] The political implication was reinforced by the placement of the Altar on the Campus Martius in relation to the gigantic Solarium Augusti in such a way that the pointer of the sundial would shine directly onto the altar on September 23, Augustus' birthday.[23]

The central figure on the peace altar is Mother Earth restored, a female figure representing Rome sitting at ease with "two children and pomegranates, grapes and nuts on her lap; in front of her a cow and a sheep. . . . [She] clearly represents notions of fertility (human and agricultural), set between images of sky and sea, . . . 'earth' or 'fertility' in the sense of Italy."[24] The feminine figure of Tellus (Mater) combines features of Venus, Ceres, and Cybele, whose depiction and surroundings imply a supernatural world in which plants are larger than life and animals live in peace with one another.[25] The fused goddesses serve as guarantors of the new golden age that Augustus was seen to have restored. "For the Romans of the Augustan period, the conception of the Golden Age embodied on the Ara Pacis [altar] was essentially one of renewal—the renewal of time and the renewal of bounteous life." This was produced by "the renewal of traditional religious practices and moral values."[26]

The Ara Pacis was widely emulated as depictions of a fruitful Mother Earth came to center stage on coins and altars in the period of Augustus

---

18. Ibid., 135.
19. Zanker, *Power of Images,* 184–86.
20. Castriota, *Ara Pacis Augustus,* 139.
21. Zanker, *Power of Images,* 189.
22. Castriota, *Ara Pacis Augustus,* 138.
23. Ibid., 131.
24. Beard et al., *Religions of Rome,* 204; discussing fig. 4.6.
25. Zanker, *Power of Images,* 178, 182.
26. Castriota, *Ara Pacis Augustus,* 141, 144.

and his successors.[27] For instance, the grand public altar erected in the Augustan period near the Roman colony in Carthage features a similar "seated female figure, with children in her arms, her lap full of fruit, animals at her feet. This figure is closely based on the scene of 'Earth' on Augustus' Ara Pacis in Rome."[28] Another altar in Carthage has the figure of Earth with a "globe and cornucopia in front of her," probably adapted from a Roman design.[29] While these motifs were present on Roman coins in the decades prior to Augustus, he combined them with the theme of *pieta,* the proper honoring of the gods that would ensure the Golden Age with his victory.[30] One of his coins has the ruler with divine light streaming from his head while he stands with his foot on the globe and holds the symbols of the "return of the Golden Age," including the cornucopia.[31] Augustus and later emperors used this symbol on coins and sculpture to indicate that their regimes were the sources of plentitude. Capricorn, the nativity star of Augustus, was associated with the cornucopia, indicating that his birth inaugurated the new age of prosperity, a theme adopted from Hellenistic kingship ideology.[32] Following this tradition, "numerous Roman Caesars, queens, princes, and princesses depict themselves as bringers of salvation by means of the single or double cornucopia."[33]

While none of the subsequent emperors up until Paul's time was as successful in the propaganda that associated their reigns with the redemption of nature, the themes remained alive in poetry, art, and the civic cult. Calpurnius Siculus relates these themes to the ruling emperor (Nero):

> Rejoice, first of all, dwellers in the forests, rejoice, O my people. Though all your flocks wander without a guardian, and the shepherd neglect to close them in at night, . . . yet no thief shall lay his traps near the sheep-fold nor loosen the tethers of the beasts of burden to drive them off. The golden age of untroubled peace is born again, and kindly Themis returns to earth freed from stain and rust. The happy times are ruled by a youth [Nero] who won the victory while still in his mother's arms. When he shall himself reign as a god, . . . peace will appear, . . . and clemency has broken

---

27. See Ilona Opelt, "Erde," *RAC* 5 (1962): 1136–38.

28. Beard et al., *Religions of Rome* 331, with the altar depicted on 332.

29. Ibid., 333.

30. Alföldi, "Der neue Weltherrscher," 376.

31. Ibid., 385, provides a number of other Roman coins containing the cornucopia motif.

32. Johannes B. Bauer, "Horn I," *RAC* 16 (1994): 544–46.

33. Ibid., 546.

in pieces the weapons of madness. . . . Full peace will come upon us, a peace which . . . shall bring back a second reign of Saturn. (*Ecl.* 1.33–99)

Since the "madness" of non-Roman warfare and the corruption of barbaric impiety had ruined the world, Nero's reign brings peace that is blessed by the gods. His magical "victory" allegedly restores nature to its original state in the primeval Age of Saturn, when beasts of the field were so tame that they herded themselves, and when the earth brought forth its harvest without the use of the plow. This imperial vision of the former corruption and current redemption of Mother Earth differs from Paul's letter to the Romans at virtually every point and provides a suitable foil for reassessing the relevance of its argument.

A Reading of Rom 8:18–23 within the Imperial Context

Romans is an epideictic letter that does not indulge in polemics. We should therefore anticipate that the relation of this passage to the prevailing Roman view of nature is implicit rather than explicit. In thinking through the implications of Paul's formulation against the foil of the imperial context, we also need to take account of the impact of the previous argument in the letter. Whereas the Roman cult touted piety and conquest as the means whereby the golden age was restored, Paul's letter rejects salvation by works in all its forms. Whereas the Roman premise was that disorderly barbarians and rebels caused the corruption of nature, Paul argues that all humans reenact Adam's fall. In place of imperial celebrations and administration as the hinge of the golden age, Paul touts the power of the gospel to convert the world. Moreover, as the wording of Rom 8:18–23 indicates, the natural world is far from idyllic, and it has certainly not been restored by the Roman imperium. Drawn from a forthcoming commentary, I translate Rom 8:18–23 as follows:

> [18]For I reckon that the sufferings of the present time are not equivalent with the coming glory to be revealed to us.
> [19]For the eager expectation of the creation awaits the revelation of the sons of God.
> [20]For the creation was subjected to futility, not voluntarily but on account of the one who subjected it in hope
> [21]because the creation itself will also be freed from the slavery to corruption and obtain the liberation consisting of the glory for the children of God.
> [22]For we know that the whole creation groans together and travails together until now,

²³and not only [the creation] but even ourselves who have the first
   fruits of the spirit,
even we ourselves, groan within ourselves as we await the redemption of our body.

While noting the sufferings to be experienced by the saints in the
eschaton (last/new age) as a traditional motif,[34] commentators tend to over-
look the contextual implications that this formulation would have carried
for the Roman believers. They had already experienced harassment and
deportation, and their everyday life as members of the Roman underclass
was anything but idyllic. Paul's formulation simply assumes, without arguing the point, that the Caesarean view about the presence of a peaceful,
magically prosperous golden age is illusory. The term *pathēmata* (passions,
sufferings) appears in Rom 8:18 with the article, indicating that the topic
is known to the audience. The plural form is typical of Pauline usage (2 Cor
1:5, 6, 7; Gal 5:24; Phil 3:10; Col 1:24), referring to the sufferings that
believers should expect in following a suffering Christ.[35] This wording follows the idea of suffering together with Christ in Rom 8:17. While in 7:5
the entire fallen world remains subject to "*ta pathēmata tōn hamartiōn* (the
sinful passions)," these particular sufferings in Rom 8:18–23 are a sign of
eschatological solidarity with Christ, whose new age is now dawning.

The expression "*tēn mellousan doxan*" should be translated in the
adjectival sense of "the future glory" rather than linking the participle with
the verb to depict the close proximity of "about to be revealed" (1:18).[36]
Paul used a similar expression in Gal 3:23, "*tēn mellousan pistin
apokaluphthēnai (the future faith to be revealed),*" indicating that such faith
became available only in the future. I find it particularly significant that
Paul uses the expression "to be revealed" in a manner parallel to the thesis
of Romans,[37] conveying an apocalyptic disclosure of the triumph of God

---

34. See, for instance, Heinrich Schlier's discussion based on *4 Ezra* 13:16–19; *2 Bar.*
(Syriac Apocalypse) 25:1–3; 2 Thess 1:4; in *Römerbrief* (HTKNT 6; Freiburg: Herder,
1977), 257. James D. G. Dunn, *Romans 1–8* (WBC 38a; Dallas: Word, 1988), 468–69,
cites Dan 7:21–22, 25–27; 12:1–3; *Jubilees* 23:22–31; *Testament of Moses* 5–10; 1QH
3:28–36; *Sibylline Oracles* 3:632–56; and Matt 3:7–12 and parallels, in support of the
contention that "Paul is taking over an earlier eschatological schema" in this verse.
Walther Bindemann, in *Die Hoffnung der Schöpfung: Römer 8,18–27 und die Frage
einer Theologie der Befreiung von Mensch und Natur* (Neukirchener Studienbücher
14; Neukirchen: Neukirchener, 1983), 82–95, claims that Paul is polemicizing here
against an apocalyptic scheme stressing the distance of God; but this argument
seems overly abstract and unrelated to the cultural context.

35. See Wilhelm Michaelis, "*pathema,*" *TDNT* 5 (1967): 930–34.

36. BAGD 501.

37. See Dunn, *Romans 1–8,* 470.

over adversity and the corruption of the cosmic order. Despite the illusions of the Roman civic cult, the originally intended glory of the creation shall yet be restored, including specifically the glory humans were intended to bear. The phrase *"eis hēmas"* that ends Rom 1:18 could be translated "for us," implying, in John Murray's view, that the glory is "to be bestowed upon us, so that we become the actual partakers; it is not a glory of which we are to be mere spectators."[38] In contrast to imperial claims, this is not a glory that shines from the head of Caesar alone.

The concept of "glory" implied in this passage is in fact quite distant from the classical Greco-Roman sense of opinion, reputation, or renown ascribed by public opinion; it is closely related to the Hebrew sense of *kābôd (doxa)* as innate weightiness, honor, beauty, fiery presence, splendor, or power.[39] This term is comparable to what moderns refer to as "stardom," the innate capacity some people have to perform with inspiration, to be intensely attractive, and to shine beyond others. The "glory of God" has the concrete meaning of "a fiery phenomenon issuing from radiance and brilliance, and an abstract meaning of honor, worthiness, and majesty."[40] Human beings were created to reflect such glory (Ps 8:1, 5), which is particularly visible in the wise (Prov 11:16; 20:3) and symbolized throughout the ancient Near East by the royal crown or diadem.[41] When persons or nations become corrupt, they lose their glory (Hos 4:7; 9:11; Jer 2:11; Ezek 24:25), but when Yahweh redeems them, their glory is restored (Isa 35:1–2). The connection in Rom 8:18 between "revelation" and the restoration of "glory" is derived from a major stream of prophetic and postexilic expectations. Isaiah 24:23 foresees the time "when the LORD of hosts will reign on Mount Zion and in Jerusalem, and before his elders he will manifest his glory." This expectation reflects Exod 24:9–10, where Yahweh revealed himself to the elders at Mount Sinai.[42] Deutero-Isaiah foresaw a universal extension of this idea in 40:5: "Then the glory of Yahweh shall be revealed, and all flesh shall see it together" (author). The revelation of divine radiance and glory, to be seen by all the nations, is also expressed in Isa 60:1–3, which reiterates the theophanic vision of Deut 33:2 and Hab 3:3–4, a vision that will one day "fill the whole world" (Isa 6:3; Num 14:21; Ps 72:19), thus demonstrating God's triumph over evil.[43]

---

38. John Murray, *The Epistle to the Romans: The English Text with Introduction, Exposition, and Notes* (NICNT; Grand Rapids: Eerdmans, 1997), 301.

39. See Gerhard Kittel, *"doxa,"* TDNT 2 (1964): 233–51, esp. 247.

40. Weinfeld, *"kābôd,"* ThWAT 4 (1982): 38.

41. Ibid., 30–31.

42. Ibid., 36.

43. See ibid., 37.

In the light of this background and of Paul's argument concerning the present experience of faith in the midst of suffering, it seems inappropriate to restrict "glory" in this passage to a future state of "immortality" to be enjoyed by the saints.[44] As evident in 8:30, where the past-tense verb, "he glorified" is employed, Paul intends the beleaguered Christ-believers in Rome to discern in the growing triumph of the gospel the initial evidence of this glory that will one day fill the creation (cf. 2 Cor 3:18).

In Rom 8:19 Paul explains the cosmic scope of divine glory by introducing the concept of *ktisis* (creation), probably referring primarily to the various nonhuman components of the universe.[45] In contrast to Greco-Roman views of the eternal Mother Earth, *ktisis* implies purposeful creation of the natural order by God at a particular moment in time. The biblical creation stories are in view, but in contrast to Genesis, there is a striking measure of personification in Paul's view of the nonhuman world; it is capable of *apokaradokia* (eager expectation), just as humans are (Phil 1:20). This word, attested only in these two passages written by Paul, conveys a positive connotation of "confident expectation,"[46] very much in contrast to the relaxed depictions of Mother Earth in the Ara Pacis. The attitude is contrasting, but the personification is similar. This personification of creation is also paralleled in an apocalyptic treatment of the flood tradition (1 Enoch 7:6) where the earth takes on human qualities as it lays accusation against

---

44. See Brendan Byrne, *"Sons of God"—"Seed of Abraham": A Study of the Idea of the Sonship of God of All Christians in Paul against the Jewish Background* (AnBib 83; Rome: Biblical Institute, 1979), 107. Similarly, Joseph A. Fitzmyer, *Romans: A New Translation with Introduction and Commentary* (AB 33; New York: Doubleday, 1993), 506, restricts glory to that which will occur "in the eschaton."

45. In Rom 1:20–25 *ktisis* referred to all created things, including birds, reptiles, and humans. But Ulrich Wilckens, *Der Brief an die Römer* (EKKNT 6; Zurich: Benziger; Neukirchen—Vluyn: Neukirchener Verlag, 1978–82), 2:152–53; and C. E. B. Cranfield, *A Critical and Exegetical Commentary on the Epistle to the Romans* (ICC; Edinburgh: Clark, 1975), 411–12, advance compelling arguments that neither non-Christian believers nor the angelic forces are implied in the formulation of 8:19. See also B. R. Brinkman, "'Creation' and 'Creature' II. Texts and Tendencies in the Epistle to the Romans," *Bijdr* 18 (1957), 359–74; and John G. Gibbs, *Creation and Redemption: A Study in Pauline Theology* (NovTSup 26; Leiden: Brill, 1971).

46. D. R. Denton, "*apokaradokia*," *ZNW* 73 (1982): 139, in contrast to Georg Bertram's problematic argument from etymology that the term carries a sense of anxious waiting, in "*apokaradokia*," *ZNW* 49 (1958): 264–70. Bertram's case was accepted by Schlier, *Römerbrief*, 259; and Ulrich Wilckens, *Römer*, 152. As noted by Gustav Adolf Deissmann, *Light from the Ancient East* (trans. L. R. M. Strachan; Grand Rapids: Baker, 1965), 374 n. 5, a verbal form of the word that lacks any sense of anxiety appears in Polybius, Hist. 18.31, "to expect earnestly *(apokaradokein)* the arrival of Antiochus."

its abusers.[47] (See also Gen 4:10; Deut 4:26; 30:19; 31:28; Josh 24:27.) Paul's idea of the natural world eagerly awaiting its own redemption moves in the direction of modern ecological theory, which is beginning to recapture an ancient view of the world as a living organism; thus, Teilhard de Chardin perceived an inchoate longing in the created order toward higher and higher levels of evolution. In a vision with extraordinary relevance for the modern world, Paul implies that the entire creation waits with bated breath for the emergence and empowerment of those who will take responsibility for its restoration, small groups of the *huioi tou theou* (sons of God),[48] which the mission envisioned in Romans hopes to expand to the end of the known world, to Spain. These converts take the place of Caesar in the imperial propaganda about the golden age, but they employ no weapons to vanquish foes. When Paul speaks of their "revelation/unveiling," there is a clear reference to God's glory advancing in the world through the triumph of the gospel. Persuasion rather than conquest is the means of their transformation. As the children of God are redeemed by the gospel, they begin to regain a rightful dominion over the created world (Gen 1:28–30; Ps 8:5–8); in more modern terms, their altered lifestyle and revised ethics begin to restore the ecological system that had been thrown out of balance by wrongdoing (Rom 1:18–32) and sin (Rom 5–7). In contrast to the civic cult, Paul does not have a magical transformation of nature in view.

The background of Paul's idea of the fall and redemption of nature is surveyed by Donald Gowan, who shows that the apocalyptic writers remain largely within the biblical parameters.[49] But like other biblical scholars, Gowan does not take account of the peculiar kind of Roman new-age ideology that provides the foil for Romans. In Paul's case the avenue of divine action is the conversion of humans rather than their enslavement under a ruler pretending to be a god. So what the creation awaits with eager longing is the emergence of this triumph of divine righteousness (cf. Rom 1:17), which will begin to restore a rightful balance to the creation,

---

47. Olle Christoffersson, *The Earnest Expectation of the Creature: The Flood-Tradition as Matrix of Romans 8:18–2* (Stockholm: Almqvist & Wiksell, 1990), 120.

48. Fitzmyer, *Romans,* 507, states the widely shared consensus: "'The revelation of the sons of God' refers to glorified Christians." Christoffersson's suggestion in *Earnest Expectation,* 120–24, that the "sons of God" are the angelic powers widely discussed in apocalyptic literature, does not comport well with the references to the "sonship" of believers in Rom 8:15 and 23. However, his study helps to highlight the fact that Paul places believers in the role of the redemptive angels of 1 Enoch and elsewhere, or in the immediate context of the Roman civic cult, in the role of Caesar.

49. Donald E. Gowan, "The Fall and Redemption of the Material World in Apocalyptic Literature," *HBT* 7 (1985): 83–103.

overcoming the Adamic legacy of corruption and disorder that fell as a calamitous curse upon the ground (Gen 3:17–19). Paul concentrates on the transformed children of God rather than on specific actions and policies they may be led to follow in carrying out the ethic of transformation (Rom 12:1–2); he assumes that the renewed mind of such groups will be able to discern what God wills for the ecological system. So the eager longing of the creation awaits the appearance of such transformed persons,[50] knowing that the sources of disorder will be addressed by them in due season. Here, as in many other portions of this letter, scholars have refrained from thinking through the implications of Paul's argument because they failed to take the mission context into account. The very barbarians that Rome believed it must subdue in order to bring about the golden age are the persons to whom Paul feels "obligated" (Rom 1:14) to share the gospel that constitutes a new method of global reconciliation (15:7–13).

In Rom 8:20, the explanation of creation's yearning for redemption is provided by allusion to the Genesis story, where the perversion of the originally good and glorious garden commenced. In this myth, it is the progenitor of the entire human race who was responsible for the corruption of the creation, not the enemies of Roman imperialism. The use of the divine passive, "*hypetagē* (was subjected)," points to God's action in response to Adam's fall.[51] In the Genesis account, the divine curse upon the ground resulted in its producing "thorns and thistles," causing chronic frustration symbolized by the "sweat" on the face of Adam's descendants (Gen 3:17–19). In this powerful symbolization, humans trying to play God ended up ruining not only their relations with each other but also their relation to the natural world (cf. Hos. 4:1–3). The Roman myth system claimed the exact opposite: that a ruler who plays god can restore the world to a paradisial condition by his piety and military dominance.

Paul's choice of the term *mataiotēs* (emptiness, vanity, fruitlessness) to depict this situation would have led hearers to think of the somber dictum of Ecclesiastes, which portrays this same dilemma:

---

50. See Bindemann, *Hoffnung der Schöpfung;* and Anton Vögtle, *Das Neue Testament und die Zukunft des Kosmos* (Düsseldorf: Patmos, 1970), 193–96; *Röm 8:19–22: Eine Schöpfungstheologische oder anthropologisch-soteriologische Aussage?* (Gemblaux: Duculet, 1970), 351–66. For a skeptical appraisal of the significance of the cosmological dimension of Paul's argument, see Jörg Baumgarten, *Paulus und die Apokalyptik* (WMANT 44; Neukirchen-Vluyn: Neukirchener Verlag, 1975), 171–74.

51. See the discussion in Wilckens, *Römer,* 154; Murray, *Romans,* 303, refers to this verse as "Paul's commentary on Gen. 3:17, 18." Dunn, *Romans 1–8,* 470, observes that there is "now general agreement" on this point.

"Vanity of vanities," says the Teacher/Preacher,
"vanity of vanities! All is vanity.'" (Eccl 1:2)

This dilemma is more basic than the resultant "corruption" to be mentioned in Rom 8:21.[52] Given the use of *mataioō* (make vain, empty) in Rom 1:21 to describe the frustration and destructiveness of persons or groups who suppress the truth and refuse to recognize God, it seems likely that Paul has in mind the abuse of the natural world by Adam and all of his descendants. The basic idea is that the human refusal to accept limitations ruins the world. By acting out idolatrous desires to have unlimited dominion over the garden, the original purpose of the creation—to express divine goodness (Gen 1:31) and reflect divine glory (Ps 19:1–4)—was emptied.[53] As in Eccl 2:1–17, it is the drive for fame, prestige, and immortal achievement that evacuates the goodness and glory of the creation and piles up endless frustrations in the human interaction with the natural environment, symbolized in Genesis by the "thorns and thistles" (3:18). With such clear allusions to this biblical tradition, Paul's audience could well have thought about how imperial ambitions, military conflicts, and economic exploitation had led to the erosion of the natural environment throughout the Mediterranean world, leaving ruined cities, depleted fields, deforested mountains, and polluted streams as evidence of this universal human vanity. That such vanity in the form of the *pax Romana* had promised the restoration of the age of Saturn appears utterly preposterous in the light of this critical, biblical tradition.

The somewhat awkward qualification that the futility of the nonhuman creation was "*ouch hekousa* (not willingly, not voluntarily)" makes clear that Paul does not subscribe to a gnostic view of the world as innately frustrating and evil. The fall of nature was "not through its own fault"[54] because it is the human race that remains responsible for the defacing of the ecological system. Paul had used this classic term for free will in Phlm

---

52. See Schlier's critique in *Römerbrief,* 260–61, of the exegetical consensus of most ancient and modern commentators, who argue for the essential identity of "vanity" and "corruption." He mentions Ambrosiaster, Theodoret, Augustinus, Thomas Aquinas, Estius, Bisping, H. W. Schmidt, Althaus, Lietzmann, and Michel; to this list one could add Chrysostom, Jülicher, Lipsius, Zahn, Kühl, and others; see Otto Kuss, *Der Römerbrief übersetzt und erklärt* (Regensburg: Pustet, 1957–78), 626.

53. Cranfield, *Romans,* 413, refers to the creation "not being able properly to fulfill the purpose of its existence." Schlier's explanation in *Römerbrief,* 260, is so subtly existential, with the creation absolutizing itself just as humans do, that the causative link between human sin and ecological futility is rendered obscure.

54. Cranfield, *Romans,* 414.

14, describing his preference for the slave owner to act voluntarily rather than under compulsion, "in order that your good deed might not be done out of necessity but out of free will *(kata hekousion)*." Here Paul continues the personified manner of speaking about nature, as if it would have preferred not to participate in the sinful futility caused by Adam and Eve and their descendants. The phrase contrasting "voluntarily" is "*dia ton hypotaxanta, eph' helpidi* ([variant: *ep' elpidi*] on account of the one who subjected it, in hope)," clearly referring to God's curse against the land in response to human sin.[55] We find the same idea derived from Genesis in 4 Ezra 7:11: "And when Adam transgressed my statutes, what had been made was judged." A later rabbi expressed the same idea: "Although things were created in their fulness, when the first man sinned they were corrupted, and they will not come back to their order before Ben Perez [the Messiah] comes."[56] The curse thus remains provisional, awaiting the dawn of a genuinely new age when nature will be restored to its original beauty and glory. Paul used the same expression *ep' elpidi* (in hope/anticipation) in Rom 5:2 with specific reference to overcoming suffering. The "hope" in this passage, to be elaborated in 8:21, is that the human race, which has defaced the world, would be redeemed and begin to participate in removing the curse from the land.[57] Paul's wording makes it absolutely clear that such redemption is a matter of future hope, and not a present political achievement as the Roman civic cult was maintaining.

In Rom 8:21 Paul formulates this hope, that the creation "itself will be set free"[58] from the Adamic distortion. This takes up a significant theme in Jewish prophetism and apocalypticism,[59] which articulate in a contrasting manner some of the themes in the Roman expectation. Isaiah's vision of a messianic future includes both a king who will restore righteousness among humans (Isa 11:4–5) and a restoration of Edenic conditions between animals and humans (Isa 11:6–9; 65:17, 25; 66:22). Jubilees envisions the

---

55. It is implausible to suggest that either Adam or Satan may be identified as the "one subjecting it in hope," because neither can be understood as acting "in hope." See Kuss, *Römerbrief,* 627–28.

56. Cited by Ernst Käsemann, *Commentary on Romans* (trans. E. W. Bromiley; London: SCM; Grand Rapids: Eerdmans, 1980), 233, from Gen. Rab. 12:6.

57. See Franz-J. Leenhardt, *The Epistle of Saint Paul to the Romans: A Commentary* (trans. H. Knight; London: Lutterworth, 1961), 125–26.

58. The emphatic "*kai autē* (also itself)" explicitly includes nature in the redemptive process, rendering implausible C. K. Barrett's comment in *A Commentary on the Epistle to the Romans* (HNTC; 2d ed.; New York: Harper, 1991), 165, that Paul "is not concerned with creation for its own sake."

59. Gowan's survey in "Fall and Redemption," 100–2, concludes that apocalyptic literature echoes but does not extensively develop the biblical theme.

time when "the heavens and the earth shall be renewed" (1:29). First Enoch speaks of regaining access to the "fragrant tree" on the seventh mountain which restores the joy and long life of Eden (chaps. 24–25; see also 91:16–17), while the Testament of Levi anticipates a messianic priest who "shall open the gates of paradise, and shall remove the threatening sword against Adam. And he shall give to the saints to eat from the tree of life, and the spirit of holiness shall be on them" (18:10–11). Fourth Ezra expects the messianic "Man from the Sea" to "deliver his creation" from the perils of violence (13:26). The Sibylline Oracles predicts a time after the day of judgment and the arrival of a just empire, when the earth will once again become "the universal mother who will give to mortals her best fruit in countless store of corn, wine and oil. . . . And the cities shall be full of good things and the fields rich" (3.744–745, 750–751). These oracles reiterate Isaiah's vision of wolves and lambs eating grass together, with no creature harming others (3.788–795).

As we have seen, Paul's version of this Edenic hope features the converted "children of God" (Rom 8:19) in place of the righteous king, priest, or empire whose ministration would overturn the Adamic curse. Although the future tense of the verb Paul selects in verse 21, "*eleutherōthēsetai* (it will be freed)," clearly correlates with the "revelation of the sons of God" in verse 19,[60] the inference is rarely drawn concerning the means by which God intends to restore the natural world. Heinrich Schlier is exceptional in referring to the "responsibility that Christians have not only for themselves but also for the realm of pure creatureliness."[61] Overcoming ecological disorder is depicted here as a divine gift enacted as a result of God's restoration of humanity to its position of rightful dominion, reflecting God's intended glory. Instead of a Caesar with a sunburst about his head, the glory proclaimed by Paul will be shared by every converted person, whether slave or free, male or female, Roman or barbarian. In this passage, as Otto Michel points out, "Bondage stands in opposition to freedom, corruption to glory."[62] In verse 21, the term *phthora* (corruption, decay, destruction) refers to the consequence of the perverse "vanity" of the human race, namely, the disruption and death of natural ecological systems. This occurs in a process that takes a course

---

60. Cranfield, *Romans*, 415.

61. Schlier, *Römerbrief,* 262–63, restricts this responsibility to the arena of a proper existential attitude toward nature, refraining from any discussion of ethical responsibility.

62. Otto Michel, *Der Brief an die Römer* (KEK 4; 14th ed.; Göttingen: Vandenhoeck & Ruprecht, 1978), 268.

of its own, thwarting human efforts at dominion and producing a veritable "bondage to corruption."[63]

A correlative inference is drawn in 8:21b, that the restored creation will serve the purpose of the liberation of the children of God. This is a puzzling reversal, because on the basis of 8:19, it had appeared that the revelation of such liberation on the part of the redeemed would become the divinely appointed agency for the restoration of nature. But if the achievement of "*tēn eleutherian tēs doxēs* (liberation consisting of glory)"[64] is understood in terms of humans regaining a proper dominion over the creation, participating responsibly in the "righteousness of God," whose scope is cosmic (see Rom 1:17), this corollary is understandable. For Paul, it is inconceivable that humans could exercise any absolute form of liberation, related only to themselves.[65] Freedom must be responsibly embodied in the real world as the "new creation" manifests itself in the lives and actions of believers.[66] Again, there are ecological insights that fit this perspective, that no one can be free if the environment is poisoned, that human fulfillment is contextual and cosmic. Murray states the theological corollary, that "the glory of the people of God will be in the context of the restitution of all things" (cf. Acts 3:21).[67] Despite the interpretive difficulties in understanding Rom 8:21b, it provides a barrier against the chronic individualizing of salvation that has marked the tradition of Pauline theology just as it stood against the glorification of Caesar.

In Rom 8:22–23 Paul moves on to place human suffering within the context of the creation's groaning for redemption. "Whereas elsewhere Paul always emphasizes the contradiction between nature and the new

---

63. I take the second genitive in the phrase "*apo tēs douleias tēs phthoras*" as an objective genitive, "from the bondage to corruption," following Lipsius, who refers to corruption as "a ruling power." For an argument in favor of a genitive of quality, see Günther Harder, "*phtheiro ktl,*" *TDNT* 9 (1974): 104; and Leon Morris, *The Epistle to the Romans* (Pillar New Testament Commentary; Grand Rapids: Eerdmans, 1988), 322.

64. See Cranfield's argument in *Romans,* 415–16, against the adjectival construal of "*tēs doxēs (of glory)*"; he wishes to preserve the correspondence with the phrase "bondage to corruption" in 8:21a and to retain the dependence of the genitive "*tōn teknōn* (of the children)" on the adjacent word "glory" rather than on the more distant word "freedom." The genitive "of glory" thus becomes epexegetical, "liberty-resulting-from-glory."

65. See Samuel Vollenweider, *Freiheit als neue Schöpfung: Eine Untersuchung zur Eleutheria bei Paulus und in seiner Umwelt* (FRLANT 147; Göttingen: Vandenhoeck & Ruprecht, 1989), 331–36, 402–6.

66. See Vollenweider's argument in *Freiheit,* 386–88, that freedom in this passage is both a present and a future reality.

67. Murray, *Romans,* 305.

man, here he uncovers a profound correspondence—a common longing that joins 'nature' and the spirit."[68] The wording, *"oidamen gar hoti* (for we know that)" (see 2:2; 3:19) makes clear that Paul assumes the Roman Christ-believers are acquainted with the idea of nature's corruption. It had played a decisive role in the Roman civic cult, as we have seen, and was explained in another way by the Genesis story. The expression *"pasa hē ktisis* (the whole creation)" includes the entire range of animate and inanimate objects on earth and in the heavens. The personification of creation noted earlier is continued in this verse by the birth metaphors of groaning and travailing. These metaphors resonate with Greco-Roman images of Mother Earth. Once again, the personification stands parallel to Roman usage, but in place of nature's joy at its deliverance through Augustus and his successors, Paul hears only agonized groans. The verb *stenazō* (cry out, groan), used here in the compound form of *sustenazō* (cry out, groan together), appears with a similar meaning in Job 31:38–40, where the link established in Gen 3:17–18 between human sin and the groaning of nature provides the basis for Job's protestation of innocence:

> If at any time the land has groaned *(estenazen)* against me, and if its furrows also have mourned together *(eklausan homothymadon),* and if I alone have eaten its yield without payment, and if I have grieved the soul of the owner by expropriation, let nettle grow up instead of wheat, brambles instead of barley! (LXX)

The idea that the earth "languishes," "mourns," and suffers "pollution" under the burden of human exploitation also appears in Isa 24:4–7 and Hos 4:1–3. Within the Roman context, it is important to observe that this mourning is a present reality. Nothing whatsoever remains of the illusion that the golden age has already arrived and that nature "rejoices" in Caesar's victories.

The theme of birth pangs is frequently employed as a metaphor for the painful prospect of divine judgment (Isa 13:8; 21:3; 26:17–18; Jer 4:31; 22:23; Hos 13:13; Mic 4:9–10; 1 Enoch 62:4; 4 Ezra 10:6–16; 1 Thess 5:3). Both the inevitability of punishment and the happy outcome of the establishment of divine justice, sometimes in the form of the messianic era (Mark 13:8; John 16:21), may be conveyed by this metaphor. A Greco-Roman writer can also refer to the regeneration of nature after the groaning of winter's dormancy: "The groaning earth gives birth in travail to what

---

68. Gerd Theissen, *Psychological Aspects of Pauline Theology* (trans. J. P. Galvin; Philadelphia: Fortress, 1987), 333.

has been formed within her?"[69] Paul's usage at this point is somewhat reminiscent of the later rabbinic concept of the "messianic woes,"[70] except that such woes were expected to be intensified in the period just before the coming of the Messiah, and they were anticipated to fall upon humans rather than on the creation as a whole. The exclusive concentration on humans is also visible when birth pangs are used to depict the suffering of the innocent at the hands of the wicked (1QH 3.7–18) or the painful birth of Israel (Isa 66:7–8).

Paul moves beyond this familiar range of usage in two ways, by imagining nature as a whole undergoing such birth pangs, and by the anaphoric reduplication of *syn* (with), that brings the expression "*systenazei kai synōdinei* (groans together and travails together)" into a rhetorically unified expression (Rom 8:22). The first of these verbs recalls the more commonplace reference in Euripides, *Ion* 935: "*hōs systenazein g' oida gennaiōs philois* (indeed, I genuinely know how to groan with friends)." In Paul's formulation the "together" refers to the shared experience of believers and the creation as a whole, both yearning for the future restoration. There is an unparalleled coherence in this expression that combines the suffering of creation from the time of Adam with a metaphor of hope—travail, the agony that leads to a new birth. In Schlier's words, "All of the pain of the creature in the entire world . . . is not a proclamation and beginning of death, but of salvation, and all the sighs of the entire world . . . signify its glorification, the glorification of the 'children of God' in the glory of Christ."[71] Paul views the creation as a holistic, interdependent system with a life and development of its own, yet anticipating appropriate human intervention to counter Adam's fall. The emphatic reference to the "whole" creation and the unique use of the compound verbs with *sus-/syn-* points to the option preferred by Origin, Athanasius, Schlatter, Asmussen, and Lipsius,[72] that human beings along with the rest of creation appear to be included in this groaning. Perhaps it would be better to say that these clues provide rhetorical hints at human participation, which becomes explicit in 8:23.[73] The

---

69. BAGD 793, from Heraclitus Stoicus, *Questiones Homericae* (ed. societatis philologae Bonnensis sodales; Leipzig, 1910), c. 39, p. 58; cited by Fitzmyer, *Romans,* 509, with reference to A.-M. Dubarle, "Le gémissement des créatures dans l'ordre divin du cosmos (Rom 8:19–22)," *RSPT* 38 (1954): 445–65.

70. See Schlier, *Römerbrief,* 263–64; Cranfield, *Romans,* 416.

71. Schlier, *Römerbrief,* 264, referring to Paul Claudel's discussion in *Conversations dans le Loir-et-Cher* (Paris: Gallimand, 1935), 255.

72. See the refutation in Kuss, *Römerbrief,* 629.

73. See F. R. Montgomery Hitchcock, "'Every Creature,' Not 'All Creation' in Romans viii. 22," *ExpT* 8 (1916): 372–83.

mainstream interpretation rejecting this option[74] aims to improve the logic of Paul's argument by making the wording of 8:22 consistent with 8:19, at the expense of denying its rhetorical suggestiveness for the audience. That the groaning of 8:22 lasts "*achri tou nyn* (until now)" echoes the eschatological emphasis of 8:18[75] while including the suffering presently experienced and witnessed in the natural world within the painful legacy of the Fall.[76] If the groaning really lasts "until now," this would exclude the Augustan premise that the golden age had been inaugurated by the Saecular Games of 17 B.C.E., or that Nero had ushered in a "golden age of untroubled peace."

That believers are included in the suffering of creation, the theme of Rom 8:18, is developed in verse 23 with the contrasting formula "*ou monon de, alla kai* (not only, but also)," which serves to eliminate any exceptionalism for those who have the supreme gift of the Spirit. I take the participle "*echontes*" in the simple attributive sense of believers "having" the firstfruits of the Spirit, rather than in a strictly causal[77] or concessive[78] sense. The elimination of any exception is emphatically driven home by the repeated "*autoi . . . kai autoi* (ourselves, . . . even ourselves)," closing the door to the kinds of charismatic enthusiasm Paul had earlier encountered in Thessalonica and Corinth that understood the gift of the Spirit as a form of apotheosis, rendering believers invulnerable to suffering. This concern probably also explains the expression "*tēn aparchēn tou pneumatos* (firstfruits of the Spirit),"[79] a unique Pauline combination of the Hebrew concept

---

74. See Kuss, *Römerbrief,* 629–36; Dunn, *Romans 1–8,* 472.

75. Barrett, *Romans,* 166, and Dunn, *Romans 1–8,* 473, move beyond a verbal echo to contend that this expression conveys a unique eschatological emphasis.

76. See Cranfield, *Romans,* 417; Wilckens, *Römer,* 2:156.

77. Kuss, *Römerbrief,* 638, argues for the causal sense, "because we have the firstfruits," following Gutjahr and Bernard Weiss. Dunn, *Romans 1–8,* 473, accepts this view.

78. Käsemann, *Romans,* 237, follows Jülicher's line in arguing that "Christians do not sigh because they do not yet have the Spirit totally but in spite of the fact that they have him."

79. I feel that the context favors the possessive genitive here, in which the Spirit remains the active force of God within believers, a theme elaborated in 8:26–27. Käsemann's advocacy of an epexegetical genitive (*Romans,* 237) has a similar implication. The active role of the Spirit is downplayed by the theory of the partitive genitive, advocated by Bardenhewer, Bisping, and Lietzmann, implying that the firstfruits is only partially represented by the work of the Spirit; and also downplayed by the theory of a genitive of apposition, advocated by Gutjahr, Kühl, Michel, Bernard Weiss, Zahn, and Kuss, which identifies the present experience of the Spirit as constituting the firstfruits.

of the firstfruits of the harvest to be dedicated to God[80] and the early church's concept of the Spirit as the identifying mark of believers.[81] The odd feature of this expression is that "the relationship of giver and recipient is reversed,"[82] since it is not humans who give the firstfruits to God, but God who bestows them on believers. Although the expression "firstfruits of the Spirit" is highly evocative, with numerous implications,[83] Paul's point is that no matter how charismatically they may be endowed, believers continue to participate in the suffering to which the entire world has been subjected as a result of sin. Christ-believers also "groan," with the expression *en heautois* specifying the arena as being "within ourselves," in the inner life of individual believers, where the tension between the "already" and the "not yet," between the hope of righteousness and the weight of corruption, is most intensely felt. Paul referred in Rom 5:5 to the heart as the locale of the Spirit's action and in 7:21–24 to the inner conflict that will not be completely set aside until the eschaton; he goes on in 8:26–27 to describe how the Spirit sustains believers in the meanwhile within the secret places of their hearts. By associating the charismatic Spirit with human vulnerability, Paul effectively eliminates any project of apotheosis such as he had confronted in Corinth. This is highly relevant for the Roman context, where the city's civic cult centered on the apotheosis of Caesar.

At first glance it is rather puzzling that Paul would refer to "awaiting sonship" as a future fulfillment when he had spoken so clearly in 8:15 of the Spirit confirming the sonship of believers as a present experience. The clue is in his repetition of *apekdechomai* (await), which had been used in 8:19 to refer to awaiting the "revelation of the sons of God."[84] The content of the

---

80. See the extensive discussion in Dunn, *Romans 1–8*, 473, citing Deut 12:6; 26:2; Exod 22:29; 23:19; Lev 2:12; 23:10; Num 15:20; 18:12–13, 30; 2 Chron 31:5; Neh 10:37, 39; Mal 3:8; Jdt 11:13. Whether the association of firstfruits with Pentecost, and of Pentecost with the gift of the Spirit, influenced this expression is possible but not demonstrable.

81. For the somewhat more distant Greco-Roman parallels to the use of *tēn aparchēn* (firstfruits), see Arrian, *Cynegeticus* 33.1; Theopompos 115 (frg. 334); Porphyry, *De abstinentia* 2.61. Fitzmyer, *Romans*, 510, identifies these sources on the basis of Rafal Taubenschlag, *Opera minora* 2 (Warsaw: Pánstwowe Wydawn Naukowe, 1959): 220–21; C. C. Oke, "A Suggestion with Regard to Romans 8:23," *Int* 11 (1957): 455–60; and H. Stuart Jones, "SPILAS—APARCHĒ PNEUMATIKOS" *JTS* 23 (1922) 282–83. The latter infers from the legal use of *aparchē* in Egyptian papyri that it is "the birth-certificate of a free person."

82. Gerhard Delling, "*aparchē*," *TDNT* 1 (1964): 486.

83. See Dunn, *Romans 1–8*, 473–74.

84. This is an instance where the literal language of "sonship" needs to be preserved despite its chauvinistic implications, because if the less offensive term "adoption" is used in 8:15 and 23 as in the NRSV and Dunn, *Romans 1–8*, 452, 474, the link

future hope is that the full and undistorted dominion of God's children will one day manifest itself in the context of a restored creation. In the Roman context, this futurity has decisive significance. Thus the phrase Paul selects to explain this restoration is "*ten apolutrosin tou somatos hemon* (the redemption of our body)," since body is the basis of communicating and interacting with the world.[85] Paul does not hope for "redemption from the body,"[86] or as the peculiar singular reference to "body" seems to suggest, for a resurrection of the body in some individualistic sense of being detached from the creation and its corruptibility,[87] but for a socially transformed corporeality within the context of a transformed creation that is no longer subject to "corruption."[88] The verb *apolutrōsis* ordinarily has a military connotation, referring to the redemption of captives or prisoners of war either by victory or by paying a ransom.[89] In the Roman context only persons with status and means could hope for that kind of redemption; here Paul speaks of all members of the community, who share in the groaning as well as in the future release.[90]

---

with "the revelation of the sons of God" in 8:19 is obscured. The translation "adoption" is in any case a secondary choice, since adoption places a person in the category of sonship. For a discussion of the use of *huiothesia* in the sense of legal adoption, see G. H. R. Horsley, "*kath huiothesian*," *NewDocs* 4 (1987): 173; the reflections of Greek legal practice render implausible Francis Lyall's contention in "Roman Law in the Writings of Paul—Adoption," *JBL* 88 (1969): 458–66, that Paul's usage reflects only Roman practice. In "Petition to a Prefect," *NewDocs* 3 (1982): 16–17, G. H. R. Horsley discusses an alternate term for adoption not used by Paul, *technothesis*, indicating the adoption of a girl.

85. See Robert Jewett, *Paul's Anthropological Terms: A Study of Their Use in Conflict Settings* (AGJU 10; Leiden: Brill, 1971), 218–19, 254–79.

86. See Hans Lietzmann, *An die Römer* (HNT 8; 3d ed.; Tübingen: Mohr Siebeck, 1971), 85.

87. See the discussion of individual resurrection without the cosmic context in Morris, *Romans*, 324. Some of the older commentaries by Beck, Zahn, Nygren, and Schmidt stress the redemption of individual believers from temptation, corruption, and mortality. See the critique in Schlier, *Römerbrief*, 266.

88. See John A. Ziesler, *Paul's Letter to the Romans* (TPINTC; London: SCM; Philadelphia: Trinity Press International, 1989), 222.

89. See Friedrich Büchsel, "*apolutrōsis*," *TDNT* 4 (1967): 351: "to set free for a ransom"; Karl Kertelge, "*apolutrōsis*," *EDNT* 1 (1990): 138: redemption "of prisoners and slaves." The military context is clear in Posidonius, fr. 213.20; Diodorus Siculus 37.5.

90. Kertelge, "*apolutrōsis*," 139, offers an abstraction in place of a contextual explanation that might have arisen out of the consideration of the Roman context: "The completed form of redemption is given when this mortal body is 'further clothed' with that new corporeality which God has prepared for his own (2 Cor 5:1–5; cf.1 Cor 15:37f)."

The "new creation" of 2 Cor 5:17 and Gal 6:15 is clearly in view here, but not merely in the traditional form of an inaccessible theological ideal; the guiding metaphor is provided in Rom 8:19, where the disclosure of rightful, future dominion is announced. Sons of God demonstrate their sonship by exercising the kind of dominion that heals rather than destroys. Although the tension between the "already" and the "not yet" will not be overcome until the Parousia, Paul's purpose is to encourage the Roman church members to begin enacting their sonship right now, in refusing to conform to the fallen age, and resolutely acting rightly toward the groaning creation, of which their bodies are a part. The arena for such action was narrower for the members of Roman house and tenement churches than for later Christian communities; it probably consisted mainly of the spheres of bodily responsibility in work, family, congregational life, and, given the purpose of Romans, the sphere of mission. By participating in the projected Spanish mission, Paul is offering the Romans a concrete opportunity to enact their rightful sonship and contribute to the ultimate restoration of the creation. Given the presumption of powerlessness on the part of the underclass represented by most of the Roman house and tenement churches in a dictatorial society, such prospects would have appeared grandiose and unrealistic if undertaken without the foundation of eschatological hope. However, compared with believing that the Roman gods had already ushered in the golden age through a victorious Caesar, Paul's hope could lead to a far more realistic form of collective responsibility for the creation.

– 2 –

"UNMASKING THE POWERS"

Toward a Postcolonial Analysis of 1 Thessalonians

Abraham Smith

Popularly read for more than a century as the basis for fanciful specula-
tion about a "rapture," 1 Thessalonians has more recently been touted
as a warm, friendly letter that expresses "longing for absent friends" (2:17;
3:6).[1] The standard conceptual apparatus of Pauline studies, however, may
have blocked our view of both the broader context of the letter and of one
of its principal concerns. Once our view is less obstructed, we can see that in
1 Thessalonians Paul was taking an adamant stand against the Roman imperial order. Paul was "unmasking the powers" operative in Thessalonica.[2]

Reading Paul against the Empire: A Postcolonial Move?

Recent scholarship has suggested that Paul be read as opposing the
Roman Empire. Religion and politics were not separate. Paul's diction is
political as well as religious. He understands the movement he is spreading as an alternative to the Roman imperial order, which stands under

---

1. Abraham Malherbe, "Did the Thessalonians Write to Paul?" in *The
Conversation Continues: Studies in Paul and John: In Honor of J. Louis Martyn,* ed.
Robert Fortna and Beverly Gaventa (Nashville: Abingdon, 1990), 249, 250. Cf.
Johannes Schoon-Janβen, "On the Use of Elements of Ancient Epistolography in 1
Thessalonians," in *The Thessalonians Debate: Methodological Discord or
Methodological Synthesis?* ed. Karl P. Donfried and Johannes Beutler (Grand Rapids:
Eerdmans, 2000), 179-93.

2. On the expression, see Walter Wink, *Unmasking the Powers: The Invisible Forces
That Determine Human Existence* (Philadelphia: Fortress, 1986).

God's judgment.[3] First Thessalonians figures prominently in this new scholarship. Key terms such as *parousia* ("coming" or "presence," 2:19; 3:13; 4:15; 5:23); *apantēsis* ("meeting," 4:17) and *asphaleia* ("security," 5:3) were not politically innocuous. Such terms portrayed Jesus' "coming" or "return" as that of an emperor greeted by a ceremonial delegation that pours out of the city to meet him (4:14–18).[4] In Paul's view the grand ceremonial Parousia of the Lord is "an event that will shatter the false peace and security of the Roman establishment."[5] The city officials of Thessalonica cultivated Roman beneficence.[6] But in an allusion to the official propaganda of the *pax Romana*, its "peace and security," Paul focuses on the eschatological battle in which God will bring the imperial order under judgment (1 Thess 5:3, 8).[7] With an allusion to the prophecy of Isa 59:17, Paul suggests that the role once reserved for God as a warrior seeking the restoration of creation is now transferred to his Thessalonian assembly in their resistance to the Roman imperial order.[8]

This recent scholarship on Paul, including the essays on 1 Thessalonians, opens toward a postcolonial analysis of Paul.[9] With roots in the earlier work of W. E. B. DuBois, many artists of the Harlem Renaissance, C. L. R. James, and Frantz Fanon, the postcolonial criticism of Chinua Achebe, Wole Soyinka, Wilson Harris, and many others has received more theoretical formulation recently by Edward Said, Gayatri Spivak, and Homi Bhabha. Generally speaking, postcolonial analysis examines the *historical* and *discursive* ways in which the colonial or imperial powers seek to subdue other peoples, and the *historical* and *discursive* means available to subjected

---

3. Richard A. Horsley, "General Introduction," in *Paul and Empire: Religion and Power in Roman Imperial Society* (ed. R. A. Horsley; Harrisburg, Pa.: Trinity Press International, 1997), 1–8. On the inseparability of politics and religion in the ancient world, as in Philo, see Dieter Georgi, *Theocracy in Paul's Praxis and Theology*, trans. David Green (Minneapolis: Fortress, 1991), 14. On the communal nature of salvation, see Georgi, 20, 29.

4. Helmut Koester, "Imperial Ideology and Paul's Eschatology in 1 Thessalonians," in *Paul and Empire* (ed. Horsley), 158–66; cf. Helmut Koester, "From Paul's Eschatology to the Apocalyptic Schemata of 2 Thessalonians," in *The Thessalonian Correspondence*, ed. Raymond F. Collins (Leuven: University Press, 1990), 446.

5. H. Koester, "From Paul's Eschatology," 447.

6. Karl P. Donfried, "The Imperial Cults of Thessalonica and Political Conflict in 1 Thessalonians," in *Paul and Empire* (ed. Horsley), 215–23.

7. Georgi, *Theocracy*, 28.

8. Ibid., 27.

9. Postcolonial studies is a broad umbrella term for many types of studies across a wide range of periods, places, persons, and practices, as discussed by Bart Moore-Gilbert, *Post-Colonial Theory: Contexts, Practices, Politics* (London: Verso, 1997).

peoples to resist such domination. The recent work on 1 Thessalonians and this essay represent some first steps toward a postcolonial analysis insofar as we examine *historical* and *discursive* ways in which the Roman Empire sought to subdue the Jewish people, including those small "spin-off" communities that Paul helped form in cities of the eastern Mediterranean.[10] From postcolonial criticism biblical scholars can learn to trace the shadow of the Empire within and beyond biblical texts. Postcolonial critics insist that besides tracing the historical forms of colonialism, it is crucial to appreciate also the discursive forms of colonialism that "imply a relation of structural domination."[11]

Moreover, a closer look at Paul's writings may reveal the *historical* and *discursive* means available to Paul as he resisted the Empire. Thus, a postcolonial analysis may help us both to recover "submerged history" and to reread 1 Thessalonians against some of the conventions of power in the Roman imperial world. The analysis below unfolds in three steps. First, to explore the historical and discursive means through which Paul could resist the Roman imperial order, it is necessary to situate Paul in a larger context of resistance to the Empire. Next, we must appreciate the pro-Roman forces in the Greco-Roman world, mainly the local urban aristocracies and provincial elites, with which resistance had to contend, with a focus on Judea and Thessalonica. Finally, we examine two key passages to see how Paul sharply criticized pro-Roman stances of those forces that most likely bore on the Thessalonians. In 1 Thess 2:13–16 and 5:1–11, in particular, Paul was criticizing the controlling aristocracy of Thessalonica for their accommodation to the Roman imperial order and their persecution of his assembly in Thessalonica. First Thessalonians 2:13–16 is not an interpolation, but Paul's critique of the dominating pro-Roman elite in Thessalonica through an analogy with the pro-Roman priestly aristocracy

---

10. Postcolonial criticism has been criticized on a variety of fronts, especially for its perpetuation of the anti-foundationalist perspectives of poststructuralism (à la Derrida and Foucault), for the apparent lack of appreciation for political agency in some brands of postcolonialism, and the aversion to any "totalizing theory" or "grand narrative." See Rosalind O'Hanlon and David Washbrook, "After Orientalism: Culture, Criticism, and Politics in the Third World," in *Comparative Studies in Society and History* 34 (1992): 141–67. For self-criticism by a postcolonial critic, see Tejumola Olaniyan, "On 'Post-Colonial Discourse': An Introduction," *Callaloo* 16 (1993): 743–49. Critics of postcolonial discourse are not opposed to "the emancipation of previously submerged colonial histories and identities" (O'Hanlon and Washbrook, 141). On the use of the work of Michel Foucault, see Abraham Smith, "'I Saw the Book Talk': A Cultural Studies Approach to the Ethics of an African American Biblical Hermeneutics," *Semeia* 77 (1997): 115–38.

11. Laura E. Donaldson, "Postcolonialism and Biblical Reading: An Introduction," *Semeia* 75 (1996): 3.

in Judea. First Thessalonians 5:1–11 unmasks the supposed "peace and security" offered by Roman power in the light of the eschatological events that are about to bring permanent "peace and security" for Paul's assembly, which he calls to maintain its corporate solidarity in resistance to the dominant imperial order.

Postcolonial analysis also exposes not only established Western scholarship's separation of politics from religion, but also the peculiar Christian-centric conceptual apparatus with which it operates.[12] Like most other academic fields, NT studies originated in western Europe during the heyday of its imperial domination of other peoples; hence, its orientation and conceptual apparatus often betray its Western imperial origins.[13] It has thus been difficult for Western biblical scholarship to become critically aware of the shadow that European empire casts across biblical criticism itself, particularly the distinctively Christian, or more narrowly, Protestant character of its questions, concepts, and solutions.[14] The postcolonial exposure of Western biblical studies will be more implicit than explicit here, given the limitations of space.

Historical and Discursive Resistance to Roman Power: Judeans and Philosophers

In both historical and discursive ways, Paul's contemporaries resisted Rome, and Paul would likely have drawn on similar social and literary conventions to indicate his opposition to the Roman government. Having spent time in Jerusalem and Judea prior to his commissioning as an apostle of Jesus Christ, Paul would surely have been familiar with various historical and discursive forms of resistance in Judea. And as a Jew who was widely traveled in the cities of the eastern Roman Empire, he seems likely to have been familiar also with various forms of discursive resistance among Hellenistic philosophers. If some scholars and popular interpreters of Paul have seen him as an accommodationist or as one who simply chose

---

12. S. R. F. Price, *Rituals and Power: The Roman Imperial Cult in Asia Minor* (Cambridge: Cambridge University Press, 1984), 9, 15, points to the pitfalls of interpreting ancient rituals of power with narrow Christianizing assumptions—as if the imperial ruler cult were not only not religious but also had nothing to do with imperial power.

13. On these larger imperialistic influences and socioreligious movements, see Fernando Segovia, "Biblical Criticism and Postcolonial Studies: Toward a Postcolonial Optic," in *The Postcolonial Bible*, ed. R. S. Sugirtharajah (Sheffield: Sheffield Academic, 1998), 58–60.

14. For an excellent critique of modern scholarship on Paul, see Shawn Kelley, *Racializing Jesus: Race, Ideology and the Formation of Modern Biblical Scholarship* (London: Routledge, 2002).

not to resist the ruling powers of his day, perhaps such readings are rooted in a failure to situate Paul's writings within the resistance conventions of the time.[15] While the reconstruction of the resistance and conventions given here cannot be exhaustive, they are intended to intimate *some* of the resistance means known both to Paul and his assemblies.

The Judean-Israelite Tradition of Resistance

The tradition of Israelite resistance to foreign rule was as old as origins of the people itself. Israel's foundational movement arose out of "God's liberation of Israel from bondage to the pharaoh in Egypt."[16] Subsequent retellings of the story (as, e.g., in Deutero-Isaiah) and the celebration of Passover kept the tradition alive.[17] It is little wonder that the popular prophetic movements that emerged shortly after Jesus' crucifixion modeled themselves on the exodus, Jordan, or Jericho traditions. In 44 C.E., Theudas's promise that the waters of the Jordan would part was likely an attempt to reenact deliverance on analogy with the exodus. Later, an unnamed prophet from Egypt led a popular movement that reenacted "the battle of Jericho" led by Joshua.[18] A more serious challenge to Roman rule in Judea than these nonviolent popular prophetic movements were the revolts that took the form of popular messianic movements in 4 B.C.E., following the death of Herod, and again as part of the "Jewish War" in 66–70 C.E. These resemble the "native revolts" among the other peoples subjected by the Romans, in northern Italy, Sardinia, Spain, Gaul, Africa, Britain, and even Macedonia-Thrace.[19]

Even scribal circles generated protests and movements against Roman rule in Judea. While these (e.g., the covenanters at Qumran, some Jerusalem sages and their students, and "the Fourth Philosophy") were all nonviolent prior to the 50s C.E.,[20] in the 50s and 60s the scribal-led Sicarii adopted terrorist tactics (Josephus, *Jewish War*, 7.253–255), apparently in

---

15. For critiques of these readings of Paul, see Neil Elliott, *Liberating Paul: The Justice of God and the Politics of the Apostle* (Maryknoll, N.Y.: Orbis, 1994), 3–90.

16. Richard A. Horsley, *Jesus and Empire: The Kingdom of God and the New World Disorder* (Minneapolis: Fortress, 2002), 38.

17. See, e.g., Bernhard W. Anderson, "Exodus Typology in Second Isaiah," in B. W. Anderson and W. Harrelson, eds., *Essays in Honor of James Muilenburg* (New York: Harper, 1962), 177–95.

18. Horsley, *Jesus and Empire*, 52.

19. See Stephen L. Dyson, "Native Revolt Patterns in the Roman Empire," *ANRW* 2.3 (1975): 138–75.

20. On the anti-Roman sentiment in the Qumran literature, see Geza Vermes, *Discovery in the Judean Desert* (New York: Desclee, 1956), 79–85. Cf. the Qumran War Rule (1QM 11.8; 13.2; 15.1; 18.3; 19.29).

response to the increasingly repressive measures taken by the Roman governors.[21] The Sicarii carried out assassinations and took hostages among the Judean aristocracy, who were collaborating in Roman rule.

Paul's ministry in Thessalonica took place just as political conflict intensified in Judea. While Paul in no way shared the violent tactics of the Sicarii, he can hardly be interpreted as acquiescent in the Roman imperial order or socially conservative. Like others before him, Paul drew *discursively* on the Israelite tradition of resistance in his appropriation of Scripture. While Paul's use of Scripture was varied, it is clear that he at least read "Scripture as a vast network of typological pre-figurations of himself and his communities."[22] Paul understood his call and commission to the Gentiles within the prophetic tradition, for his description of his call and commission in Gal 1:15 is reminiscent of Isa 49:1–6 and Jer 1:4–5.[23] And as Jeremiah (11:20; 12:3) spoke of God as one who "tests the heart," Paul speaks of God as one "who tests our hearts" (1 Thess 2:4). It is also likely that Paul drew his understanding of the "gospel" (cf. Rom 10:15–16) from Deutero-Isaiah, a text that repeatedly speaks about the "good news" of God's salvation in its LXX (Septuagint) form (cf. Isa 52:7; 61:1).[24] Perhaps Paul saw his collection for the saints in Jerusalem as a fulfillment of the Isaianic "prediction that Gentiles would bring their gifts (60:11) in that final eschatological grand procession" of the last days.[25] Likewise, perhaps Paul's repeated diction of consolation (1 Thess 4:18; 5:11; 2 Cor 1:3–7) is an echo of that theme in Isa 40:1–11; 57:18.[26] Furthermore, Paul's construal of God's action of reconciliation, as announced in "new creation" diction of 2 Cor 5:17–6:2, clearly echoes the "second exodus/restoration/new creation perspective" of Isa 43:18–19, which was designed to encourage the exiles.[27]

---

21. Horsley, *Jesus and Empire*, 43.

22. Richard Hays, "The Role of Scripture in Paul's Ethics," in *Theology and Ethics in Paul and His Interpreters: Essays in Honor of Victor Paul Furnish*, ed. Eugene H. Lovering Jr. and Jerry Sumney (Nashville: Abingdon, 1996), 41.

23. See J. Christiaan Beker, *Paul the Apostle: The Triumph of God in Life and Thought* (Philadelphia: Fortress, 1982), 115. Cf. Hays, "Role of Scripture," 33.

24. Cf. Beker, *Paul the Apostle*, 116.

25. Calvin Roetzel, *Paul, The Man and the Myth* (Minneapolis: Fortress, 1999), 63.

26. Ibid., 79. Cf. Karl L. Donfried, "The Epistolary and Rhetorical Context of 1 Thessalonians 2:1–12," in *The Thessalonians Debate: Methodological Discord or Methodological Synthesis?* ed. Karl P. Donfried and Johannes Beutler (Grand Rapids: Eerdmans, 2000), 49.

27. S. Hafemann, "Paul's Argument from the Old Testament on 2 Cor 1–9: The Salvation-History/Restoration Structure of Paul's Apologetic," in *The Corinthian Correspondence*, ed. R. Bieringer (Leuven: University Press, 1996), 301 n. 46. On "new creation," also cf. Isa 65:17–25; 66:22–23, as noted in Hays, "Role of Scripture," 34.

If Paul is drawing on the prophetic tradition and especially Deutero-Isaiah in 1 Thessalonians and throughout his corpus, he assuredly is writing resistance literature. That is, Paul reads events in light of an eschatological vision of God bringing a new era of justice for those who have faced alienation and oppression. Paul's language of consolation in 1 Thessalonians then is not simply another reminder of Paul's friendliness toward the Thessalonians. Rather, it is an affirmation of the consolation and salvation of God in the tradition of words once spoken to oppressed exiles.

Resistance and Alternative Communities among the Philosophies

Ever since the ascent of Hellenistic kings, power had been a keen concern in the Mediterranean world. The Greek cities in which Paul conducted his mission sought power both in gods and in godlike heroes, whether local benefactors or foreign saviors who provided resources for urban buildings and public welfare. Some people, however, formed alternative communities. As alternative communities with wider connections than the usual local voluntary associations, Jewish *synagōgai* and Paul's *ekklēsiai* were similar to certain philosophies "whose promotion of good living as well as right thinking, philanthropy as well as piety, could involve sharp criticism of the ruling classes."[28] The Jewish way of life was classified as philosophy, and for apologetic reasons, some Jews adopted the classification themselves. Paul also shared much with certain philosophers of his age. There is evidence that the Cynics, Stoics, Pythagoreans, Epicureans, and others of the period embraced the psychagogic tradition of exhortation designed to transform a person. Recent comparisons of the Pauline communities with Epicurean communities of late republican times suggest not a genetic relationship but a common "communal pattern of mutual participation by community members in exhortation, edification, and correction."[29] In both Pauline and Epicurean communities, a wide variety of persons were admitted, including slaves and women, and in both, the goal was character formation in accordance with communal unity ideals.[30] Neophytes could acquire a teacher status and thus use the same reformatory ethic to help others,[31] and leaders recognized the different conditions of those in their respective communities and tailored their hortatory means to fit the varying dispositions of their charges.[32]

---

28. S. G. Wilson, "Voluntary Associations: An Overview," in *Voluntary Associations in the Graeco-Roman World,* ed. John S. Kloppenborg and Stephen G. Wilson (London: Routledge, 1996), 3.

29. Clarence Glad, *Paul and Philodemus: Adaptability in Epicurus and Early Christian Psychagogy* (Leiden: Brill, 1995), 7.

30. Ibid., 8.

31. Ibid., 105.

32. Ibid., 137-52. See Seneca, *Epistles* 52.3–4.

With respect to the dominant cultural ethos of the time, the net effect of the alternative communities was to create a viable, oppositional network of shared values across time and space. These alternative communities often shifted the loyalty of their constituents from their traditional families to the new group or philosophy.[33] Members of the groups frequently denounced the former honor they received when they achieved wealth and reputation.

Thus, Paul's creation of a network of assemblies was an *historical* means of resisting the Roman Empire. That is, the network functioned like an alternative movement designed to create solidarity in a distinctive set of values. Of course, this distinctive set of values should easily be recognized in light of Paul's apocalyptic gospel, for that gospel was not politically innocuous but was a fundamental "critique of this age and its values."[34] To the extent that the Roman government was a part of "this age," it also was subject to the critique of Paul's gospel.

Given the repressive character of the imperial order, it is not difficult to imagine that Paul would find subtle or indirect ways to direct his critique in his writings. And given the afflictions Paul notes that he experienced in Philippi (1 Thess 2:2), moreover, one could expect him to use indirect critique in order not to offend the Roman authorities in a blunt fashion.[35] Yet, Paul's production of a "brotherhood that extend[ed] beyond the city, throughout Macedonia, Achaia, and beyond (1:8–9)" constituted a strategy of resistance to the dominant order. That is, he urged all the members of the "brotherhood," his assemblies such as the one in Thessalonica, to refuse to "participate in the intricate web of local cults that gave sacred legitimation to the Empire."[36]

The *Philoromanoi* (Pro-Roman Elites)

Rome systematically established control of the ancient Mediterranean by both military conquest and self-justifying ideology.[37] After Rome successfully

---

33. Carolyn Osiek, "The Family in Early Christianity: 'Family Values' Revisited," *CBQ* 58 (1996): 7.

34. J. Paul Sampley, *Walking between the Times: Paul's Moral Reasoning* (Minneapolis: Fortress, 1991), 108.

35. See discussion of Paul's use of indirect speech by J. Paul Sampley, "'The Weak and Strong,' Paul's Careful and Crafty Rhetorical Strategy in Romans 14:1–15:13," in *The Social World of the First Christians: Studies in Honor of Wayne A. Meeks,* ed. L. M. White and O. L. Yarbrough (Minneapolis: Fortress, 1994), 43–46. Cf. Frederick Ahl, "The Art of Safe Criticism in Greece and Rome," *American Journal of Philology* 105 (1984): 174–208. What deserves attention now is Paul's use of indirect speech as a form of resistance.

36. Elliott, *Liberating Paul*, 195.

37. On Rome's establishment of its Empire, see Erich S. Gruen, *Studies in Greek Culture and Roman Policy* (Leiden: Brill, 1990), esp. 129, 138; and Peter K. Nelson,

campaigned against the Greek cities of southern Italy and Sicily, it defeated Carthage in a series of wars. Rome then expanded to the north and west, and advanced an eastern campaign that subdued Asia Minor, Armenia, and Syria. Roman warlords accrued untold sums of wealth. By the time of the Principate, Rome exercised political and economic *imperium* over the Mediterranean world and beyond.

Crucial for the justification of its imperial rule from Augustus onward were its divine expansionist claims. Virgil's *Aeneid* justified Rome's right to rule the world (279). Virgil does not simply portray Aeneas, one of the heroes of the Trojan War, as a wanderer like Odysseus; he also places the protagonist in a war to win Latium, from which Rome was established. Furthermore, Aeneas is "the executor of a divine universal plan which did not become visible until Virgil's time," in the reign of Augustus.[38] Moreover, Virgil portrays Augustus' reign as the new reign of Saturn, the Roman equivalent of Kronos, the ruler of the golden age (first mentioned in Hesiod's *Works and Days*).[39] Thus, in the *Aeneid,* Rome is depicted as divinely ordained to be ruler of the world,[40] and Augustus is depicted as the long-awaited restorer of peace (Virgil, *Aeneid* 3; Livy 1.1–2.6).

In a rapidly escalating process that began with Augustus' accession to power, the cities and provincial assemblies of Greek and Asia lavished numerous honors in multiple forms on the Roman emperors. In the form of decrees, coin issues, temples, statues, and public festivals, the emperors were honored by the subjects cities, all at their own initiative.[41] Though

---

Leadership and Discipleship: A Study of Luke 22:24–30 (Atlanta: Scholars, 1994), esp. 28–29.

38. Albrecht Dihle, *Greek and Latin Literature of the Roman Empire: From Augustus to Justinian,* trans. Manfred Malzahn (London: Routledge, 1994), 32.

39. On Virgil's adoption of Hesiod's "Ages of Metal" myth and the "Life under Kronos" myth from another Greek tradition, see Andrew Wallace-Hadrill, "The Golden Age and Sin in Augustan Ideology," *Past and Present* 97 (1982): 20. Virgil first used the golden-age theme in his fourth *Eclogue,* in a period of civil unrest. Later, when Octavian became the undisputed ruler of Rome, Virgil composed *Georgics,* which chanted a similar theme and posited Augustus as a "potential savior" (Wallace-Hadrill, 20). Then, when Augustus actually gained a tight grip on Rome, Virgil composed the *Aeneid,* which returned yet again to the *Eclogue* theme and signaled "a confident recognition of Augustus as savior" (Wallace-Hadrill, 22). Also, Wallace-Hadrill (25) notes how the golden-age theme is repeated in Nero's imperial reign through the writings of Seneca and Calpurnius Siculus.

40. Dionysius of Halicarnassus gives a similar portrait of Rome as divinely ordained to rule the world. See John T. Squires, *The Plan of God in Luke–Acts* (Cambridge: Cambridge University Press, 1993), 41.

41. See esp. S. R. F. Price, *Rituals and Power: The Roman Imperial Cult in Asia Minor* (Cambridge: Cambridge University Press, 1984); excerpts in Richard A. Horsley, "Introduction to the Gospel of Imperial Salvation," in *Paul and Empire* (ed. Horsley), 20.

anti-imperial sentiment was not uncommon, Rome's subjects, led by the local elite, accommodated themselves to Roman rule because of Rome's unavoidable presence and power.

In Judea in particular, where the movement Paul had joined originated, the ruling priestly elite acceded to Rome's domination as long as "there was no specific interference in Jewish practices of worship and laws."[42] The ruling elite sought to accommodate themselves to the Romans, moreover, even as they aimed to maintain Jewish traditions. The Idumaeans Antipater and his son Herod, principal administrator and king, respectively, of greater Judea in the first-century B.C.E., "ingratiated themselves with prominent Romans such as Julius Caesar, Mark Antony and Octavian."[43] The historian Josephus, a wealthy priest and client of the Flavian emperors, commends the Romans in lavish terms: "Without God's aid so vast an Empire could never have been built up" (*Jewish War* 2.390–391). Indeed, in its rebellion the Jerusalem populace "was warring not against the Romans only, but also against God" (*Jewish War* 5.378; cf. 5.9.3; 5.9.4; 6.2.1).[44] Correspondingly, he blames not the Romans but the Sicarii (among others) for the war against Rome and the destruction of the Jerusalem temple (*Jewish War* 1.27; 5.444; 6.251). "They outdo each other in acts of impiety toward God and injustice to their neighbors, . . . oppressing the masses, . . . bent on tyranny. . . . Violence, . . . plundering, . . . lawlessness and cruelty, . . . no word unspoken to insult, no deed untried to ruin" (*Jewish War* 7.8.1). Accommodationist practices also included violent repression of persons or groups deemed subversive.[45] New Testament literature itself provides evidence of such repressive acts by the rulers of Judea and Galilee, such as the arrest and beheading of John the Baptist and the arrest of Peter and the stoning of Stephen and James in Jerusalem. Herod Antipas likely killed John the Baptist, at least according to Josephus, because he feared "that John's followers might turn to insurrection *stasis*" (*Jewish Antiquities* 18.5.2 [116–119]).[46]

---

42. David M. Rhoads, *Israel in Revolution, 6-74* C.E.*: A Political History Based on the Writings of Josephus* (Philadelphia: Fortress, 1976), 11.

43. Richard A. Horsley, "Introduction to Patronage, Priesthoods, and Power," in *Paul and Empire* (ed. Horsley), 93.

44. On Josephus as Roman client and historian, see Per Bilde, *Flavius Josephus between Jerusalem and Rome: His Life, His Works, and Their Importance* (Sheffield: JSOT, 1998). Josephus' *Jewish War*, written to persuade Jews in the East not to resist Rome in the aftermath of the Roman reconquest of Judea, was commissioned by the emperor Titus.

45. See Richard A. Horsley, "Popular Prophetic Movements at the Time of Jesus: Their Principal Features and Social Origins," *JSNT* 26 (1986): 3–27.

46. David Fiensy, "Leaders of Mass Movements and the Leader of the Jesus Movement," *JSNT* 74 (1999): 15.

With regard to Macedonia Livy gives the account of Onesimus, a Macedonian and a pro-Roman,[47] whose speech to the Roman Senate castigates Perseus for not abiding by his father's treaty with Rome (44.16.5). This is the same Perseus (the son of Philip V) who lost the decisive battle of the Third Macedonian War with Rome, the battle at Pydna, which led to the Macedonian settlement or the division of Macedonia into four republics in 167 B.C.E.

By mid-first century B.C.E. the aristocratic rulers in Thessalonica, the provincial capital of Macedonia, cultivated Roman favor and beneficence. Despite occasional anti-Roman revolts by other Macedonians,[48] there is ample literary, numismatic, epigraphic, and statuary evidence for a rich history of honors given to the Romans by the city of Thessalonica and particular figures of wealth and power.[49] A Thessalonian inscription praises Metellus, who had quashed the revolt of the Macedonians, as a "savior" *(sōtēr)*. Another inscription honors the quaestor C. Servilius Caepio as "savior." A series of coins praises Antony and Octavian and commemorates the city's "liberation" through Antony's defeat of Brutus in 42 B.C.E. Thessalonica commemorated Antony's victory as the inauguration of a new era, complete with celebratory games. After the battle of Actium (31 B.C.E.), the city issued coinage honoring the deification of Julius. While Augustus is not deified on the coins, the coins juxtapose him with his father, and thus the issue suggests the "Thessalonians' awareness of the Imperator's status as *divi filius* [son of a God]." Some of Augustus' successors (from Gaius to Commodus) also appear on the city's coins. A partial statue of Augustus survives from the Claudian period. One inscription indicates the presence of a temple of Caesar, while others praise "Roman benefactors" or Roma in association with Roman benefactors. The inscription praising the first-century Thracian prince Rhoimetalus II, as priest and *agonothete* (judge of public games) of the Imperator Caesar Augustus, suggests that the Thessalonians were actively cultivating the patronage of the emperor and imperial figures in seeking political leverage.

---

47. On the term *philoromanoi,* see Douglas R. Edwards, *Religion and Power: Pagans, Jews, and Christians in the Greek East* (New York: Oxford University, 1996), 18.

48. Dyson, "Native Revolt Patterns,"169–70, mentions several revolts in late Republican or early imperial times.

49. Documentation for the following evidence is mainly in Holland Lee Hendrix, "Thessalonicans Honor Romans," (diss., Harvard University, 1984; on microfilm, Ann Arbor, Mich.: UMI, 1997), respectively, on 266, 156, 172, 198, 135, 192, 315, 37; Hendrix, "Benefactor/Patron Networks in the Urban Environment: Evidence from Thessalonica," *Semeia* 56 (1992): 50; Holland Lee Hendrix, "Archaeology and Eschatology," in *The Future of Early Christianity: Essays in Honor of Helmut Koester* (ed. Birger A. Pearson et al; Minneapolis: Fortress, 1991), 117; Raymond F. Collins, *The Birth of the New Testament: The Origin and Development of the First Christian Generation* (New York: Crossroad, 1993), 6.

This abundant evidence of their active cultivation of Roman power makes clear that the dominant Thessalonian aristocracy, like its counterpart in Judea, were the local instruments of the Roman order. It is critical for us to realize how visible the Roman imperial ideology would have been as a part of the everyday world of the Thessalonians when we read 1 Thessalonians.

Paul's Criticism of the Thessalonian Aristocracy

When read against the clear evidence that the aristocratic rulers of both Judea and Thessalonica were strongly pro-Roman and, indeed, the local instruments of the Roman imperial order, 1 Thess 2:13–16 and 1 Thess 5:1–11 appear to be Paul's encouragement of resistance to that imperial order.

First Thessalonians 2:13–16

Traditional readings of 1 Thess 2:13–16 hardly mention the Romans at all despite the fact that, as we have seen, the Roman imperial presence was visible everywhere in Thessalonica.[50] Indeed, the interpretation of this passage is mired in debate over whether it is an interpolation or an original part of the letter.[51] While the debate cannot be fully reviewed or settled in this essay, manuscript evidence supports the originality of the passage, and reasonable arguments can be given on other grounds—formal or theological— for its authenticity. Formally, the repetition of a thanksgiving notice (cf. 1:2; 2:13) is not problematic because the passage in question appears to repeat

---

50. The exception is the case when some scholars interpret an act of the Romans against the Jews (cf. Suetonius, *Claudius* 25.4) as the wrath of God (1 Thess 2:16). E. Bammel, "Judenverfolgung und Naherwartung," *ZTK* 56 (1959): 249–315; Robert Jewett, *The Thessalonian Correspondence: Pauline Rhetoric and Millenarian Piety* (Philadelphia: Fortress, 1986), 37–38. Cf. Josephus, *Jewish Antiquities,* 20.112; *Jewish War,* 2.224–27.

51. The earliest supporters of an interpolation hypothesis are catalogued in Werner Kümmel's "Das literarische und geschichtliche Problem des ersten Thessalonicherbriefes," in *Neotestamentica et patristica: Eine Freundesgabe, Herrn Professor Dr. Oscar Cullmann zu seinem 60. Geburtstag überreicht* (Novum Testamentum Suppl. 6; Leiden: Brill, 1962), 220–21. The most notable recent advocate is Birger Pearson, "1 Thessalonians 2:13–16: A Deutero-Pauline Interpolation," *HTR* 64 (1971): 79–94. Pearson's argument that 1 Thess 2:13–16 is an interpolation has three pivotal bases: (1) an historical one, the presumption of the destruction of the temple in 70 C.E. as the event of the wrath in 1 Thess 2:16 (94); (2) a theological one, the presumption that Paul could not have written an anti-Jewish polemic (85); and (3) a formal one, the apparent disruption that 1 Thess 2:13–16 causes between 2:12 and 2:17 (88–91). For a critique of Pearson's position, see Karl P. Donfried, "Paul and Judaism: 1 Thessalonians as a Test Case," *Int* 38 (1984): 242–53.

and amplify the earlier emphasis on imitation of suffering (1:6; 2:14), with both passages ending on a note about the wrath of God (1:10; 2:16).[52]

Theologically, some doubt that Paul could have written a passage with an anti-Jewish valence. There are at least four counterarguments to this notion. First, 2:14–16 is not directed toward all Jews, just some.[53] Second, debate and conflict between various Judean groups and movements of Jews (or between Judean groups and their rulers) was often intense in Roman times (e.g., Josephus, *Jewish Antiquities* 1.15.91; Philo *Cherubim* 17), even at points leading to violence (Josephus, *Jewish War* 1.4.3; 1.7.5; 1.29.1; 2.1.3; 2.3.1); this passage must be understood precisely in this context.[54] Third, the passage does not conflict with Romans 11, "where far from suggesting the final judgment of the Jews, [Paul] speaks concerning the continuing validity of God's covenant with them and indeed of their eventual salvation."[55] Not only must Romans be read for its own situation, but in any respect, Paul's reference to "some Jews" is an analogy designed to speak about the character of the Gentiles in Thessalonica who cause suffering for Paul's assembly.[56] Fourth, any specific referencing of "the wrath"

---

52. On 1 Thess 2:13–16 as an amplification of 1:2–10, see F. F. Bruce, *1 and 2 Thessalonians* (Word Biblical Commentary 35; ed. Ralph P. Martin; Waco, Tx.: Word, 1982), 44. On amplification, the author of *Ad Herennium* (4.54–56) says:

> Refining consists in dwelling on the same topic and yet seeming to say something ever new. It is accomplished in two ways: by merely repeating the same idea, or descanting upon it. We shall not repeat the same thing precisely—for that, to be sure, would weary the hearer and not refine the idea—but with changes. Our changes will be of three kinds: in the words, in the delivery, and in the treatment. Our changes will be verbal when, having expressed the idea once, we repeat it once again or oftener in other, equivalent terms.

See also Cicero, *Orator* 63.212; Dionysius of Halicarnassus, *Demosthenes* 48.

53. See Frank Gilliard, "The Problem of the Anti-Semitic Comma between 1 Thessalonians 2:14 and 15," *NTS* 35 (1989): 481–502. Cf. W. D. Davies, "Paul and the People of Israel," *NTS* 24 (1977): 6–9; Willi Marxsen, *Der erste Brief an die Thessalonicher* (Zürich: Theologischer Verlag, 1979), 149.

54. Luke Timothy Johnson, "The New Testament's Anti-Jewish Slander and the Conventions of Ancient Polemic," *Journal of Biblical Literature* 108 (1989): 419–41; Donald Hagner, "Paul's Quarrel with Judaism," in *Anti-Semitism and Christianity: Issues of Polemic and Faith*, ed. Craig A. Evans and Donald A. Hagner (Minneapolis: Fortress, 1993), 130–36. It is necessary to consider critically Josephus' defensive establishment viewpoint and sharp castigation of dissenting or disruptive groups.

55. Hagner, "Paul's Quarrel with Judaism," 131.

56. Abraham Smith, *Comfort One Another: Reconstructing the Rhetoric and Audience of 1 Thessalonians* (Louisville, Ky.: Westminster John Knox, 1995), 35–37.

to the (later) destruction of the temple or a massacre or something else is highly speculative.[57]

Yet, the debate likely lingers because the approach to Paul on either side of the debate examines Paul's statement in this passage so *narrowly*, that is, only with reference to (other) Jews and without considering the larger context in the Roman Empire. While the tragic history of anti-Semitism requires that we never bring closure to any scriptural passage that has been used by later Christians to support racial hatred, it is possible that the recent turn in Pauline scholarship offers us a way forward in understanding the wider polemical and political dynamics of the passage, if we assign it to Paul's hands.[58]

Given the strong pro-Roman atmosphere in Thessalonica (where Paul's assembly had suffered at the hands of other Thessalonians) and the frequent repressive action by the pro-Roman Judean rulers against Jewish groups there (including the assemblies of Christ-believers), it seems likely that in 1 Thess 2:13–16 Paul is criticizing the pro-Roman aristocracy in Thessalonica by way of an analogy with the pro-Roman rulers of Judea.[59] Three principal arguments support this suggestion.

First, the diction of 1 Thess 2:13–16 is political. For Paul, Jesus Christ, not the emperor, is "Lord" and "Son of God," in pointed contrast to the visible signs of the "lordship" and "divine sonship" of the emperor in Thessalonica.[60] Furthermore, the expression "that they might be saved"

---

57. In agreement, see George Lyons, *Pauline Autobiography: Toward a New Understanding* (SBL Dissertation Series 73; Atlanta: Scholars, 1985), 203; Abraham Malherbe, *The Letters to the Thessalonians* (Anchor Bible; New York: Doubleday, 2000); 168–69. For a sterling critique of the basic arguments against the authenticity of 1 Thess 2:13–16, see Jon A. Weatherly, "The Authenticity of 1 Thessalonians 2:13–16: Additional Evidence," *JSNT* 42 (1991): 79–98.

58. In passing, it should be noted that Thessalonica (modern-day Salonika) bears several tragic connections for the Jews. Some went there when they were forced out of Spain by Ferdinand and Isabella. During World War II, moreover, "60,000 of them were deported [from Salonika] by the Nazis and nearly all of them slain." Sherman E. Johnson, "The Apostle Paul in Macedonia," *Lexington Theological Quarterly* 19 (1987): 77.

59. On the analogy, cf. Malherbe, *The Letters to the Thessalonians*, 168. *Ioudaioi* should be read as "Judeans" rather than all "Jews," as explained by Beverly Gaventa, *First and Second Thessalonians* (Interpretation; Louisville, Ky.: Westminster John Knox, 1998), 36.

60. To Paul's insistence on Jesus Christ as Lord, and not the emperor, compare the exclusive commitment of the Fourth Philosophy to God as their sole Lord and Master versus Caesar (hence, the impossibility of paying the Roman tribute) and the insistence of the Sicarii holding out on Masada: no degree of torture could get them "to confess that Caesar was their lord" (Josephus, *Jewish War*, 2.118; 7.418).

presupposes that the Gentiles needed to be saved; they were not already saved by Caesar, despite the power of the Empire and the long-standing claim in imperial ideology that the emperor as savior had already established salvation.[61] Moreover, Paul's use of the standard political term "assemblies" *(ekklēsiai)* for his communities clearly suggests that they were an alternative to the assemblies of Greek cities such as Thessalonica. As mentioned, Christ-believers, like Diaspora Jews, saw themselves as members of alternative communities that were wider than the usual local voluntary associations. Paul's references not only to the "assembly" of the Thessalonians but to assemblies in Judea and in Macedonia and Achaia indicate that he imagines the further development of alternative communities in the Empire. Paul's assemblies may have been small, but for him they represented the power of his God's presence beyond, as well as within, the beleaguered assembly at Thessalonica.

Second, the way in which the afflictions (persecutions) are discussed in 2:13–16 indicates an apocalyptic (political) worldview in which "the Day of the Lord" is near. In the Judean apocalyptic worldview, serious afflictions would occur just before the time of God's judgment and deliverance (cf. Dan 12:1; Mark 13:19, 24; Matt 24:9–14).[62] In other words, Paul's reading of the times is that the persecution that believers are now facing is a sure indicator of the imminence of the Parousia of Christ and God's judgment of the old order. For this interpretation, of course, 1 Thess 2:16b must be translated not as "God's wrath 'has overtaken' *[ephthasen]* at last," as the NRSV reads, but as "God's wrath 'has drawn near' *[ephthasen]* at last" (cf. Luke 11:20).[63] This view of the world, however, means that Paul anticipates the imminent beginning of a new *era* for his assemblies, in pointed contrast to the official Thessalonian declarations that new *eras* had begun with the victories of the Roman warlords Antony and Octavian.

Third, the characterization of the Thessalonian persecutors (partly by analogy) as relentless in 2:13–16 appears to be a polemical indication of their lack of self-control. Various suggestions have been made regarding the character of the afflictions caused by the "compatriots" of Paul's assembly at Thessalonica.[64] Some think that "Paul was the target of (at

---

61. See, e.g., Craig R. Koester, "'The Savior of the World' (John 4:42)," *JBL* 109 (1990): 665–80.

62. On the suffering of the prophets as a sign of the end, see the Ascension of Isaiah 5:14; cf. W. H. C. Frend, *Martyrdom and Persecution in the Early Church: A Study of a Conflict from the Maccabees to Donatus* (Oxford: Basil Blackwell, 1965), 58.

63. I. H. Marshall, *1 and 2 Thessalonians* (Grand Rapids: Eerdmans, 1983), 80–81.

64. Donfried, in "Paul and Judaism," 243, thinks that the compatriots in 2:14 include Jews and Gentiles. On the one hand, Donfried's argument seems to be influenced by a desire to attenuate the disparities between 1 Thessalonians (which never

least) slanderous abuse" ("shamefully mistreated," 1 Thess 2:2).[65] Perhaps the Christ-believers were being harassed because they refused to take part in their former cultic activities (the "sufferings" in 1 Thess 1:6b; 2:2, 14–15; 3:1–5),[66] or were even being martyred.[67] In any case, Paul's charge that the Thessalonian "compatriots" are severely repressing his assembly members is a polemical accusation of a lack of self-mastery, a well-known philosophical topos. Remarkably, moreover, this topos had been adopted by Augustus and his culture shapers.[68] So, if Paul is indeed developing this topos here, the passage ironically suggests that the opponents are out of control even though they honor and collaborate in an Empire that has claimed self-control as the basis for its governance of the entire world.[69]

---

explicitly mentions Jewish opposition in Thessalonica) and Acts (which does; 17:5). Luke's tendentious portrait is known, however, not simply because Luke yields a set idealized pattern, as I have shown elsewhere (*Comfort One Another: Reconstructing the Rhetoric and Audience of 1 Thessalonians* [Louisville, Ky.: Westminster John Knox, 1995], 117 n. 53), but as well, because Luke's insistence that Thessalonica had a synagogue of the Jews simply cannot be supported. For a balanced treatment of the issue, see Collins, *Birth of the New Testament,* 111–12.

65. John Barclay, "Conflict in Thessalonica," *Catholic Biblical Quarterly* 55 (1993): 513.

66. Jeffrey Weima, "How You Must Walk to Please God," in *Patterns of Discipleship in the New Testament,* ed. Richard N. Longenecker (Grand Rapids: Eerdmans, 1996), 106.

67. Karl P. Donfried, "Imperial Cults of Thessalonica," 221. According to de Vos, however, Paul does not "specifically link these deaths [in 4:13–18] with the conflict [of 1 Thess 2:14-16]," as Donfried contends. Craig Steven de Vos, *Church and Community Conflicts: The Relationships of the Thessalonian, Corinthian, and Philippian Churches with Their Wider Civic Communities* (Atlanta: Scholars, 1997), 159.

68. Catharine Edwards, *The Politics of Immorality in Ancient Rome* (Cambridge: Cambridge University Press, 1993), 25; Abraham Smith, "'Full of Spirit and Wisdom': Luke's Portrait of Stephen (Acts 6:1–8:1a) as a Man of Self-Mastery," in *Asceticism and the New Testament,* ed. Leif E. Vaage and Vincent L. Wimbush (New York: Routledge, 1999), 100.

69. Some scholars (e.g., Hagner, 135) think Paul's description of the opponents here is similar to some of the polemical descriptions of the Jews as espoused by Gentile writers. While Gentile writers (Hecataeus of Abdera, Manetho, Apollonius Molon, Diodorous Siculus, Strabo, Pompeius Trogus, Lysimachus, Apion, and Tacitus) charged the Jews with either *misanthropy* or *xenophobia,* both polemical motifs were a part of a Greek and Roman tradition that was used by Jews, Greeks, and Romans against other ethnic groups, select persons within a group, or even single individuals. Thus, the presence of the motif does not indicate a sweeping indictment of the entire Jewish nation, whether by Paul or by a later redactor of Paul's earliest extant letter. On the tradition of *misanthropy* and *xenophobia* and its varied uses, see Peter Schaefer, *Judeophobia: Attitudes toward the Jews in the Ancient World* (Cambridge, Mass.: Harvard University Press, 1997), 173–75. See Tacitus, *Histories* 5.5.2. Josephus notes Apion's use of the polemic, in *Against Apion* 2.121.

First Thessalonians 5:1–11

Paul does not direct 1 Thess 5:1–11 at failures within the Thessalonian assembly. This is not a passage about the delay of the Parousia.[70] Paul's "us/them" rhetoric here suggests, rather, an attack on outsiders.[71] "Peace and security" in 1 Thess 5:1–11 is "a direct allusion to Roman propaganda or to Greek propagandistic responses to Roman beneficence."[72] Thus, we need here only to indicate the very real concern that people in Thessalonica had for the issue of "peace and security," and then to read 1 Thess 5:1–11 as Paul's critique of those who trusted in the Romans to provide.

The history of Macedonia and its capital Thessalonica reveals that "peace and security" was a continuous concern. On the one hand, both knew that "peace and security" entailed military action. The Roman "peace" that came to Macedonia in 167 B.C.E. arrived by virtue of Paulus's defeat of Perseus. Moreover, while that peace gave tacit overtures to freedom (e.g., use of "their own laws, and election of their own magistrates"),[73] it also came with the deportation of Macedonia's military officers, the division of the land into four republics, and restrictive laws on inter-republic trade.[74] This type of "peace and security," a propaganda slogan that simply "affirmed the existing order,"[75] did not change with the Principate.

On the other hand, imperial Macedonia and Thessalonica knew from earlier centuries of invasions that the established order might be difficult to maintain. Macedonia had been invaded several times, by the Skordiskoi to the north in 119 and 110 B.C.E., by several groups inspired by Mithridates in 87 B.C.E., and again by the Skordiskoi, with the Madoi and the Dardanians, in 84 B.C.E.[76] Thessalonica itself came under direct threat

---

70. As demonstrated convincingly by H. Koester, "From Paul's Eschatology," 16–17. Cf. Hendrix, "Archaeology and Eschatology," 109-10. With Hendrix, I think Paul's "peace and security" does not stem from the Septuagint because the reference in 1 Thessalonians has a temporal and causal force that is not found in LXX prophetic denunciations and because the two terms never appear together in the Hebrew Scriptures.

71. For a different opinion, see Abraham Malherbe, *The Letters to the Thessalonians*, 303.

72. Hendrix, "Archaeology and Eschatology," 114.

73. N. G. L. Hammond and F. W. Walbank, *A History of Macedonia*, vol. 3: *336–167 B.C.* (Oxford: Clarendon, 1988), 559–67.

74. Hammond and Walbank, 564.

75. Klaus Wengst, *Pax Romana and the Peace of Jesus Christ*, trans. John Bowden (Philadelphia: Fortress, 1987), 78.

76. David W. J. Gill, "Macedonia," in *The Book of Acts in Its First-Century Setting*, vol. 2 of *The Book of Acts in Its Graeco-Roman Setting* (ed. David W. J. Gill and Conrad Gempf; Grand Rapids: Eerdmans, 1994), 403. By the time Paul wrote his letter, Macedonia and Achaia were two separate senatorial provinces, a change put into place by Claudius in 44 C.E.

during the governorship of L. Calpurnius Piso, leading to the fortification of the citadel (Cicero, *De provinciis consularibus* 2.4; *L. Calpurnium Pisonem oratio* 17.40). The effect of such incursions left Thessalonica with a bit of a siege mentality up to the beginning of the civil wars.[77] Then during the civil war period, by shifting their loyalty from one warlord to another in their search for security, the Thessalonian aristocracy developed a habit of backing the losers. Feeling vulnerable, therefore, after Octavian's ascendancy following his victory at Actium, they quickly heaped lavish honors on "Augustus," and received benefits from him.[78]

In 1 Thess 5:1–11, therefore, Paul is likely referring to the Thessalonian aristocracy's continuing obsession with "peace and security," with which his assembly at Thessalonica was all too familiar.[79] Furthermore, Paul sets "peace and security" within the framework of apocalyptic battle imagery (children of light vs. children of darkness, 5:4–5) similar to that in the *Community Rule* and the *War Rule* of the Qumran covenanters (1QS 3.13–4.26; 1QM 1.1, 3). Assuming that the Qumran covenanters were referring to the Romans as the "Kittim" (1QM 2.1; 15.4; 16.13; 18.5; 19.1), they show that Paul's Jewish contemporaries were expecting the eschatological battle to be against the Romans. Continuing the battle imagery (5:8), Paul insists on sober deportment that reflects belonging to the day as opposed to the night (cf. 5:6–7). Moreover, with the earlier triad of faith, love, and hope (cf. 1:3), he portrays his Thessalonian assembly's "weaponry for the eschatological battle."[80] Critical for us to note, however, is that the aorist or past-tense participle—usually translated (as in the NRSV) as "let us . . . put on" (*endysamenoi*, 5:8), as if it were present—should be translated as "already having put on." Hence, the sobriety is a *consequence* of the believers' having been clothed in battle gear.

The mention of the eschatological weaponry is likely an echo of Isa 59:17, where Yahweh is depicted as a "man of war."[81] Now, however, the assembly has the eschatological weaponry. The "Day of the Lord" imagery, with which 5:1–11 begins (5:2), is also an echo from Isa 2:12, where it "describes God's decisive intervention."[82] Paul's allusion to the "Day of the

---

77. De Vos, *Church and Community Conflicts*, 125.

78. Ibid., 126.

79. Cf. Jouette Bassler, "Peace in All Ways: Theology in the Thessalonian Letters: A Response to R. Jewett, E. Krentz, and E. Richard," in *Thessalonians, Philippians, Galatians, Philemon*, vol. 1 of *Pauline Theology* (ed. Jouette Bassler; Minneapolis: Fortress, 1990), 84.

80. H. Koester, "From Paul's Eschatology," 451.

81. Malherbe, *Letters to the Thessalonians*, 297.

82. Ibid., 290.

Lord" imagery and his general dependence upon Isaiah (especially Deutero-Isaiah) again suggests that he is not simply communicating warm feelings of encouragement to his friends. Rather, he is speaking the diction of resistance as he reflects on eschatological events that have already occurred (e.g., the preparation of his assembly with eschatological weaponry) and those which will shortly come to pass when the Day of the Lord arrives. The realization of the Day of the Lord will consummate God's intervention in the world. Rome will no longer hold power. God alone will rule.

This profusion of battle imagery, moreover, suggests that the ignorance of the pro-Roman aristocracy is that they have placed their trust in forces that cannot provide the stable "peace and security" which they had sought for so long. Instead of "peace and security," they would face "sudden destruction." For Paul, of course, the ignorance of the pro-Roman aristocracy extends further. They belong to the sphere of the night (cf. 5:4) because they do not know that the new age has already begun. Already the battle is engaged; already Paul's band of believers are clothed in battle armor. Salvation does not come from the emperor, as if the emperor were a true savior. Rather, for Paul, salvation comes from God, who has not destined the foundational team and Paul's assembly for wrath, but to obtain salvation through Jesus Christ (5:9; cf. Phil 3:19–21). Furthermore, by connecting 5:1–11 and 4:13–18 with the repetition of the expression "with" *(syn)* the Lord (4:17; 5:10), Paul indicates that the permanence of the salvation has already begun; for the earlier verse indicates that, with the Parousia,[83] the assemblies of Christ will "always" or "forever" be with the Lord (4:17).[84] What Paul guarantees for his assembly is an alternative society of mutual love and support, dramatically different from the security in their dominant positions sought by the Thessalonian elite who placed their faith in the imperial order.

---

83. The word "parousia" has two essential meanings: "presence" (2 Macc 15:21; 3 Macc 3:17; 2 Cor 10:10; Phil 2:12); and "arrival" (Jdt 10:18; 2 Macc 8:12; 1 Cor 16:17; 2 Cor 7:6–7). Tracy Howard, "The Literary Unity of 1 Thessalonians 4:13–5:11," *Grace Theological Journal* 9 (1988): 176, notes that the word "came to have particular associations with the arrival of a central figure" and indicated both "the physical act of arrival" and "the attendant circumstances in which the ruler was honored." It is generally believed that the early followers of Jesus adopted these "particular associations" to speak about Christ's coming as his Parousia. It is likely, moreover, that the term "would have evoked the image of the return of a triumphant conqueror in the Hellenistic world and the idea of a coronation on that occasion" (Collins, *Birth of the New Testament,* 112).

84. First Thess 4:13–18 also exploits military imagery. Note the "cry of command" and "the sound of God's trumpet" (4:16).

Conclusion

A more thorough postcolonial analysis would require more self-reflective analysis about the pre-interpretive reading constraints of students of 1 Thessalonians (in line with Price's caveats about Christianizing assumptions). Nevertheless, this essay is a modest first step in revealing the mixture of politics and religion that Paul and the auditors of 1 Thessalonians likely shared about their movement and the ruler cult at Thessalonica as well. Paul's earliest extant letter, while friendly in its efforts to console a beleaguered assembly, offers a harsh critique of those who have stood in the way of his formation of assemblies among the Gentiles across the provinces of the Mediterranean world. In 1 Thess 2:13–16, Paul criticizes pro-Roman Thessalonian aristocrats who have persecuted his assembly through an implicit comparison with the pro-Roman aristocracy in Judea. For Paul, both evince a lack of self-control even while they align themselves with the Romans, who justify their right to rule the world on the putative claim that they have self-control. In the case of 1 Thess 5:1–11, Paul criticizes the pro-Roman aristocracy yet again because of their ignorance about "peace and security" and about the real eschatological battle that has already begun with the death and resurrection of Jesus. For Paul, the "peace and security" that has eluded the Thessalonian elite for centuries cannot be found in the Romans. Genuine peace can only come from Paul's deity, the "God of peace" (1 Thess 5:23), and that deity's representative, the Lord Jesus Christ, through whose death God brings salvation and a permanent union of believing assemblies at Jesus' Parousia (1 Thess 4:15, 17).

– 3 –

THE APOSTLE PAUL'S SELF-PRESENTATION
AS ANTI-IMPERIAL PERFORMANCE

Neil Elliott

Roman imperial ritual and propaganda filled the environment in which the apostle Paul worked.[1] In convergent ways, recent studies of the imperial cult, on the one hand, *and* of Paul's "theology," on the other, are moving away from the individualistic, cognitivist concerns of classical Christian theology, and toward an understanding of the meaning of symbols and the function of rituals in representing relationships of power. I argue here that *both* imperial imagery and cult, *and* the performance of Paul's apostolic *parousia* (presence), constituted ritual representations of power.

Further, the evidence of Paul's Letters tells us that, despite the vaunted "religious tolerance" of the Empire,[2] these two ritual strategies did not

---

1. Dieter Georgi and Stanley K. Stowers regard Roman imperial ideology as a more relevant context for understanding the letter to the Romans than a presumed debate with Judaism: See Georgi, *Theocracy in Paul's Praxis and Theology* (trans. David E. Green; Minneapolis: Fortress, 1991); and Stowers, *A Rereading of Romans: Justice, Jews, Gentiles* (New Haven, Conn.: Yale University Press, 1994). Holland Lee Hendrix, "Archaeology and Eschatology at Thessalonica," in *The Future of Early Christianity: Essays in Honor of Helmut Koester* (ed. Birger A. Pearson; Minneapolis: Fortress, 1997), 107–18, has used archaeological and numismatic evidence in a systematic reconstruction of the imperial context for 1 Thessalonians. See also the important collection of essays in Richard A. Horsley, ed., *Paul and Empire: Religion and Power in Roman Imperial Society* (Philadelphia: Trinity Press International, 1997).

2. Richard Gordon, "The Veil of Power: Emperors, Sacrificers and Benefactors," in *Pagan Priests: Religion and Power in the Ancient World* (ed. Mary Beard and John North; Ithaca, N.Y.: Cornell University Press, 1990], 207, notes that one ideological function of religion in the early Principate "was to insulate Rome from the cultural consequence of her own imperialism: the religion of Rome became a guarantee not merely of her supremacy but also of her freedom from contamination by her

coexist peacefully. That is, they did not keep to neatly segregated "political" and "religious," or public and private, spheres (as citizens of modern Western democracies are too prone to imagine, on the analogy of our division between "church and state"). Instead, Paul's apostolic performance constituted a *rival* representation of power, even if that representation was realized on the public landscape of the Roman city only rarely (and in paradoxical ways, as we shall see below).[3] Informed by the covenantal and apocalyptic traditions of Israel, and by the *apokalypsis* of Jesus Christ (Gal 1:15–16), Paul understands his *parousia* to actualize an invasive power that is at odds—indeed, at war!—with the imperial power of "the rulers of this age" (1 Cor 2:8).

Ritual Representations of Power in the Roman Civic Landscape

Recent studies bring valuable light to bear on the symbolic representations of power in Hellenistic-Roman society. Especially important in this regard is S. R. F. Price's work on power and ritual. Price demonstrates that in Paul's day, imperial rituals had saturated public life throughout the provinces, including long-standing local festivals which took on new imperial aspects, as well as new celebrations and games, festivals, and sacrifices offered to, or on behalf of, the imperial family. These rituals were not irregular and passing events, but cults institutionalized on a regular basis. Further, they were not simply occasional accommodations imposed on an indifferent population by imperial fiat. Usually, rituals celebrating Roman power were "created and organized by the subjects of a great empire" themselves—in the absence of the emperor or even his representative—"in order to represent to themselves the ruling power."[4]

Price argues that "Christianizing" assumptions still hinder an adequate understanding of the imperial cult. These misapprehensions include, first, privileging the individual's feeling at the expense of ritual action. "With the imperial cult, the processions and the sacrifices, the temples and the images fill our sources. They are the crucially important collective constructs to which the individual reacted. Ritual is what there was."[5] Another

---

subjects. . . . Rome was different from her Empire and her religion was an emblem of that difference. The so-called tolerance of the indigenous religions of the provinces is rather to be understood as a consequence of this colonial attitude."

3. Compare Georgi, *Theocracy,* 83–88, and Stowers, *Rereading,* 14–15. Raymond Pickett's program in *The Cross in Corinth: The Social Significance of the Death of Jesus* (JSNTSup 143; Sheffield: Sheffield Academic, 1997), 9–36, is very similar to what I wish to accomplish here on a smaller scale.

4. S. R. F. Price, *Rituals and Power: The Roman Imperial Cult in Asia Minor* (Cambridge: Cambridge University Press, 1984), 1.

5. Ibid., 11.

Christianizing bias is the "theological" focus on the question of how wide-spread and how sincere was belief in the emperor's divinity, a question abstracted from the social matrix of the Roman city in which the imperial cult took place. Price criticizes a scholarship too often preoccupied with a presumed skepticism on the part of the Roman elite—a presumption that reduces imperial rituals to a cynical political manipulation of religious symbolism.

Instead, Price argues, imperial rituals constituted "a public cognitive system," a social "embodiment of thinking," an attempt on the part of the Greek cities "to represent to themselves their new masters in a traditional guise," and thus "to come to terms with a new type of power." He finds the origins of the imperial cult in public Hellenistic cults for rulers and prominent citizens. The transitions to cults of Roma—of the "Roman benefactors" in general, or of Roman individuals in particular—represent "clear-sighted perception of the new situation" of Roman hegemony, expressed in Greek idiom.[6] Taking seriously Price's attention to the *cultural* mechanisms of imperialism does not mean we should minimize the role of brute force in establishing Roman hegemony, of course. Paul's insistence that in one particular act of Roman brutality—the humiliation and crucifixion of Jesus of Nazareth—the "rulers of this age" had exposed their own fraudulence and folly (1 Cor 2:4–6), requires that we who seek to understand the apostle not divert our gaze from imperial violence, in the ancient world or in our own. Rather, Price points us to the thickly textured cultural process by which provincial elites sought to accommodate themselves to a force that would have been "otherwise unmanageable."[7]

Price's study of imperial cult in Asia Minor has found important echoes in other recent works[8] that demonstrate the aggressive, pervasive, and systematic representation of imperial power in public space. The redesign of city squares, the construction of new temples, the appropriation or transfer of existing shrines, monumental architecture, dedicatory inscriptions, and the proliferation of standardized images of the emperor all served the interests of the Roman government, clearly enough. Yet the imperial cult was enthusiastically produced and maintained by the provincial elites, who were eager to participate in the new networks of power,

---

6. Ibid., 8–9; 25–43.

7. Ibid., 52.

8. For example, Susan E. Alcock, *Graecia Capta: The Landscapes of Roman Greece* (Cambridge: Cambridge University Press, 1993); also worthy of note is Ramsay MacMullen, *Romanization in the Time of Augustus* (New Haven, Conn.: Yale University Press, 2002). On the Romanization of the Mediterranean economy, see Greg Woolf, "Imperialism, Empire, and the Integration of the Roman Economy," *World Archaeology* 23 (1992): 283–93.

privilege, and prestige. The cult served as "a system of exchange," linking Greek and provincial elites to Rome; it "enhanced the dominance of local elites over the populace, of cities over other cities, and of Greek over indigenous cultures."[9]

Public rituals served as the medium through which the image of the emperor came to represent the network of military, economic, and social relationships of Roman hegemony. Most persons in the empire of Rome knew the emperor only through the proliferation of images throughout the provinces, and these dominated the celebration of the cult. Ceremonial processions frequently involved the carrying-about of images of the emperor; producing the image for the reverential gaze of the citizens was a sacred action. The omnipresence of imperial images, and their strategic manipulation through ritual, produced a considerable effect, providing a constant reminder of who ruled the world.[10] The ritualized maintenance of public order was in the imperial era focused increasingly on the person of the emperor himself, in Rome; and on the successful manipulation of his image, in the provinces.[11]

Several aspects of the imperial cult merit particular note. First, while the production of imperial images was a propaganda project from the center, Rome, their *manipulation and representation* in civic ritual, public ceremonial, and everyday conversation was enthusiastically carried on at the "periphery," by the Greek elites in the provinces.[12] Second, the rise of Augustus marked an abrupt end to the proliferation of cults to human benefactors *and* a consolidation of cults to the gods with the imperial cult, transparently a reflection of the colonial relationship.[13] Third, following his dramatic triple triumph in 29 B.C.E., Octavian, later called Augustus, consistently refused the Senate's offers of triumphs in his honor, and in a

---

9. Price, *Rituals and Power*, 65–77, 248; Alcock, *Graecia Capta*, 215–30. See also G. W. Bowersock, "The Imperial Cult: Perceptions and Persistence," in *Self-Definition in the Greco-Roman World*, vol. 3 of *Jewish and Christian Self-Definition* (ed. Ben F. Meyer and E. P. Sanders; Philadelphia: Fortress, 1982); and Clifford Ando, *Imperial Ideology and Provincial Loyalty in the Roman Empire* (Berkeley: University of California Press, 2000), a work that came to my attention too late to be considered in this paper.

10. Bowersock, "Imperial Cult," 173–74; Price, *Rituals and Power*, 170–206. Price relies explicitly (7–9, 239–40) on Clifford Geertz, *The Interpretation of Cultures: Selected Essays* (New York: Basic Books, 1973), for his understanding of ritual.

11. See Wilfried Nippel, *Public Order in Ancient Rome* (Cambridge: Cambridge University Press, 1995), 4–17 (on Republican Rome), and 85–119 (for the early Principate); and Paul Zanker, *The Power of Images in the Age of Augustus* (Ann Arbor: University of Michigan Press, 1990).

12. Price, *Rituals and Power*, 172–76.

13. Ibid., 49–51; 54–56; Gordon, "Veil of Power," 206–7.

deliberate and unified political program, restricted the official triumphs, celebrated by others, to his own potential successors. At the same time, he actively promoted the use of the image and title of *triumphator* in other rituals (acclamations, supplications) and other media (architecture, coins, statues). The result was an effective *imperial monopoly on the imagery of triumph*.[14] The effect in Roman cities was that sacrifices by individual emperors in specific rituals increasingly became manifestations of *a generalized and distinctly Roman piety*, practiced and promoted by the emperors in the name of the Empire. Thus the emperor was able to accumulate "symbolic capital" for himself, and piety in the provinces became saturated with the symbolized presence of the emperor.[15]

Power and Rhetoric in Paul

To the extent that Roman imperial power and ideology found ritualized representation on the Roman civic landscape, we should expect that Paul's apostolic work on that same landscape would engage imperial ritual, at least obliquely. Until recently, however, imperial ritual and symbolization have been curiously underappreciated in Pauline studies.[16] This is curious, since

---

14. Frances V. Hickson, "Augustus *Triumphator:* Manipulation of the Triumphal Theme in the Political Program of Augustus," *Latomus* 50 (1991): 124–38.

15. Gordon, "Veil of Power," 205, 208, 219.

16. Important recent efforts include Georgi, *Theocracy:* and the essays collected in *Paul and Empire* (ed. Horsley). Recent interpretation of the Corinthian correspondence has also focused on apparent competition within the *ekklēsia* over power, especially as represented in eloquence ("wise speech"), and upon social stratification and friction between classes. The relationship between imperial ideology and codes of "vertical reciprocity" in Roman patronage has been ably investigated by Peter Marshall, *Enmity in Corinth: Social Conventions in Paul's Relations with the Corinthians* (Tübingen: J. C. B. Mohr [Paul Siebeck], 1987), and John K. Chow, *Patronage and Power: A Study of Social Networks in Corinth,* JSNTSup 75 (Sheffield: JSOT Press, 1992); also David G. Horrell, *The Social Ethos of the Corinthian Correspondence: Interests and Ideology from 1 Corinthians to 1 Clement* (Edinburgh: T. & T. Clark, 1996). The notion of a "new consensus" regarding the social setting of the Pauline *ekklēsiai*, depending on the work of Gerd Theissen (*The Social Setting of Pauline Christianity: Essays on Corinth* [trans. John Schütz; Philadelphia: Fortress, 1977]) and Wayne A. Meeks (*The First Urban Christians: The Social World of the Apostle Paul* [New Haven, Conn.: Yale University Press, 1983]), has been challenged regarding its implicit functionalism and overgeneralizing from the particular situation in Corinth. See Mary Ann Tolbert, "Social, Sociological, and Anthropological Methods," in *Searching the Scriptures*, vol. 1 (ed. Elizabeth Schüssler Fiorenza; New York: Crossroad, 1993), 255–71; Richard A. Horsley, "Paul's Counter-Imperial Gospel: Introduction," in *Paul and Empire* (ed. Horsley), 140–47; idem, *1 Corinthians* (ANTC; Nashville: Abingdon, 1998); Justin J. Meggitt, *Paul, Poverty, and Survival* (Studies of the New Testament and Its World; Edinburgh: T. & T. Clark, 1998); and Stephen Friesen, "Poor Paul," at the Paul and Politics Section of the SBL, 2002.

Paul does not merely *speak about power:* he intended his letters to function within a larger public, apostolic strategy that *represented and expressed power and power relations* in a way different from, and often subversive of, imperial symbol and ritual. An adequate rhetorical criticism will not be content to interpret Paul's Letters as vehicles for conveying theological concepts; they are instruments of persuasion within a larger apostolic strategy.

Paul describes his own apostolic activity as the manifestation of divine power. I focus below on several key metaphors: the triumphal procession, the spectacle of the arena, and combat imagery, metaphors through which Paul seeks to represent the death and resurrection of Jesus as the decisive manifestation of divine power. First, however, we must attend to some aspects of the rhetorical *performance* of Paul's Letters.

Though the Hellenistic world was far from a purely oral culture, it is nevertheless true that reading was *oral performance.*[17] In dictating letters to be read aloud to his communities, Paul sought to extend the presence of his apostolic authority and power, his "apostolic *parousia,*" in circumstances where his personal presence, the primary medium through which he preferred to make his authority effective, was impossible. Paul's Letters did more than maintain personal contact over distance. In contrast to our visual way of taking in the text of a letter, holding it quite literally "at arm's length," *oral* performance situates people in the midst of "a world of voices." The effect of Paul's message *performed orally* would have been to create an atmosphere of effectual energy, an orbit of power. We expect the creation of this "acoustic space" to have been the responsibility of the associate to whom Paul entrusted his letter; thus, Paul would presumably have taken care to prepare this messenger to *perform* the letter as a part of his apostolic strategy, for the letter had only done its work once it was performed.[18]

---

17. As Paul Achtemeier declares, late antiquity knew nothing of the "silent, solitary reader"; "*Omne verbum sonat:* The New Testament and the Oral Environment of Late Western Antiquity," *JBL* 109 (1990): 16–19.

18. See Robert W. Funk, "The Apostolic *Parousia:* Form and Significance," in *Christian History and Interpretation: Studies Presented to John Knox* (ed. W. R. Farmer, C. F. D. Moule, and R. R. Niebuhr; Cambridge: Cambridge University Press, 1964), 249, 258; William G. Doty, *Letters in Primitive Christianity* (Philadelphia: Fortress, 1973), 45–47; Bengt Holmberg, *Paul and Power: The Structure of Authority in the Primitive Church as Reflected in the Pauline Epistles* (Philadelphia: Fortress Press, 1978), 57–93; Werner Kelber, *The Oral and Written Gospel: The Hermeneutics of Speaking and Writing in the Synoptic Tradition, Mark, Paul, and Q* (Philadelphia: Fortress, 1983), 140–83; Stanley K. Stowers, *Letter Writing in Greco-Roman Antiquity* (Philadelphia: Westminster, 1986): 23; David E. Aune, *The New Testament in Its Literary Environment* (Philadelphia: Westminster, 1987), 192; Pieter Botha, "The Verbal Art of the Pauline Letters: Rhetoric, Performance and Presence," in *Rhetoric and the New Testament: Essays from the 1992 Heidelberg Conference* (ed. Stanley E.

Ancient rhetorical handbooks gave specific instructions regarding the body and hand gestures most effective in oral performance. Even if Paul had no direct contact with those handbooks, we may expect that Paul's colleagues would have arrived in a city like Corinth prepared to present a vivid performance of his letters. The troubled interactions recorded in the Corinthian correspondence show the high esteem in which some in the Corinthian *ekklēsia* held polished rhetorical performance, such as that attributed to Apollos of Alexandria (Acts 18:24–28; cf. 1 Cor. 1:17–18, 2:1–5). Also evident is the reaction of these same Corinthians to what they came to regard as Paul's inadequate rhetorical performance, and the consequent crisis for an apostle compelled to restore his authoritative *parousia* (his strategic presence) through an effective counterperformance by an apostolic colleague (or colleagues).[19]

If (as 2 Cor 10:10 indicates) some of the Corinthians found Paul's performance disappointing, the challenge facing him was to establish the authenticity of his own apostolic presence *without participating in the same self-commendation that he condemns in his rivals.* His strategy in both letters—heightened in the second—is to represent himself, not merely as a particularly able speaker among others, but as an agent of the "power of God," distinct from mere practitioners of rhetoric (so 1 Cor 4:19–20).[20] Using terminology

---

Porter and Thomas H. Olbricht; JSNTSup 90; Sheffield: JSOT Press, 1993), 415–23; Joanna Dewey, "Textuality in an Oral Culture: A Survey of the Pauline Traditions," *Semeia* 65 (1994): 37–65; Arthur J. Dewey, "A Re-Hearing of Romans 10:1–15," *Semeia* 65 (1994): 109–28; Vernon K. Robbins, "Oral, Rhetorical and Literary Cultures: A Response," *Semeia* 65 (1994): 75–91; Richard Ward, "Pauline Voice and Presence as Strategic Communication," *Semeia* 65 (1994): 102–3.

19. Quintilian, *Inst.* 1.11; Ward, "Pauline Voice," 99–101; Hans Dieter Betz, *Galatians: A Commentary on Paul's Letter to the Churches in Galatia* (Hermeneia; Philadelphia: Fortress, 1979), 131; Antoinette Clark Wire, "Performance, Politics, and Power: A Response," *Semeia* 65 (1994): 129. The argument that a Corinthian disparagement of Paul's rhetoric was a key issue in the correspondence was first made by Johannes Munck, *Paul and the Salvation of Mankind* (trans. Frank Clarke; Atlanta: John Knox, 1959), 135–67; compare Nils Dahl, *Studies in Paul: Theology for the Early Christian Mission* (Minneapolis: Augsburg, 1977), 40–61; Hans Dieter Betz, "The Problem of Rhetoric and Theology according to the Apostle Paul," in *L'Apôtre Paul: Personnalité, style et conception du ministère* (ed. A. Vanhoye; Bibliotheca ephemeridum theologicarum lovaniensium 73; Louvain: Louvain University Press/Peeters, 1986), 24–39; Meeks, *First Urban Christians,* 117–18.

20. On the challenge and Paul's response, see Steven J. Kraftchick, "Death in Us, Life in You: The Apostolic Medium," in *1 and 2 Corinthians,* vol. 2 of *Pauline Theology* (ed. David M. Hay; Minneapolis: Fortress, 1993), 166; Elizabeth Castelli, "Interpretations of Power in 1 Corinthians," *Semeia* 54 (1991): 205–6; Antoinette Clark Wire, *Corinthian Women Prophets: A Reconstruction through Paul's Rhetoric* (Minneapolis: Fortress, 1990), 176–80; Elisabeth Schüssler Fiorenza, "Rhetorical

familiar from the rhetorical handbooks, Paul calls his own performance among the Corinthians a "demonstration *[apodeixis]* of the Spirit and of power" (1 Cor 2:4), not mere "persuasive words of wisdom" (NASB). One might say his rhetoric is *apodeictic*—"demonstrative of power"—rather than *epideictic* (rhetorical display). God's power is at work in Paul: thus Paul is not ashamed of the gospel because it is "the saving power of God" (Rom 1:16; cf. 1 Thess 1:5). Paul's "signs and wonders" are the work of Christ (Rom 15:18–19), or of the Spirit (Gal 3:3–5); they are "the signs of a true apostle" (2 Cor 12:12).[21]

Recognizing what I am calling the "apodeictic" character of Paul's rhetoric means shifting attention from the apostle's "consciousness, that is, what Paul *thought*" about a subject, to the *effects* he wished to achieve— including the work he intended his letters to perform, through divine power. Through them he means to fulfill his own calling as apostle *and* to realize the calling of his hearers as "holy ones," by securing their faithful obedience (Rom 1:5) and thus the sanctity of "the offering of the nations" (Rom 15:14–16, author).[22] But this means that the conventional rhetorical-critical approaches to Paul's letters must be expanded. The "rhetorical situation" addressed in any letter is more than the network of relationships and expectations that connect the apostle with his audience. The "deep exigence" of Paul's Letters is nothing less than the apocalyptic horizon of God's coming triumph in power. This "deep exigence" necessarily impinges

---

Situation and Historical Reconstruction in 1 Corinthians," *NTS* 33 (1987): 175–86. In 1 Corinthians, Castelli, Wire, and Schüssler Fiorenza detect Paul's effort to curtail the autonomy, authority, and power of charismatic women in the Corinthian congregation, an assessment depending heavily on the authenticity of 1 Cor 14:34–35 and its alignment with 11:2–16. I suspect the first passage is an interpolation, and regard Paul's rhetorical power-play as aimed at a different segment of the Corinthian church; see Neil Elliott, *Liberating Paul: The Justice of God and the Politics of the Apostle* (Maryknoll, N.Y.: Orbis Books, 1994), 52–54; 204–14.

21. Betz, "Rhetoric and Theology," 35–37; Schüssler Fiorenza, "Rhetorical Situation," 392; Holmberg, *Paul and Power*, 74–75.

22. Compare Pickett, *The Cross in Corinth*, 9–36; similarly Jouette M. Bassler speaks of Paul's mission as *activity*: "Paul's Theology: Whence and Whither?" in *1 and 2 Corinthians*, vol. 2 of *Pauline Theology* (ed. Hay; Minneapolis: Fortress, 1993), 3-17. See also Nils Dahl, "Paul's Letter to the Galatians: Epistolary Genre, Content, Structure," in *The Galatians Debate* (ed. Mark Nanos; Peabody, Mass.: Hendrickson, 2002); idem, *Studies in Paul*, 73; Kelber, *Oral and Written Gospel*, 145, 148–51; Neil Elliott, *The Rhetoric of Romans: Argumentative Constraint and Strategy and Paul's Dialogue with Judaism*, (JSNTSup 45; Sheffield: JSOT Press, 1990), 94–104; Holmberg, *Paul and Power*, 70–74; John L. White, "New Testament Epistolary Literature in the Framework of Ancient Epistolography," *ANRW* 2.25.2 (1984): 1745.

directly on the "near exigence" of the letter's audience, for Paul clearly wrote in anticipation of God acting in the congregation.[23]

We must not let our orientation to the Pauline *text* restrict the horizon of Paul's *parousia*. While we have no direct access to Paul's own oral performance, we do have the apostle's characterization of his performance. The fact that Paul repeatedly uses powerful metaphors drawn from the sphere of public ceremonial and the display of imperial power merits close examination, to which I now turn.

The Apostle "Led in Triumph"

In 2 Cor 2:14–16 Paul takes up the language of the imperial triumph to describe his own apostolic presence:

> But thanks be to God, who in Christ always leads us in triumphal procession, and through us spreads in every place the fragrance that comes from knowing him. For we are the aroma of Christ to God among those who are being saved and among those who are perishing; to the one a fragrance from death to death, to the other a fragrance from life to life.

While earlier generations of translators and commentators regarded as "most unsuitable" the implication that Paul had been "conquered" by God,[24] more recently interpreters have emphasized precisely this theme as a key to Paul's rhetorical strategy in 2 Corinthians 8–9. Lexical evidence from the period indicates that *thriambeuein* plus accusative has the sense "to celebrate a victory already won" over someone, specifically, in a triumphal procession. To be led in such a procession means being subjected to humiliation and, routinely, to be led to one's death. The term could thus be used as

---

23. Compare J. Louis Martyn's comments regarding Galatians: "Events in Galatia," in *Thessalonians, Philippians, Galatians, Philemon*, vol. 2 of *Pauline Theology* (ed. Jouette M. Bassler; Minneapolis: Fortress Press, 1991), 161. Martyn speaks of a "theological event" (163; 178–79) where Paul speaks of *God's action*. See also Ernst Käsemann, "The 'Righteousness of God' in Paul," in *New Testament Questions of Today* (trans. W. J. Montague; Philadelphia: Fortress, 1969), 168–82. On "rhetorical situation," see Lloyd A. Bitzer, "The Rhetorical Situation," *Philosophy and Rhetoric* 1 (1968): 1–14; Scott Consigny, "Rhetoric and Its Situations," *Philosophy and Rhetoric* 7 (1974): 175–86. On the "deep exigence" of Paul's letter to the Romans, Elliott, *Rhetoric of Romans*, 17–21, 70–93.

24. G. Findlay, "St. Paul's Use of *thriambeuo*," *Expositor* 10 (1879): 404–5; C. K. Barrett, *A Commentary on the Second Epistle to the Corinthians* (London: Black; New York: Harper & Row, 1973), 97–98.

a metaphor of shame and humiliation, and Paul relies on just that meaning as he confronts the enmity of a social elite among the Corinthians.[25]

Paul's opponents have accused him of breaching a relationship of reciprocal friendship based on faith. They may suspect him of initiating the collection for his own profit; further, they may even regard his subsequent imprisonment and mortal trial in Ephesus (2 Cor. 1:8–10) as evidence of God's punishment for his attempt to "fleece" the church.[26] Paul responds that his conduct toward the Corinthians has been open and transparent, and that his own humiliation and mistreatment is in fact evidence that he is a genuine apostle! The triumphal metaphor allows Paul to reconfigure his apparent disgrace: even if God *has* displayed him as a figure of shame and ridicule, it redounds to God's triumph; the apostle remains the locus of God's power!

Paul relies upon the imagery of triumphal or epiphany processions elsewhere in 2 Corinthians: "The love of Christ has taken us captive" (5:14, author). Paul's presence is a fragrant substance such as the aroma spread in epiphany processions, to indicate the god's presence (2:14–16). Paul and his co-workers "carry about in the body the dying of Jesus, so that the life of Jesus may also be manifested in our bodies" (4:10, author). Paul bids the Corinthians "make way" as for a ceremonial procession (7:2). Paul Duff detects in this proliferation of ritual images a single strategic purpose:

> Paul . . . "plays" with the definition of *thriambeuein,* expanding it. . . . Although Paul might look like he is being "led in triumph," a victim of defeat, the object of the vengeance of God, he is in fact a captive of the "love of Christ." He is a participant not in a military victory parade but in an epiphany procession. He has been captured, not as a prisoner of war, but as a devotee of the deity. . . . He describes himself with an image which would be eagerly embraced by his opponents; but throughout the course of the letter fragment,

---

25. Lamar Williamson, "Led in Triumph: Paul's Use of *Thriambeuo,*" *Int* 22 (1968): 321; Cilliers Breytenbach, "Paul's Proclamation and God's '*thriambos*' (Notes on 2 Corinthians 2:14–16b)," *Neotestamentica* 24 (1990): 259–62; Jan Lambrecht, "The Defeated Paul, Aroma of Christ: An Exegetical Study of 2 Corinthians 2:14–16b," *Louvain Studies* 20 (1995): 170–86 (with survey of interpretation); Peter Marshall, "A Metaphor of Social Shame: *thriambeuein* in 2 Cor. 2:14," *NovT* 25 (1983): 302–17; Scott Hafemann, *Suffering and the Spirit: An Exegetical Study of II Cor. 2:14–3:3 within the Context of the Corinthian Correspondence* (WUNT 2/19; Tübingen: J. C. B. Mohr [Paul Siebeck], 1986), 33.

26. Victor P. Furnish, *II Corinthians* (AB 32A; Garden City, N.J.: Doubleday, 1984), 369; Paul Brooks Duff, "Metaphor, Motif, and Meaning: The Rhetorical Strategy behind the Image 'Led in Triumph' in 2 Corinthians 2:14," *CBQ* 53 (1991): 86–89.

he subtly redefines it, using metaphors and allusions drawn from the processions of the Greco-Roman world.[27]

This is not mere rhetorical "play," of course. While part of Paul's purpose is to address Corinthian charges that he has proved false by delaying his return to them (2 Cor 1:15–17; 1:23–2:4; 2:12), he must also revise their understanding of the "affliction" he suffered (1:8–10; see below). By taking up key images from the imperial ritualization of power (the triumph procession), Paul acknowledges that *he* has been made the object of public ridicule and shame in civic representations of Roman power (he refers obliquely to receiving "the sentence of death," 1:9). Indeed, the later Pauline tradition uses the language of triumphs and processions precisely in the context of public spectacles of torture, expulsion, or execution.[28] But Paul insists that the Corinthians must perceive in his humiliation the decisive display of *God's* power; wherever he goes, the "fragrance of the knowledge of God" is spread (2:14, author, cf. 2:12). The peculiar double effect of this fragrance—to those perishing, "a fragrance from death to death"; to those being saved, "a fragrance from life to life"—is clearly an invitation and a challenge to the Corinthians to discern Paul's conduct from God's perspective.

Paul's "Afflictions"

All of 2 Corinthians 1–9 stands under the themes of "affliction" and "consolation" (1:3–7). Paul was "afflicted" in Asia (1:8), most probably at mortal risk during an Ephesian imprisonment;[29] he was subsequently "afflicted" in Macedonia, enduring "combats without and fears within" (7:5, author). Even his solicitude toward the Corinthians has been an "affliction" (2:4, 13)! Paul repeatedly lists his afflictions: in 4:8–12, where being "afflicted, . . . perplexed, . . . persecuted, . . . struck down, . . . always being given up to death for Jesus' sake" is characterized, in terms of the epiphany procession, as "carrying about in the body the death of Jesus so that the life of Jesus may be manifested in our bodies" (4:10, author). The triumph/epiphany metaphor in 2 Cor 2:14 and the allusion to the epiphany procession in 4:10 reveal a parallel structure: In both cases the afflictions of

---

27. Duff, "Metaphor," 87, 91.

28. Heidelberg and Hamburg Papyri: see Edgar Hennecke and Wilhelm Schneemelcher, *Writings Relating to Apostles, Apocalypses, and Related Subjects,* vol. 2 of *New Testament Apocrypha* (rev. ed.; trans. R. McL. Wilson; Louisville, Ky.: Westminster John Knox, 1992), 244–45, 253.

29. Furnish, *II Corinthians,* 122–25.

the apostolic workers are characterized as the public, ceremonial manifestation of the knowledge or power of God.[30]

Again in 6:4–10, Paul protests that his party of God's servants have conducted themselves with openness and purity in the face of "afflictions, hardships, calamities, beatings, imprisonments, riots, labors, sleepless nights, hunger"; he then appeals to the Corinthians to "make way" *(chōrēsate)* for these afflicted ministers, as for a sacred procession (7:2),[31] and thus to fulfill their sacred service *(diakonia)* to God (6:3–4). In 1 Cor 4:9–13, Paul presents another "affliction list" under a different though related metaphor, that of the ritualized spectacle of the arena:

> I think that God has exhibited us apostles as last of all, as though sentenced to death, because we have become a spectacle *[theatron]* to the world, to angels and to mortals. . . . To the present hour we are hungry and thirsty, we are poorly clothed and beaten and homeless, and we grow weary from the work of our own hands. When reviled, we bless; when persecuted, we endure; when slandered, we speak kindly. We have become like the rubbish of the world, the dregs of all things, to this very day.

As in the passages from 2 Corinthians, the afflictions suffered by the apostles are here represented in ritual terms: first, the ghastly rehearsals of imperial power in the arena; then also the (often violent) public expulsions of ritual victims *(perikatharmata, peripsēma)* in apotropaic rituals.[32] While Paul's reference to fighting "wild animals at Ephesus" (1 Cor 15:32) should perhaps not be taken literally (as it was, however, by the author of the Acts of Paul!), neither is the phrase merely an extravagant metaphor for facing opposition.[33] In Jewish and Christian tradition, the metaphor of facing wild beasts was clearly associated with confronting ruling authorities, and with the possible

---

30. Duff, "Metaphor," 89-90; Hafemann, *Suffering*, 73; on the affliction lists in general, J. T. Fitzgerald, *Cracks in an Earthen Vessel: An Examination of the Catalogues of Hardships in the Corinthian Correspondence* (Atlanta: Scholars, 1988).

31. Duff, "Metaphor," 87–88.

32. The NRSV translates with "rubbish" and "dregs," but the Greek words are technical terms from apotropaic rituals; see B. Hudson McLean, *The Cursed Christ: Mediterranean Expulsion Rituals and Pauline Soteriology* (JSNTSup 126; Sheffield: JSOT Press, 1996), 98–99, 107. On the arena, see Roland Auguet, *Cruelty and Civilization: The Roman Games* (New York: Routledge, 1972).

33. Anthony Tyrrell Hanson, *The Paradox of the Cross in the Thought of Paul* (JSNTSup 17; Sheffield: JSOT Press, 1987), 115–16, wrongly retreats from the "theatrical" connotations of Paul's language here. On the Acts of Paul, see Hamburg Papyrus 1–5; Hennecke and Schneemelcher, *Writings*, 251–54.

prospect of martyrdom.[34] The overall effect of Paul's language is to cast himself and his apostolic colleagues as those who consistently are *humiliated, ritually mistreated, and expelled* in public events that represented the prevailing order of power, and distinguished citizens from subjects.[35]

Paul "at War"

We do not exhaust the significance of Paul's affliction lists by determining their tradition—historical background, either among Stoic and Cynic traditions or the prophetic and apocalyptic traditions. Nevertheless, one aspect of Paul's apocalyptic perspective is his occasional identification of the power behind his opponents as "the dominion of the god of this age." He is engaged, not merely in a controversy with rival opinions, but in a war of darkness against light.[36]

Paul's use of triumph imagery (2 Cor 2) and his use of affliction lists cohere in the fundamental understanding of his apostolic *parousia* as participation in warfare.[37] The language of combat recurs in Paul's Letters: he calls upon the Romans to "demobilize" themselves from service to sin and to "surrender their members to God as weapons for right" (Rom 6:13, author).[38]

Paul describes himself as "at war" in 2 Cor 10:3–6:

> We do not wage war according to human standards; for the weapons of our warfare are not merely human, but they have divine power to destroy strongholds. We destroy arguments and every proud obstacle raised up against the knowledge of God, and we take every thought captive to obey Christ. We are ready to punish every disobedience when your obedience is complete.

This language derives from Cynic and Stoic discussions of the wise person's "warfare" with the passions. Contesting a Corinthian deprecation

---

34. Dan 6; Ignatius, *Rom.* 5.1. Hanson, *Paradox,* 119, gratuitously introduces "the strict party among Christian Jews" or even "the Pharisaic party among Jews" as the referent for the "wild animals."

35. Nippel, *Public Order,* 6: "Exemption from the humiliation of corporal punishment underlined the distinction between citizens and Roman subjects . . . as well as between citizens and slaves."

36. A point ably made by Susan R. Garrett, "The God of This World and the Affliction of Paul: 2 Cor 4:1–12," in *Greeks, Romans, and Christians: Essays in Honor of Abraham J. Malherbe* (ed. David L. Balch, Everett Ferguson, and Wayne A. Meeks; Minneapolis: Fortress, 1990), 117.

37. Similarly Lambrecht, "Defeated Paul," 185; Hanson, *Paradox,* 99.

38. Ernst Käsemann, *Commentary on Romans* (trans. G. W. Bromiley; Grand Rapids: Eerdmans, 1980), 177, considers a military sense "the most likely."

of his humble self-presentation, Paul declares that his warfare "consists in his manner of life. Far from being abject, the Paul who is *tapeinos* [humble] is combative. In this respect he is like the Cynic who appears in humiliating circumstances and garb but is actually at war." This "humble warrior" image stands in contrast to the image of "the self-sufficient, self-confident Stoic, secure in the fortification of his reason," an image with which Paul implicitly characterizes his opponents.[39]

All these metaphorical domains—the imagery of triumph, the afflictions of the arena or the expulsion ritual, the metaphor of combat—cohere in a common rhetorical strategy on Paul's part. He wishes, first, to call attention to his apostolic *parousia* as the public manifestation *(phanerōthēnai)* of divine power (Rom 1:16–17; 15:18–19). Second, he acknowledges that his *parousia* is normally characterized by both humility and public humiliation. In the context of the Corinthian correspondence, this is in part an acknowledgment of his unimpressive rhetorical skill, but also of his "afflictions," which may have been interpreted (by others) as divine punishment. Third, Paul insists, through use of a range of metaphors, that it is precisely through his apostolic *parousia as humbled* that God is glorified and God's power in Christ displayed. This paradoxical claim is the point of the triumphal image: "God will continue on his triumphal way though Paul appears only as a figure of shame in his procession."[40]

But how can *weakness* and humiliation manifest *power*?

Representing the Body of the Crucified

I emphasize again that Paul's metaphorical strategy is not "mere" metaphor. The affliction list in 2 Cor 11:23–27 is the most specific of these passages:

> Are they ministers of Christ? I am talking like a madman—I am a better one: with far greater labors, far more imprisonments, with countless floggings, and often near death. Five times I have received from the Jews the forty lashes minus one. Three times I was beaten with rods. Once I received a stoning. Three times I was shipwrecked; for a night and a day I was adrift at sea; on frequent journeys, in danger from rivers, danger from bandits, danger from my own people, danger from Gentiles, danger in the city, danger in the wilderness, danger at sea, danger from false brothers and sisters;

---

39. Abraham J. Malherbe, "Antisthenes and Odysseus, and Paul at War," *HTR* 76 (1983): 170–71. Hanson's derivation of Paul's language from Isa 40:2 and Zech 9:12 (LXX) is doubtful (*Paradox,* 99–101), and importing "unbelieving Jews" into 2 Cor 10 is unwarranted.

40. Marshall, *Enmity,* 316.

> in toil and hardship, through many a sleepless night, hungry and thirsty, often without food, cold and naked.

Note that first named among these very real "afflictions" are ritual punishments: the corporeal discipline of the synagogue, and the civic floggings of the Roman *polis* (city).[41] Indeed, Paul declares that his body has been inscribed with the marks of torture: "I carry the marks of Jesus branded on my body" (Gal 6:17).

The apostles' afflictions are one medium through which the crucified Jesus is publicly embodied. They are simultaneously manifestations of God's power. If Paul and his apostolic colleagues are put forward as a humiliated spectacle (1 Cor 4:9–13), they also thus reveal that "the kingdom of God depends not on talk but on power" (4:20). If the apostles "carry about the dying of Jesus" in their very bodies, it is "so that the life of Jesus may also be made visible in our bodies" (2 Cor 4:10, NRSV).

Similarly, Paul considers his proclamation of the gospel to be a medium through which the crucified Jesus is manifested publicly. Again and again in his letters, Paul speaks of representing the body of the crucified Jesus, and from what we have seen, Paul considers just these events to be manifestations of power and life. When he first came to the Corinthians, he resolved to "know nothing among [them] except Jesus Christ, and him crucified"; this was "a demonstration of the Spirit and of power" (1 Cor 2:2, 4). Paul heatedly reminds the Galatians that "it was before your eyes that Jesus Christ was publicly exhibited as crucified!" (Gal 3:1); do they now really misunderstand *how* God supplied them with the Spirit and worked miracles among them (3:5)?

By speaking of the public exhibition of Christ crucified (Gal 3:1), Paul calls upon his Galatian audience as "eyewitnesses."[42] But, of course, they saw not the actual crucifixion of Jesus, but *its representation in performance*. We cannot know what this representation looked like. As indicated in the ancient rhetorical handbooks, contemporary rhetorical practice involved vivid and impressive deliveries, so that (as Quintilian recommended) listeners "imagined the matter to have happened right before their eyes. All kinds of techniques were recommended to achieve the effect,

---

41. In 2 Cor 11:25, the "rods" *(rhabdoi)* with which Paul was beaten *(erabdisthen)* were carried publicly before Roman magistrates; they were at once instruments of coercion and symbolic of Roman power (Nippel, *Public Order,* 13–16).

42. On the rhetorical echoes here see Betz, *Galatians,* 131–32. In Gal 3:1, as Betz points out, *prographein* can mean either "proclaim publicly" (so the Jerusalem Bible: "in spite of the plain explanation you have had of the crucifixion of Jesus Christ"), or "portray publicly" (RSV; NEB translates, "Jesus Christ was openly displayed upon his cross"). Betz argues effectively for the second interpretation.

including impersonations and even holding up painted pictures" (though Quintilian frowned upon this latter practice). Giving an argument "presence" could mean bringing forward realia such as the marks of injury or torture. Minimally, the evidence of Paul's Letters suggests that Paul's apostolic performance included some visual representation of Christ as crucified. Further, Paul wanted others to *see* his apostolic presence, particularly in its weakness, affliction, and humiliation, as a representation of Christ— literally, a making-Christ-present-again—as crucified.[43]

This does not mean that, for Paul, the crucifixion may be regarded *in isolation* as the "demonstration of God's power." Statements to the effect that the proclamation of the cross *is* "the power of God" (e.g., 1 Cor 1:17–18) are elliptical. Therefore, it is potentially misleading to say that "it is precisely in the death of Jesus, represented to the world in the mortality and suffering of Christian apostles, that 'the life of Jesus' is manifested"; nor can recognizing the power of God be reduced to "perceiving the meaning *of Christ's death* and identifying oneself with that."[44] To the contrary, Paul never perceives weakness and suffering as meaningful in and of themselves.[45] Rather, for Paul, the cross manifests God's power because of *its inseparable connection with the resurrection of Christ. No contemplation of the cross alone would have turned its horror into blessing.* As J. Christiaan Beker observes,

> [In Paul's thought,] the cross of Christ does not permit a passion mysticism, a contemplation of the wounds of Christ, or a spiritual absorption into the sufferings of Christ *(conformitas crucis)*. Paul never sanctifies or hallows death, pain, and suffering. There is no hint of a masochistic delight in suffering. *The death of Christ is efficacious only because it stands within the radius of the victory of the resurrection.* . . . Although the death of Christ qualifies the resurrection of Christ as that of the Crucified One, the death of Christ does not in and by itself inaugurate the new age or in and by itself legitimize and sanctify suffering and death as the way in which God executes his lordship in an evil world, that is, as suffer-

---

43. Supposed distinctions between a "Semitic" orality and a "Greek" knowing through vision (e.g., Marianne Sawicki, *Seeing the Lord: Resurrection and Early Christian Practices* [Minneapolis: Fortress, 1994], 80-81) are overdrawn. Neither am I prepared to subsume visual terminology in 2 Corinthians as "susceptible of explanation in terms of the oral gospel" (Kelber, *Oral and Written Gospel,* 141). The goal of Paul's visual imagery is *not* "interiorizing the essentially invisible" (ibid., 142), but *the manifestation of God's power in public space.*

44. Against Furnish, *II Corinthians,* 189 (emphasis added to quotation).

45. Pickett, *The Cross in Corinth,* 141.

46. J. Christiaan Beker, *Paul the Apostle: The Triumph of God in Life and Thought* (Philadelphia: Fortress, 1980), 196, 199–200 (emphasis added).

ing love.[46]

Paul proclaims, and through his *parousia* represents, the crucified Christ as the manifestation of God's power *because this is the One whom God has raised.* Paul's wretched apostolic presence, wafting an odor suggesting death to those who do not believe, is for believers "not the stench of death at all but the 'sweet aroma of [the resurrected!] Christ.'" Paul can know his "carrying about in the body the dying of Jesus" also manifests the life of Jesus (2 Cor 4:10–11, author) *because* he knows "that the one who raised the Lord Jesus will raise us also with Jesus, and will bring us with you into his presence" (4:14).[47] Thus carrying about the dying of Jesus is not *itself* the full manifestation of God's power: rather, it points to Paul and his colleagues as those who still contend in "Christ's battle."[48] Put another way, the embodied showing-forth of the crucified Jesus is an apostolic strategy for representing the *risen* Christ.[49]

Knowing the risen Christ is, for Paul, neither remembering a past event—the resurrection—*as past,* as "dead" history; nor is it the present experience of ecstatic communion with the Lord. In Jürgen Moltmann's words, "'The resurrection of Christ' is a meaningful postulate only if its framework is the history which the resurrection itself throws open: the history of the liberation of human beings and nature from the power of death." The structure of this history is evident in Rom 8:11: "If the Spirit of the One who has raised Jesus from the dead dwells in you, the One who has raised Christ Jesus from the dead will give life to your mortal bodies also through the power of the Spirit which dwells in you" (author). Here Paul "links the perfect tense of Christ's resurrection with the present tense of the indwelling of the Spirit, and the present tense of the Spirit with the future tense of the resurrection of the dead."[50]

The point of examining imperial rituals of power in the Roman polis is that these were the prevalent "strategies of knowing" elsewhere in Paul's day. The *ekklēsia's* "proclaiming the Lord's death until he comes," and the apos-

---

47. Calvin J. Roetzel, "'As Dying, and Behold, We Live,' Death and Resurrection in Paul's Theology" *Int* 46 (1992): 5–18; Pickett, *The Cross in Corinth,* 140–41.

48. Hanson's phrase, *Paradox,* 114–15; see Kraftchick, "Death in Us, Life in You," 174–75.

49. Compare Marianne Sawicki's discussion of early Christian "strategies for recognizing the risen Lord," the "protocols of approach," which defined within the early *ekklēsiai* "what 'resurrection' itself means." As Sawicki puts it, "risen life is that mode of availability of Jesus to the church that results from the enactment or realization" of a particular protocol of praxis (Sawicki, *Seeing the Lord,* 1, 10, 79). I find it curious that Sawicki's discussion ignores Paul.

50. Jürgen Moltmann, "The Resurrection of Christ: Hope for the World," in *Resurrection Reconsidered* (ed. Gavin D'Costa; Oxford: Oneworld Publications, 196), 80–81.

tles' "carrying about the dying of Jesus in the body," are alike representations of the power of God because the crucified one so shown forth *is* the resurrected Jesus. That is, precisely the body exhibited by the Empire as tortured and crucified has been decisively *counter-exhibited* by God's act in raising Jesus from the dead; and that counter-display continues to be re-presented by apostolic and ecclesial performance as the locus of God's life-giving power. "Showing forth the Lord's death" thus constitutes a ritual gesture of defiance, a refusal to allow the Empire's exhibition of a crucified corpse to be determinative of the future of Jesus, or of the creation.

Habeas corpus Christi: An Ecclesiological Postscript

What I have just described as the strategic intent of Paul's self-presentation has, I think, profound implications for the way we read Paul's Letters today. Our own world, after all, is no stranger to imperial representations of power—representations often made in and upon the very bodies of subject peoples. Moreover, contemporary discussions of intentional counter-representations of power on the part of church groups present a provocative analogue to what I have described as Paul's apostolic performance.

Terrorism has been the focus of intense discussion, and the target of tremendous military action, since the spectacular terrorist attacks against the United States on September 11, 2001. We must nevertheless recognize that terrorism is neither new, nor does the strategy exclusively belong to avowed enemies of the United States. In the "national security states" developed and reinforced as an integral part of avowed U.S. policy since the 1980s, torture has routinely been used to dismember and disappear both human bodies and the body politic.

The development of torture as an instrument of terror, and thus of social control, at the level of military policy is one of the most salient aspects of our age. Latin American analysts speak of the creation of a "culture of fear" that isolates individuals and fragments the body politic so as to render a population passive and incapable of resistance.[51] The systematic effort of military strategists and architects of security policy to fund, train, equip, and coordinate military and paramilitary regimes over the decades since

---

51. On "fear as a cultural and political construct," see Juan E. Corradi, Patricia Weiss Fagen, and Manuel Antonio Garretón, eds., *Fear at the Edge: State Terrorism and Resistance in Latin America* (Berkeley and Los Angeles: University of California Press, 1992); on the psychological effects of institutionalized terrorism, Ignacio Martín-Baró, *Writings for a Liberation Psychology* (ed. Adrianne Aron and Shawne Corne; Cambridge, Mass.: Harvard University Press, 1994).

52. On state terrorism as an integral component of U.S. policy, see William Blum, *Killing Hope: U.S. Military and CIA Interventions since World War II* (Monroe, Maine: Common Courage Press, 1995); Edward S. Herman, *The Real Terror Network*

World War II is well documented, but is especially evident since the 1980s.[52]

State-sponsored terrorism is not a peculiarly Western phenomenon. Nevertheless, the increasingly steep upward gradient of Western power in the wake of the Soviet Union's collapse, and the apparently greater availability of democratic avenues of redress in Western democracies and the United States in particular, have led some Western activists to concentrate their efforts on ending Western support for terror regimes. Jack Nelson-Pallmeyer, for example, has argued eloquently that the stated Pentagon policy of low-intensity conflict constitutes nothing less than a "confessional situation" for Christians in the United States today; and his published indictment of the U.S. School of the Americas condenses a much larger protest movement in the United States.[53]

My purpose here is not to assess questions of relative blame, but to lift up the relevance of Paul's subversive theology and praxis to a modern world in which terror regimes thrive. In a theological analysis of explicitly eucharistic strategies of resistance in Agosto Pinochet's Chile, William Cavanaugh has argued that when Christian doctrine and liturgy have envisioned the church as the "*mystical* Body of Christ," somehow transcending the physical plane of public space, Christ has remained politically disembodied. In such circumstances the body of Christ may be successfully "disappeared" by the torture regime.[54] However, his investigation of "the actual and potential impact of the Eucharist on the dictatorship" of Pinochet leads Cavanaugh to regard the Eucharist as "the Church's counterpolitics to the politics of torture."

Cavanaugh discusses the Sebastián Acevedo Movement against Torture in Chile to show "what it means for the church to perform liturgically the body of Christ in opposition to the state's liturgy of torture":

What was so different and disruptive about the Sebastián Acevedo Movement was its sense of liturgy, the public ritual acts of solidar-

---

(Boston: South End Press, 1982); Edward S. Herman and Gerry O'Sullivan, *The "Terrorism" Industry* (New York: Pantheon, 1989); Noam Chomsky, *Pirates and Emperors: International Terrorism in the Real World* (London: Spokesman, 1987); Alexander George, ed., *Western State Terrorism* (New York: Polity, 1991); Jack Nelson-Pallmeyer, *War against the Poor: Low-Intensity Conflict and Christian Faith* (Maryknoll, N.Y.: Orbis Books, 1989) and *School of Assassins* (Maryknoll, N.Y.: Orbis Books, 1997); Eqbal Ahmad, David Barsamian, and Greg Ruggiero, *Terrorism, Theirs and Ours* (New York: Seven Stories Press, 2001).

53. Nelson-Pallmeyer, *War against the Poor*; idem, *School of Assassins*.

54. William Cavanaugh, *Torture and Eucharist: Theology, Politics, and the Body of Christ* (Challenges in Contemporary Theology; London and New York: Routledge, 1998), especially chs. 3, 4.

ity and denunciation that members would perform with their
bodies. Locations were chosen for their symbolic importance:
places of torture, the courts, government buildings, media head-
quarters. Exactly at a prearranged time, members of the
Movement—sometimes as many as 150—would appear out of the
crowds, unfurl banners and pass out leaflets, often blocking traffic
[and performing brief liturgies]. . . .

This type of street liturgy precisely reverses the anti-liturgy of
torture in that it irrupts into and disrupts the public places of the
city which the regime has so carefully policed. New spaces are
opened which resist the strategy of place which the regime has
imposed. . . . In an astonishing ritual transformation, clandestine
torture centers are revealed to the passersby for what they are, as if
a veil covering the building were abruptly taken away.[55]

Organized rituals of remembrance for the disappeared, taking place in
public, and especially outside the chambers where bodies were tortured,
defied the regime's disposition of human bodies. Recitals of the names of
the disappeared ritually re-presented the tortured and demanded that the
regime account for their bodies in a communal act of habeas corpus. The
regime's covert application of terror to human bodies is brought to light,
"not . . . by mere denunciation in words and song. The repressive apparatus is made visible on the very bodies of the protesters as they are beaten,
tear gassed, hosed down, and dragged away to prison." That is, the demon-
strators "use their bodies as ritual or theatrical instruments."[56]

As I have argued was the case for Paul, Cavanaugh writes that "the
body becomes the battleground between evangelical and anti-evangelical
forces." Such public eucharistic liturgies thus work to reconstruct the dis-
membered body politic:

The logic of Eucharist [is] an alternative economy of pain and the
body. . . . Where torture is an anti-liturgy for the realization of the
state's power on the bodies of others, Eucharist is the liturgical
realization of Christ's suffering and redemptive Body in the bodies of his followers. Torture creates fearful and isolated bodies,
bodies docile to the purposes of the regime; the Eucharist effects

---

55. Ibid., 274–75. Cavanaugh also discusses the Vicaría de Solidaridad, on which
see also Hugo Fruhling, "Resistance to Fear in Chile: The Experience of the Vicaría
de la Solidaridad in Chile," in *Fear at the Edge* (ed. Corradi et al.), 121–41.

56. Ibid., 276.

the Body of Christ, a body marked by resistance to worldly power. Torture creates victims; Eucharist creates witnesses, *martyrs*. Isolation is overcome in the Eucharist by the building of a social Body which resists the state's attempts to disappear it.[57]

Cavanaugh stresses that this understanding of the Eucharist is based on Paul's theology in 1 Corinthians. In the light of my preceding discussion, I would go further to suggest that the public liturgies Cavanaugh has analyzed do not merely appropriate Pauline concepts or language for discrete political purposes. They embody an anti-imperial understanding of the future of human bodies and bodiliness that is structurally analogous to the "liturgical" aspects of Paul's apostolic praxis.

The "work" of the Pauline *ekklēsia* was to "show forth the Lord's death until he comes" (1 Cor 11:26, author), to hold before public gaze the representation of the Empire's victim *as the One whom God had vindicated bodily* through resurrection. This strategy, a *habeas corpus Christi*, refuses to surrender the body of Jesus to the disposition of the Empire. Nor does it render that particular body irrelevant, however, by a spiritualization of Jesus' memory. The body *as tortured, as crucified*, must be carried about, represented, embodied in the persons of his apostles, until the deadly representations of the Empire's power are brought to an end by the One to whom all powers will ultimately be subjected (1 Cor 15:24).[58] Cavanaugh sums up this understanding of apostolic and ecclesial liturgy as I have discussed it above—but he is describing the strategy of the Sebastián Acevedo Movement's public actions:

> Christ's Body reappears precisely as a suffering Body offered in sacrifice; Christ's Body is made visible in its wounds. But this Body is also marked with future glory, for Christ has suffered in order to triumph over suffering and defeat the powers of death. The space it creates is therefore a space crossed by the Kingdom of God. We witness a liturgical anticipation of the end of history and the resurrection of the body.[59]

Today, no less than in the ancient Roman environment, the crucifor-

---

57. Ibid., 278–81.
58. As Pickett observes in *The Cross in Corinth*, 141, for Paul, the cruciform life "is the appropriate mode of existence only until the apocalyptic resurrection of the dead."
59. Ibid., 277.

mity of an apostolic performance like Paul's—a praxis that makes present the body of Christ on the public landscape—will inevitably subvert the ideology and ritualization of actual or aspiring empires. Those who wish not only to study Paul's apostolic praxis, but to take on a contemporary community discipline informed and shaped by it, may find themselves in the company of those already struggling to expose and contend against the imperial instrumentalities of terror in our own world.

– 4 –

RESISTING IMPERIAL DOMINATION
AND INFLUENCE

Paul's Apocalyptic Rhetoric in 1 Corinthians

Rollin A. Ramsaran

Studies of Greco-Roman rhetoric have done much to illuminate how Paul draws on the standard rhetorical forms in formulating the arguments in his letters. Yet how Judean apocalyptic traditions inform or possibly provide the backbone to Paul's arguments have not been adequately examined. Paul moves between two rhetorical registers,[1] that of the Jewish apocalyptist and that of the Greco-Roman rhetor. Indeed, this investigation of 1 Corinthians may suggest that Paul "mixes" registers, as presumably has already happened in his personal history as a Diaspora Jew and, more recently, as one called by Christ as an apostle to the Gentiles.

In 1 Corinthians, Paul claims that he does not preach the gospel "with eloquent wisdom" or in "lofty words or wisdom" (1 Cor 1:17; 2:1). Measured against the canons of Greco-Roman rhetoric, however, Paul's ensuing words are persuasively shaped and argued.[2] Hence, it is probably not correct to relate "eloquent wisdom" and "lofty words or wisdom" in a

---

1. More likely, Paul mixes three primary registers: the Jewish apocalyptist, the Greco-Roman rhetor, and the Hellenistic moralist. Here I confine myself to the first two. On Paul as moralist, see my "In the Steps of the Moralists: Paul's Rhetorical Argumentation in Philippians 4," in *Rhetoric, Ethics, and Moral Persuasion in Biblical Discourse: Essays from the Heidelberg 2002 Conference* (ed. Tom H. Olbricht and Anders Eriksson; Harrisburg, Pa.: Trinity Press International, forthcoming). For a discussion of "registers" in the context of orally performed speech, see Richard A. Horsley, "Recent Studies of Oral-derived Literature and Q," in *Whoever Hears You Hears Me: Prophets, Performance, and Tradition in Q* (by R. A. Horsley with Jonathan A. Draper; Harrisburg, Pa.: Trinity Press International, 1999), 164–66.

2. Important studies treating the context of 1 Corinthians 1–4: Duane Lifton, *St. Paul's Theology of Proclamation: 1 Corinthians 1–4 and Greco-Roman Rhetoric* (Cambridge: Cambridge University Press, 1994); Stephen M. Pogoloff, *Logos and Sophia: The Rhetorical Situation of 1 Corinthians* (SBLDS 134; Atlanta: Scholars,

one-to-one correspondence to "rhetoric" as a monolithic entity.[3] Rather, Paul contrasts (1) persuasive words based in the educationally, religiously, and politically developed power structures of the Greco-Roman world with (2) persuasive words based in the apocalyptic intervention of God and God's revealed destiny for "set apart" humanity. Paul engages the Corinthians in a "war of myths" or a collision in "worldviews."[4]

Analysis of "apocalyptic rhetoric," which is now in its initial sounding, remains largely undefined.[5] For purposes of analysis here, "apocalyptic" refers to a worldview, a symbolic universe that articulates an interpretation of reality.[6] The apocalyptic worldview is purportedly established by revelation: visionaries learn that God will move to "rectify a world gone awry" by delivering it from the present evil age into a coming age of peace and harmony.[7] "Rhetoric," then, is persuasive argumentation to promote that worldview. Paul is an apocalyptic thinker[8] who operates in a world where rhetorical conventions are a given—part of the Zeitgeist.[9]

Paul uses the conventions of rhetoric in what he believes is an appropriate framework: the inbreaking of God's power in new human communities through the Christ-event and its subsequent release of Spirit. In so doing, Paul refuses to be identified with any type of rhetoric lodged in a

---

1992); Rollin A. Ramsaran, *Liberating Words: Paul's Use of Rhetorical Maxims in 1 Corinthians 1–10* (Valley Forge, Pa.: Trinity Press International, 1996); Bruce W. Winter, *Philo and Paul among the Sophists* (Cambridge: Cambridge University Press, 1994).

3. One need only note the disagreements within the first-century world concerning style, technique, and presentation of the orator. On sophist and antisophist differentiation, see Winter, *Philo and Paul,* 19–115, 145–202.

4. Amos N. Wilder, "Apocalyptic Rhetorics," in *Jesus' Parables and the War of Myths* (Philadelphia: Fortress, 1982), 157–64.

5. See Gregory L. Bloomquist and W. Gregory Carey, eds., *Apocalyptic Rhetoric* (St. Louis: Chalice Press, 1999), esp. the concluding essay by Bloomquist: "Methodological Criteria for Apocalyptic Rhetoric: A Suggestion for the Expanded Use of Sociorhetorical Analysis," 181–203.

6. See a full discussion of the distinctions between apocalypse as genre, apocalyptic eschatology, and apocalypticism in John J. Collins, *The Apocalyptic Imagination: An Introduction to the Jewish Matrix of Christianity* (2d ed.; Grand Rapids: Eerdmans, 1998), 1–42.

7. Martinus C. de Boer, "Paul and Apocalyptic Eschatology," in *The Encyclopedia of Apocalypticism* vol. 1 (ed. John J. Collins; New York: Continuum, 1998), 349–53. De Boer carefully defines and then labels this perspective as "apocalyptic eschatology."

8. J. Christiaan Beker, *Paul the Apostle: The Triumph of God in Life and Thought* (Philadelphia: Fortress, 1987), 135–81.

9. George A.Kennedy, *New Testament Interpretation through Rhetorical Criticism* (Chapel Hill: University of North Carolina Press, 1984), 3–12; Ramsaran, *Liberating Words,* 147 n. 14; James L. Kinneavy, *Greek Rhetorical Origins of Christian Faith* (Oxford: Oxford University Press, 1987), 56–90.

framework of human boastfulness and power manipulation.[10] Here, then, I ask: how would an *apocalyptist*, in this case Paul, argue using Greco-Roman rhetoric? With that question in mind, an analysis of Paul's *dispositio*, or arrangement of the material, in 1 Corinthians is in order.

Paul's Two Modes of Arrangement in 1 Corinthians

Much attention has been given to the rhetorical aspect of arrangement (dispositio) in terms of the various parts of a speech, that is, "disposition *internal* to the discourse," or "text-internal dispositio."[11] A deliberative speech, for example, consists of an exordium, (optional) narration, proposition, partition, proof, and peroration.[12] A variety of text-internal arrangement patterns developed in antiquity from different social, cultural, and political institutional settings.[13] The arrangement pattern for deliberative discourse, for example, arises from the social setting of the assembly (i.e., the "parts of speech model" we recognize from the rhetorical handbooks as slightly different from the judicial pattern).[14] In 1 Corinthians Paul follows a straightforward[15] deliberative pattern for an assembly.[16]

What needs more attention with regard to 1 Corinthians is "the disposition external to the discourse," the "text-external dispositio,"[17] a

---

10. Winter, *Philo and Paul,* 179–202.

11. Wilhelm Wuellner, "Arrangement," in *Handbook of Classical Rhetoric in the Hellenistic Period: 330 B.C.–A.D. 400* (ed. Stanley E. Porter; Leiden: Brill, 1997), 52, 78–79, closely following H. Lausberg, *Elemente der literarischen Rhetorik* ([1st ed., 1963] 8th ed.; Munich: Hueber, 1984).

12. Kennedy, *Rhetorical Criticism,* 23–24. Cf. Burton L. Mack, *Rhetoric and the New Testament* (Minneapolis: Fortress, 1990), 41–42.

13. Wuellner, "Arrangement," 52–53.

14. The parts of the deliberative speech are: exordium, (optional) narration, proposition, partition, proof, and peroration (see note 12, above). For a discussion of the history of "arrangement" in Greek and Latin traditions, including the rhetorical handbooks (Aristotle, *Rhetorica Anaximenes, Rhetorica ad Herennium;* Quintilian, *Institutio oratoria*), see Wuellner, "Arrangement," 52–73.

15. With respect to text-internal discourse, "arrangement of parts as a whole can be found in two types: (1) arrangement in *two* parts for tension and polarity, contrast or balance (as in thesis/antithesis); or (2) *three* parts for beginning, middle, and end of the whole, . . . which is *utilitas*—appropriate. By amplifying the middle part of the tripartite arrangement, one achieves a five-part whole, as in the parts of discourse (proem, *narratio,* proofs, refutation, epilogue). This quinquepartite system greatly influenced the order of the classical handbooks of the rhetorical *technai*" (Wuellner, "Arrangement," 78–79).

16. Margaret M. Mitchell, *Paul and the Rhetoric of Reconciliation: An Exegetical Investigation of the Language and Composition of 1 Corinthians* (Louisville, Ky.: Westminster John Knox, 1992), 182–94 and passim.

17. Wuellner, "Arrangement," 52; 79–80, with note 12, above.

speaker/writer's particular perspective, worldview, partiality, or bias. This external disposition comes from social circumstances and a shared ideology: pertinent examples are educational schools and their practice of declamation; philosophical schools with their protreptic outreach and paraenetical maintenance; or philosophic and religious teachers with their concern for psychagogic personal and spiritual development, as well as the maintenance of a coherent worldview or "sacred canopy."[18] "This orientation . . . constitutes the ordering principle of the discourse and guarantees its structural unit as a whole."[19]

First Corinthians 1:10 states the main point in the argument of 1 Corinthians: lay aside divisions and become unified.[20] But what is Paul's larger "external order," framework, worldview, "sacred canopy" (Paul's bias, if you will[21]) that provides a warrant or motivation for reconciliation and unity? What informs Paul's "text-external dispositio"?

Paul's bias is set out succinctly in the first paragraph of 1 Corinthians. What gives shape to reality is the *thelēma theou*, the "will of God" (1:1), which calls *hagioi* (set-apart ones) in the name of the Lord Jesus Christ (not Caesar; 1:2), gives this assembly in Corinth and presumably "set-apart"

---

18. Ibid., 53–55. On the concept of "sacred canopy" as "world-construction" and "world maintenance," see Peter L. Berger, *The Sacred Canopy: Elements of a Sociological Theory of Religion* (New York: Doubleday, 1967), 3–51.

19. Wuellner, "Arrangement," 79–80 (again following Lausberg, 1984). This text-external dispositio based on partiality also finds variety in its final patterns: "Lausberg defined partiality as the main principle of arrangement. He distinguishes three types of oratorical tactics: (1) the straightforward tactic *(ductus simplex)* working with perspicuity as means of expression; (2) the tactic with deceptive approaches of three subtypes *(ductus subtilis, figuratus,* and *obliquus);* and (3) the tactic using a mixture of these previous four types *(ductus mixtus)*" (Wuellner, 79).

    In what follows below, it becomes apparent that Paul employs the *ductus mixtus*. With regard to his apocalyptic bias/partiality he can be quite straightforward *(ductus simplex)* at 1 Cor 2:7–8; 7:31b; and 15:24–28. In his critique of Corinthian "leaders" who connected themselves to "worldly power/wisdom," Paul advances the critique with an oblique argument *(meteschematisa,* "covert allusion"; *ductus obliquus)* in 1 Cor 1–4. In his employment of an apocalyptic topos (critique of rulers, restoration of the people of God, and vindication of the martyrs; see directly below) as a story frame for 1 Cor 1–15, Paul subtly *(ductus subtilis)* encases the letter in a form that reinforces the Corinthian believers' common worldview. Paul's use of *ductus figuratus* is evident throughout the letter, but especially see 1 Cor 3 (field, building, temple) and 1 Cor 12 (the body image).

20. Mitchell, *Rhetoric of Reconciliation,* 198–200.

21. "All arrangement arises either *from the nature of the case* [minimize divisions in the Corinthian community], or *from the instinct of the speaker* [Paul's apocalyptic worldview], which follows the two *genera dispositionum* of *Rhetorica ad Herennium*" (Wuellner, "Arrangement," 70; emphases added). I am suggesting that Paul works from both perspectives at once in 1 Corinthians.

assemblies in every place gifts that sustain community (1:5–7a), and finds its completion in the revealing of the Lord Jesus Christ on the day of judgment (1:7b–8). Thus God's will is faithful (1:9), and it calls forth unity among those who really are "set apart." As is apparent, this *thelēma theou*, this will of God, is expressed within an apocalyptic worldview.

Paul's Rhetoric: Finding an Apocalyptic Topos

If, indeed, "disposition external to the discourse" blends invention and arrangement into a mutual process,[22] then it is fitting to ask at what "place" Paul might find material to advance his "text-external dispositio"—now defined as the working out of God's will in an apocalyptic schema. What from Paul's Jewish heritage might be called (to use Greco-Roman rhetorical terms) a topos (place, traditional topic/theme) around which apocalyptic expression took place? From what apocalyptic topos does Paul draw? Stated in this manner, our concern, then, is with an element of Paul's "native or indigenous rhetoric."[23]

In an insightful reading of Galatians, Robert Hall suggests that Second Temple apocalyptists recognized a "revelatory topos" that was fundamental in undergirding the validity of their argumentation, that is, an argumentation for "the worldview disclosed when God reveals his judgments."[24] The revelatory topos consists of four elements: "(1) a claim to inspiration, (2) a revelation of divine judgment ordering the world into righteous and wicked camps, (3) a call to join the righteous realm God rules and to repudiate the

---

22. "At this point [disposition external to the text] arrangement is seen as closely related to inventio"; Wuellner, "Arrangement," 79.

23. The terms "native" and "indigenous" are taken from Robert G. Hall, "Arguing Like an Apocalypse: Galatians and an Ancient *Topos* outside the Greco-Roman Rhetorical Tradition," *NTS* 42 (1996): 434–53. Hall's work provides a balance in perspective often overlooked in the rhetorical study of Paul's letters: "Orators trained in the handbook tradition, recollecting frequent admonitions to use whatever persuades, had freedom to utilize local styles of argumentation when required. Perhaps the logical argument in Galatians puzzles rhetorical critics because they have relied too heavily on the styles of argumentation chosen as examples in the Greco-Roman rhetorical handbooks and have largely neglected forms of argumentation developed by apocalyptists and other ancient Jewish and Christian writers" (435).

Of course, the question of other native apocalyptic *topoi* within the Hellenistic world is quite appropriate apart from the Jewish heritage. On apocalypticism as a prominent movement in the cultures of the larger Hellenistic world, see John J. Collins, "Jewish Apocalyptic against Its Hellenistic Near Eastern Background," *BASOR* 220 (1975): 27-36. Cf. Collins, *Apocalyptic Imagination*, 33–37.

24. Hall, "Arguing Like an Apocalypse," 436, 437–39. Hall's primary sources are *1 Enoch* 72–82 (Astronomical Book); *1 Enoch* 85–90 (Animal Apocalypse); and *Jubilees* 15 (a revealed argument for the necessity of circumcision).

wicked realm ruled by other forces, and (4) an implication that this choice includes a course of action the author advocates."[25]

Here, with regard to 1 Corinthians, I move in a slightly different direction. What topos sums up the apocalyptic worldview—a worldview beginning with the movement of God (the will of God) that intersects human history through time? Rather than focusing on the elements of argumentation per se or the argumentation's validity, I seek a topos that details (provides a pattern for) a shared apocalyptic worldview: the text-external *dispositio*, the arrangement of a shared story.[26]

Richard Horsley provides a descriptive scheme common to Judean apocalyptic literature that is not based on "a synthetic construct of typical elements or features abstracted from a variety of Jewish 'revelatory' literature ranging over several centuries from the third century B.C.E. to late antiquity."[27] Rather, Horsley's scheme is derived from sources prior to the New Testament (namely, Dan 7–12; the early sections of *1 Enoch;* and the conclusion of the *Testament of Moses*). These sources derive from a common social setting of imperial domination.[28] Hence, these writings advocate a "critical demystifying of the pretenses and practices of the dominant order."[29] Scholars are quickly learning that this is a perspective not lost on the apostle Paul.[30]

Horsley's proposal is attractive: God is the initiator in a movement from problem to encounter and on to full resolution—a story.[31] In other

---

25. Hall, "Arguing Like an Apocalypse," 436.

26. On worldviews as represented in "story" both in documents from the Second Temple and early Christian periods, see N. T. Wright, *The New Testament and the People of God* (Christian Origins and the People of God 1; Minneapolis: Fortress, 1992), 47–80.

27. Richard A. Horsley, "The Kingdom of God and the Renewal of Israel: Synoptic Gospels, Jesus Movements, and Apocalypticism," in *Encyclopedia of Apocalypticism* vol. 1 (ed. John J. Collins; New York: Continuum, 1998), 303.

28. Ibid., 304–9.

29. Ibid., 309.

30. See the important work by Richard A. Horsley, ed., *Paul and Empire: Religion and Power in Roman Imperial Society* (Valley Forge, Pa.: Trinity Press International, 1997); along with Dieter Georgi, *Theocracy in Paul's Praxis and Theology* (trans. David E. Green; Minneapolis: Fortress, 1991); Neil Elliott, *Liberating Paul: The Justice of God and the Politics of the Apostle* (Maryknoll, N.Y.: Orbis Books, 1994); and James R. Hollingshead, *The Household of Caesar and the Body of Christ: A Political Interpretation of the Letters from Paul* (Lanham, Md.: University Press of America, 1998). Now with more detail, Peter Oakes, *Philippians: From People to Letter* (SNTSMS 110; Cambridge: Cambridge University Press, 2001), 129–74; and Mikael Tellbe, *Paul between Synagogue and State: Christians, Jews, and Civic Authorities in 1 Thessalonians, Romans, and Philippians* (ConBNT 34; Stockholm: Almqvist & Wiksell, 2001), 238–59.

31. Compare de Boer, "Paul and Apocalyptic Eschatology," 352–54.

words, Judean apocalyptic literature arranged a worldview for its hearers, advocated a "text-external dispositio" (in rhetorical terms), told a "story" with the subsequent components (following Horsley): "[1] God would soon judge oppressive rulers, foreign and/or domestic; [2] restore the 'kingdom' to the people themselves; and [3] vindicate those who had died in defense of the traditional way of life."[32] This, then, is an apocalyptic topos fit for "text-external disposition" at the time of Paul: critique of rulers, restoration of the people, vindication of martyrs. Might this "story" have informed the thinking and arguments of Paul?

⸗The question can be asked: Why might Paul select a topos from his "native Judean rhetoric" over options from the Greco-Roman rhetorical tradition? A quick survey of the rhetorical handbooks indicates the steps in developing the *dispositio,* or arrangement of one's speech, are entrenched in a literate, elite, Greco-Roman value structure: advantage as security; honor; might; crafty use of money, promises, and deception, if necessary; and wisdom, temperance, and self-control as values, always based on one's high social standing, never apart from partiality.[33] Rhetorical handbook advice on arrangement would not support (1) Paul's view of God as the one who destroys the wise, the crafty, and the powerful (1 Cor 1:19–20, 28; 3:19–20); (2) Paul's view of the people God calls: "not many of you were wise according to worldly standards, not many were powerful, not many were of noble birth" (1 Cor 1:26, RSV); (3) Paul's view of the exemplary nature of his own life before God: "when reviled, we bless; when persecuted, we endure; when slandered, we try to conciliate; we have become, and are now, as the refuse of the world, the offscouring of all things" (4:12b–13, RSV). First Corinthians is clearly a battle between worldviews; at one level then, even technical rhetoric is subject to that clash.[34]

Text-External Arrangement in 1 Corinthians

The apocalyptic topos identified above, essential in all of Paul's thinking and writing, fits 1 Corinthians as a whole when slight adjustments are made for the revised "now/not yet" perspective of Pauline believers in Jesus. Judean apocalyptic literature spoke of an "old time" moving through judgment into a "new time," with critique and judgment of rulers, restoration of the people, and vindication of the faithful as the pivotal turning

---

32. Horsley, "The Kingdom of God," 341.

33. Here following headings and subheadings in *Rhetorica ad Herennium* 3.2.3–3.3.6. For consideration of other rhetorical handbook traditions, see note 14, above.

34. The text-*internal* dispositio may remain as expected (the "parts of speech" structure; see notes 14 and 15, above), but one should expect a clash at the value structure level within the discourse. This is what we find in 1 Corinthians.

point of the ages. Paul and the followers he sought to influence, on the other hand, thought in terms of the old and new times overlapping (1 Cor 10:11).[35] Critique, restoration, and vindication have already gotten under-way between the times and would continue until the "coming" of Jesus (1 Cor 15:23–28).

First Corinthians 1–4: Critique of Rulers and Their Domination System

In 1 Corinthians 1–4, Paul explicitly censures "the rulers of this age," retainers such as "the wise person, the scribe, the debater," and any who depend on craftiness, worldly wisdom, trained speech, or boasting. In doing so, he criticizes Corinthian leaders and their followers implicitly (ever more explicitly as the section develops, as in 3:1–4; 4:6–8, 18–21). These people pattern their lives, leadership, and rhetoric on a Greco-Roman domination system rather than the pattern or mind of Christ demonstrated in and through the cross (1 Cor 2:7–8, 14–16; 3:4). Paul finds the value system inherent in Greco-Roman rhetoric to be aligned with (and complicitous in promoting) this domination system.[36] Therefore, in constructing his counter-rhetoric, Paul leans heavily upon a text-external *dispositio* that appropriates a Jewish apocalyptic *topos* instead of Greco-Roman aristocratic values.

Paul's ensuing rhetoric is countercultural.[37] He takes aim at those he views as inappropriate leaders and also members of the community who follow them, trying to obtain high status. First, in 1 Cor 1:17–2:5, Paul employs a "cross rhetoric" that overturns Greco-Roman aristocratic ideals and power relations. He asserts that the cross has demonstrated definitively that God has again delivered the weak and brought down the mighty (1:26–29). Second, in 1 Cor 2:6–16, Paul utilizes a "Spirit rhetoric" in the form of apocalyptic wisdom.[38] Such an apocalyptic wisdom implies inspiration and revelation as a community experience rather than the domain of the highly educated, rhetorically trained, and status-seeking elite.[39]

---

35. "Upon whom the ends of the ages have arrived" (author; *eis hous ta telē tōn aiōnōn katēntēken*). See J. Paul Sampley, *Walking between the Times: Paul's Moral Reasoning* (Minneapolis: Fortress, 1991), 7–24.

36. David A. deSilva, "Investigating Honor Discourse: Guidelines from Classical Rhetoricians," in *SBLSP 1997* (Atlanta: Scholars, 1997), 491–525.

37. Ibid., 511–14.

38. For "Spirit-inspired rhetoric," see John R. Levinson, "Did the Spirit Inspire Rhetoric? An Exploration of George Kennedy's Definition of Early Christian Rhetoric," in *Persuasive Artistry: Studies in New Testament Rhetoric in Honor of George A. Kennedy* (ed. Duane F. Watson; Sheffield: JSOT Press, 1991), 25–40.

39. Argued as a persuasive thesis in Allen R. Hunt, *The Inspired Body: Paul, the Corinthians, and Divine Inspiration* (Macon, Ga.: Mercer, 1996).

Third, in 3:5–4:5, Paul begins a "freedom rhetoric" that counsels mutual cooperation over against status-seeking attachments to human leaders. Rather than claiming status through "enslavement" (cf. 7:23) to an individual or faction, believers are reminded that "all things are yours" (including leaders) and accountability is to Christ and God alone.[40] Finally, in 4:8–13, Paul returns to "cross rhetoric" by advancing his personal example within a hardship catalog: apostles are sentenced to death, led in parade, held in disrepute (1 Cor 4:9–13).[41]

In sum, in 1 Corinthians 1–4, Paul insists that his assembly in Corinth, both leaders and members, are not to take their cues from the Roman imperial order dominated by the city and provincial aristocracy, but from the crucified Christ, in whom God has brought the dominant order under imminent judgment. "Paul's *ekklēsiai* are thus [to be] local communities of an alternative society to the Roman imperial order."[42] I now briefly consider the shape of these alternative communities.

First Corinthians 5–14: Renewal of Community Life among Gentiles

The second key theme in Judean apocalyptic literature is God's restoration of sovereignty to "the people of the holy ones of the Most High" (Dan 7:27), that is, a renewal of the oppressed people of God. In his own *apokalypsis,* Paul became convinced that the restoration of Israel had already started. Since the promises to Abraham had now been fulfilled in Christ, moreover, he himself had been commissioned to bring the good news to other peoples subject to the Roman imperial order and to catalyze new communities "in Christ."

Structurally, 1 Cor 5–14 is commonly marked off from 1–4 by a turn from addressing divisions among the Corinthians focused on rival leaders, to answering Corinthian inquiries or responding to reported problems. Paul responds to reports of improper sexual and litigious behavior in chapters 5 and 6, and then in chapters 7–14 and 16 he takes up a series of Corinthian questions commonly marked by the *peri de* (now concerning) formula.[43]

---

40. For "freedom rhetoric" based on Paul's maxim usage in 1 Cor 1–4 and, then, reinforced throughout 1 Cor 1–10, see Ramsaran, *Liberating Words.*

41. On hardship catalogs in general and this text in particular, see John T. Fitzgerald, *Cracks in an Earthen Vessel: An Examination of the Catalogues of Hardships in the Corinthian Correspondence* (SBLDS 99; Atlanta: Scholars, 1988).

42. Richard A. Horsley, "Building an Alternative Society: Introduction," in *Paul and Empire* (ed. Horsley), 209.

43. The *peri de* formula occurs at 7:1, 25; 8:1; 16:1; and 16:12. On the *peri de* formula as a marker, see the discussion in Margaret M. Mitchell, "Concerning *PERI DE* in 1 Corinthians," *NovT* 31 (1989): 229–56. Of course, Paul responds to other reported items throughout 1 Cor 7–16 as well (e.g., chs. 11 and 15).

There is ostensibly a certain amount of discussion and debate in Corinth concerning how the fulfillment of God's promises and access to God's presence would be achieved. In Paul's opinion, anyhow, the implementation of "the people of God" in its Corinthian locale had gone askew at points and a sense of restoration/renewal was needed. In 1 Cor 5–14, Paul, like other apocalyptic writers, reasserts the group's boundaries and insists that the people maintain holiness as a distinctive community separate from the dominant oppressive order. He argues that the community's exclusive loyalty to God cannot be compromised by affiliation with other "lords" and their sacrificial communities. Properly ordered and acceptable worship before God is marked by common confession, active participation and inclusion among members, and expressions of spiritual gifts that lead to a true love within the common group.

For Paul—after Christ's death and resurrection, in which the fulfillment has begun—the Spirit of God is the force that brings the presence of the new time within the framework of an old time now passing away (Rom 8:23; 2 Cor 1:21–22; 5:5).[44] The building and discipline of community is empowered by the presence and activity of the Spirit (e.g., Gal 3:1–5). (1) First Corinthians 5–14 describes the inspiration and guidance of the Spirit's power as fundamental to individual discipleship and to the community discipline and solidarity of *the people of God*. In chapter 5, the community's disciplining of an errant member is accomplished "when . . . my spirit is present with the power of the Lord Jesus"; here, "power" is a reference to the Spirit.[45] (2) In chapter 6, it is again the Spirit that empowers individual and community discipline: "You were washed, . . . sanctified, . . . justified . . . in the Spirit of our God" (6:11); "Your body is a temple of the Holy Spirit" (6:19). (3) In chapter 7, Paul claims that his own advice on marriage and sexual relations is authorized by the Spirit: "I think that I also have the Spirit of God" (7:40, NASB). (4) In chapters 12–14, Paul marks the functioning of the restored people of God by an active life in the power of the Spirit: "No one can say, 'Jesus is Lord' except by the Holy Spirit" (12:3); the Spirit is the source of all giftedness such that the goal is full participation of all, not competition (12:12); true manifestations of the Spirit build up the community (12:14). This "life in the Spirit" marks the visitation of God to the people of God and the resulting renewal of God's presence.[46]

---

44. Gordon D. Fee, *Paul, the Spirit, and the People of God* (Peabody, Mass.: Hendrickson, 1996), 49–56.

45. Richard B. Hays, *First Corinthians* (Interpretation; Louisville, Ky.: John Knox, 1997), 84.

46. Fee, *Paul, the Spirit, and the People of God*, 9–23.

In sum, then, Paul in 1 Corinthians spends the majority of his time explicating the middle item of the apocalyptic topos: the restoration of the people of God. This is a restoration/renewal that is already underway. Paul does not simply gauge the present place of the Corinthian community before God, based on a backward glance at the Hebrew Scriptures (though he certainly does use the Scriptures, e.g., 1 Cor 10:1–13; also cf. 5:7b, "our paschal lamb"). He also looks back to the death and resurrection of Jesus (with its re-presentation in the Lord's Supper traditions of 10:14–22; 11:17–34). And he looks forward to the ongoing community experience of the Spirit as sanction for the restoration and marking of God's people in the present. Precisely because the "already" cannot encompass the fullness of the "not yet," much exhortation and correction is in order.

First Corinthians 15: Vindication of the Faithful

The third theme in the apocalyptic topos is the vindication of the faithful in the resurrection of the dead, precisely what Paul insists upon in 1 Cor 15. Three issues are important to recognize in Paul's argument about the vindication of the faithful. First, his argument is cast as *apocalyptic* wisdom, covering the key "events" of the resurrection of the body, the defeat of death, the "coming" of Christ, and the consummation of God's plan.[47] As he had stated toward the beginning of the letter, apocalyptic wisdom is not a "wisdom of this age," which is passing away. Corresponding to the "wisdom in a mystery" of 2:6–8, in which God has outsmarted "the rulers of this age, who are doomed to perish," so now the "mystery" he discloses in 15:51 pertains to the apocalyptic resurrection of the dead, the focus of his whole argument in chapter 15.

Second, this "mystery" is not simply for intellectual reflection. It entails a strong moral perspective. It enables the faithful to endure. The believers can walk faithfully amid the threat of death or into death itself, because God vindicates the faithful after the pattern of Jesus at the time of final judgment and completion of the events of fulfillment begun in Christ's crucifixion and resurrection (15:3–5, 20–28). One can be part of the (renewed) people of God, an alternative society[48] in a hostile world, because God will imminently vindicate the faithful. If this were not so, Paul suggests, then we might as well follow the common wisdom, "Let us eat and drink, for tomorrow we die" (15:32b). But since bodies count later, they therefore count now: believers are morally responsible for just and

---

47. Martinus C. de Boer, *The Defeat of Death: Apocalyptic Eschatology in 1 Corinthians 15 and Romans 5* (JSNTSup 22; Sheffield: JSOT, 1988), 93–140.

48. Note 42, above, and its reference in the text.

constructive social relationships. Simply put, believers are responsible for demonstrating "love." So Paul's conclusion for the section is a moral one: "Be steadfast, immovable, always excelling in the work of the Lord" (15:58). And the final summary in the letter echoes the same: "Be watchful, stand firm in your faith, be courageous, be strong. Let all that you do be done in love" (16:13–14, RSV).

Finally, Paul brings the apocalyptic topos to completion in 1 Cor 15 by outlining the consummation of God's plan. First, he does this by detailing it in breadth: "Then comes the end, when he [Christ] delivers the kingdom to God the Father after destroying every rule and every authority and power. For he must reign until he has put all his enemies under his feet. The last enemy to be destroyed is death. . . . [Then] God may be everything to everyone" (15:24–28, RSV). Second, Paul brings the apocalyptic topos to completion by detailing every believer's ongoing place within the fullness of the "new time": "We shall all be changed, . . . put on immortality, . . . [and be given] the victory" (15:51–57, RSV).

The apocalyptic topos—critique of rulers, renewal of the people, and vindication of the faithful—is what provides the very structure of Paul's overall arrangement and argument in 1 Cor 1–15: (1) a criticism of the Roman imperial order and Corinthian leaders who aspire to its aristocratic ideals (1 Cor 1–4); (2) the deliverance and discipline of the people of God (1 Cor 5–14); and (3) vindication of the faithful through resurrection from the dead (1 Cor 15). The changes from previous Jewish apocalyptic literature, when noticeable, are slight and in every case appear to be related to an eschatological shift in perspective: God's reign is now already present in a partial and defining way through the Spirit. Paul in 1 Cor 15 is providing assurance and exhortation to proper living for those Corinthians who have *already* been called into God's renewed people and away from compromise with the world.

Conclusions

The story of the crucified Christ reveals the divine condemnation and imminent destruction of the imperial rulers, power relations, aristocratic codes, and unrighteous influences embedded in the ruling structures; it provides renewal and power for the faithful people of God; and it sets a pattern for the vindication and transformation of the faithful, including martyrs. Paul clearly combines two registers, that of the Jewish apocalyptist and that of the Greco-Roman rhetoric. Attention to both registers is necessary for gaining a clearer picture of Paul's persuasive techniques. Paul's apocalyptic rhetoric in 1 Corinthians strives to maintain the integrity of the Spirit-guided community in Corinth by casting his deliberative argument *into* the larger framework of God's intervention through judgment and renewal.

Paul's use of the register of Jewish apocalypticist should be fully recognized and not underplayed. This register is a key organizing principle of his worldview—and hence, a prominent component in his "native" rhetoric that leads to a choice in the arrangement of his materials in 1 Corinthians. Worldviews are powerful structuring vehicles—a perspective, as we have seen, recognized by rhetorical handbooks that articulate worldviews of their own. Because Judean apocalyptic can be analyzed as a worldview, it provides an excellent test case for examining the rhetorical aspect of text-external dispositio, or arrangement, in 1 Corinthians. Future studies along similar lines as this one may uncover additional "native" rhetoric codes in Paul. For example, what kind of power relationships or aristocratic value codes are embedded in the handbook discussions on *elocutio*, or style? What statements in Paul's letters hint at this subject? And what does previous Jewish literature before Paul have to say about appropriate expression?

Finally, Paul's arrangement of 1 Corinthians according to the apocalyptic topos outlined above might suggest a more precise explanation for the positioning of 1 Cor 15 (the resurrection) at the end of the letter. This chapter is the "climax" of the letter because it is the climax of the "story," pointing both to the "final triumph [and renewal] brought by God" and to a courageous moral stance in the face of death-dealing powers (15:30–31), which brings assurance of *participating* in God's final triumph over, and renewal of, the present order.[49]

---

49. As insightful as I find J. Christiaan Beker's discussion of 1 Cor 15, my argument here would cast some doubt on reading 1 Corinthians as a set of addressed contingencies that find their climax only in chapter 15. Nor is a strong disjunction between chapters 1 and 2 (Christ's death with no resurrection emphasis) and chapter 15 (Christ's resurrection with no death emphasis) so theologically telling. See the discussion in Beker, *Paul the Apostle*, 163–81.

– 5 –

PATRONAGE AND COMMENDATION, IMPERIAL AND ANTI-IMPERIAL

Efrain Agosto

Patronage and Commendation in the Roman Imperial Order

Patronage was a fundamental form of social relations in Roman society by the time of the early Empire, especially among the elite. Both at the seat of imperial power in Rome and in the provinces among local magnates vying for Rome's favor, the exchange of social and political power depended upon patron-client relations. "The place of a Roman in society was a function of his position in the social hierarchy," a position positively or negatively affected by his or her "involvement in a web of personal relationships," including patronal relations.[1] In fact, "patron-client relations supply part of the answer to how such a large empire was governed by so small an administration."[2] The need to rely on patronal ties to fill leadership positions, especially in the more distant provinces, increased as Augustus and his successors coalesced more power in Rome. As G. E. M. de Ste. Croix put it, "As political authority became concentrated in the hands of the Emperor, the new role of patronage assumed great importance, above all through the dignity and influence it brought to the patron, through his ability to recommend—and often make sure of procuring appointment to all sorts of posts that could be honorific and lucrative."[3]

---

1. Peter Garnsey and Richard Saller, "Patronal Power Relations," in *Paul and Empire: Religion and Power in Roman Imperial Society* (ed. Richard A. Horsley; Harrisburg, Pa.: Trinity Press International, 1997), 96.

2. Richard A. Horsley, "Patronage, Priesthood and Powers: Introduction," in *Paul and Empire* (ed. Horsley), 88–89.

3. G. E. M. de Ste. Croix, *The Class Struggle in the Ancient World* (Ithaca, N.Y.: Cornell University Press, 1981), 342.

One of the key reasons that the patronage system became central to imperial power relations was that provincial and urban elites used their wealth to sponsor the imperial cult, as one of the principal means of securing Rome's favor. Simon Price has shown that the imperial cult became an important vehicle for political-religious expression of support and solidarity with Roman imperialism in the provinces.[4] Patronage relations rather than bureaucracy fueled the creation and functioning of local imperial cults. The imperial cult was often associated with diplomatic approaches to the emperor. Offers of cult were sometimes made in association with requests concerning privileges and other matters. Ambassadors to the emperor were frequently imperial priests.[5]

Thus, patronage and the imperial cult functioned hand-in-hand in the social relations that secured the exchange of power in imperial society between Rome and the provinces. The provincial elites made certain that the imperial cult was visible for all to see through frequent festivals and the strategic location of the cultic space in civic space.[6] "The visual expression of the emperor was incorporated into the regular life of the communities through public celebrations," including the imperial cult.[7] As provincial leaders sought to "construct" the reality of the emperor in their lives, they did so by intertwining the imperial cult into the fabric of their cities.

Patronage in the Roman Imperial Order

Patronage entailed an exchange of benefits and obligations that served to enhance the status of its participants and thereby to perpetuate the power of the elite—those with wealth, power, and privilege who benefited from, and controlled, the Roman imperial order. Seneca described the type of benefits patrons should confer on their clients:

> Do not falter, finish your task, and complete the role of the good man. Help one with money, another with credit, another with influence, another with advice, another with sound precepts. (*De beneficiis* 1.2.4–5).[8]

---

4. See Simon R. F. Price, *Rituals and Power: The Roman Imperial Cult in Asia Minor* (Cambridge: Cambridge University Press, 1984), excerpted in "Rituals and Power," in *Paul and Empire* (ed. Horsley), 47–71.

5. Ibid., 69.

6. Ibid., 57–65.

7. Ibid., 49.

8. All citations from classical Roman and Greek texts are from the LCL.

Patrons provided money, loans, and influence to those under their charge. In addition, clients attached to well-connected patrons added luster to the client's own status.

However, Seneca also emphasized the importance of reciprocity in patronage:

> No matter what the issue of former benefits has been, still persist in conferring them upon others; this will be better even if they fall unheeded into the hand of the ungrateful, for it may be [that] either shame or opportunity or example will some day make these grateful. (*Ben.* 1.2.4)

Sooner or later in imperial society, patrons could expect a payback for a benefit conferred. Clients owed their patrons an "obligation." Their response to the patron's benefits entailed loyalty. Clients understood that acceptance of benefits from a patron announced to all the client's dependency and, therefore, inferior status in comparison to the patron and the latter's peers. The greater number of clients attached to a particular patron, the greater the status of the patron in the eyes of others. Again, this worked both ways. Clients dependent on worthy and wealthy patrons benefited from such connections. However, it was the preservation of patron status and power that was the ultimate benefit in patronage relationships and exchanges.

Patronal relations served to build the reputations of both patrons and clients, and this was true throughout the Empire among the elite classes. Plutarch encouraged provincial leaders to take advantage of the benefits of Roman principles of patron:

> And not only should the statesmen show himself and his native State blameless towards our rulers, but he should also have always a friend among the men of high station who have the greatest powers as a firm bulwark, so to speak, of his administration; for the Romans themselves are most eager to promote the political interests of their friends; and it is a fine thing also, when we gain advantage from the friendship of great men, to turn it to the welfare of our community. (Plutarch, "Precepts of Statecraft," *Moralia* 814C–D)

In fact, the farther one got from Rome and its immediate bureaucracy, the more Roman provincial governors and local leaders depended on patronal exchange of benefits and obligations in order to carry out the functions of government and enhance their status. Friendly relations were critical in the exchange of gifts, power, and benefits.

Pliny (the Younger), writing to the emperor Trajan in the early decades of the second century C.E., when he was provincial governor of distant Bithynia in Asia Minor, exemplified well the benefits of good patron-client relations:

> As a result of your generosity to me, Sir, Rosianus Geminus became one of my closest friends; for when I was consul he was my quaestor. I always found him devoted to my interests, and ever since then he has treated me with the greatest deference. . . . I there-fore pray to you to give your personal attention to my request for his advancement; if you place any confidence in my advice, you will bestow on him your favor. He will not fail to earn further pro-motion in whatever post you place him. . . . I pray you, Sir, most urgently to permit me to rejoice as soon as possible in the due pro-motion of my quaestor—that is to say, in my own advancement in his person. (Pliny, *Epistolae* 10:26)

Several elements in this letter illustrate the dynamics of patron-client relations at the provincial level. The loyalty and "deference" of Geminus to Pliny made possible this endorsement to the Roman emperor. Pliny and Geminus had a patron-client relationship. Pliny's relationship to the emperor also helped. Pliny had not failed to make good recommendations in the past; so this one should be no different. Pliny had the emperor's "confi-dence." Finally, a promotion for Pliny's client was an "advancement" for Pliny himself. The status of patrons benefited from the enhanced status of their clients. Although Pliny referred to Geminus as a "close friend," the latter's deference and dependence on Pliny's largesse for his leadership advancement definitely made Geminus the client in this relationship of patronage.[9]

Such patronal relations spread rapidly among the Greek elite in the late Republican and early imperial periods, coming virtually to constitute the web of power by which the Roman imperial order held together. Yet we lack sufficient evidence for the more widespread practices of patronage among the non-elites and the poor in the provinces. Perhaps the *collegia,* trade or cultic associations that had common meals and often burial for

---

9. See Hannah Cotton, *Documentary Letters of Recommendation in Latin from the Roman Empire* (Königstein/Ts: Verlag Anton Hain, 1981), especially 19–23, where she discusses the "decorum" necessary in a letter of recommendation, such that "friend-ship" language was used for the relationship with the commended rather than explicit language of "patronage." See also Peter Marshall, *Enmity in Corinth: Social Conventions in Paul's Relations with the Corinthians* (Tübingen: J. C. B. Mohr [Paul Siebbeck], 1987), 91–129, for an extensive discussion of friendship in commendation.

members, provide examples of how patronal ideology and practice might have spread to at least some of the non-elite orders in many of the provinces. Since membership required fees, only "modestly prosperous men" could afford to belong, while the "impoverished" could only expect "unceremonious" burials in mass graves.[10] To support their common meals and other expenses, voluntary associations often depended at least in part on the financial support of well-to-do patrons. In exchange, they honored their patrons, for example, by celebrating their birthdays, thus enhancing their status and honor in the local community.

Commendation Letters: Form and Function

One of the principal means by which the imperial patronage system was facilitated was letters of recommendation. Richard Saller, a major historian of Roman patronage, has argued that "scholars have not always taken sufficient notice of the Republican tradition of recommendations."[11] Powerful and wealthy patrons wrote commendations on behalf of peers and protégés in order to advance the status of both patron and client in the eyes of other prominent persons. These commendations were thus instruments of power in the Roman Empire. They were what fueled patron-client relations.

Such Roman luminaries as Cicero and Pliny employed commendation letters to advance the fortunes of their friends and clients, sending letters to powerful individuals, including the emperor. They wrote so many such letters that we have extensive collections of them. In addition, their letters, especially those of Cicero, became the models of commendation letter-writing for generations to come. In the middle of the second century, Fronto, the teacher of Marcus Aurelius, considered himself a loyal critic of the Ciceronian traditions in letter-writing and sought to improve the tradition. However, "Cicero['s] and Fronto's *commendationes* to provincial governors look very much alike." Such similarity suggests that "exchange relationships remained essentially unchanged from the Republic" to the Empire.[12] Thus, patronage and its principal vehicle of communication, the commendation letter, were significant instruments for a long period of time in the cohesion and durability of the ruling class of the Roman imperial order.

When Pliny wrote to the emperor Trajan on behalf of his quaestor Geminus, he not only illustrated the importance and spread of the Roman patronage system; he also illustrated the nature of a commendation letter as a

---

10. Garnsey and Saller, "Patronal Power Relations," 101.

11. Richard Saller, *Personal Patronage under the Early Empire* (Cambridge: Cambridge University Press, 1982), 108.

12. Saller, *Personal Patronage*, 193.

vehicle for exercising patronage. In praising Geminus for his leadership skills and loyalty, Pliny commended him to the patron of patrons, the emperor.

Both Greek and Roman commendation letters shared similar components. The writer identified the subject of the commendation, usually with some reference to family or household relationships. He or she also indicated the qualities that commended this individual, including personal, social, and financial criteria: what character traits he or she had; what family, business, and political connections they bore with them; and the state of their, or their family's, economic well-being. At the end of a letter, the writer made a formal commendation request, usually some kind of general hospitality, employment opportunity, and/or advancement in rank or status.[13]

Perhaps the most critical component of any commendation letter was its catalogue of virtues. In particular, letters written by elite patrons on behalf of their protégés included, for example, *modestia* (moderation, restraint, obedience to authority), *humanitas* (humanity, kindness, refinement, education, culture), and *probitas* (honesty, uprightness). Such qualities, however, rather than being objective criteria of a candidate's merit, as in modern assessments of a job-seeker's qualities, reflected a common set of patronal values, those expected of anyone "irrespective of the office, honor or privilege requested."[14]

> In Roman *commendationes*, . . . the personal relationship between patron and client is stressed, and there is no attempt to appear impartial. This is because the aristocratic qualities sought were manifested largely in the context of friendship and patron-client relationships. In other words, the recommender illustrates his client's loyalty, integrity, and industry by reference to this display of those qualities in their mutual friendship.[15]

For example, Cicero endorsed a candidate for a consulship as a "most admirable and gallant of citizens *(optimus et fortissimum civis)*; a man of great influence *(summa auctoritate)* and soundest sentiments *(optime sentiens)*." Cicero concluded that people like this were "leaders of public policy" *(auctores consili publici)*. He decried the paucity of such character traits in most other Roman consular candidates (*Epistulae ad familiares* 12.2.3).

---

13. For a discussion of these and other elements in ancient commendations, especially those from the Greek papyri, see Chan Hie-Kim, *Form and Structure of the Familiar Greek Letter of Recommendation* (SBLDS 4; Missoula, Mont.: Scholars, 1972).

14. Saller, *Personal Patronage*, 108.

15. Ibid., 108–9.

However, Cicero considered the personal relations behind this commendation even more important:

> For myself, I never fail, and I never shall fail, to protect those dear to you: and whether they appeal to me for advice or whether they do not, I can in either case guarantee my love and loyalty *(benevolentur fidesque)* to yourself. *(Ep. ad fam.* 12:2:3)

Cicero's personal relationship to the letter recipient, as well as to the subject of the letter, stood behind the dynamics of this commendation letter. Patron-client relations were motivated by persons of similar status and aristocratic tastes supporting each other and their clients and protégés. Thus, "the message" of each commendation letter tended to be the same: "This man is a friend or client of mine and hence of worthy character."[16]

Commendation in Paul's Letters

Recent studies of the apostle Paul and his churches have argued that Paul may have been more subversive in his stance against the Empire than has been heretofore assumed.[17] For example, by using the term *ekklēsia* for his communities, Paul reestablishes, for the poor residents of Greek cities, a replacement for the old Greek democratic assemblies, which the Romans had attempted to eliminate. Similarly, he takes terms from Roman imperial ideology—such as *euangelion* (good news, gospel), *pistis* (faith, loyalty), *dikaiosynē* (justice, solidarity), *sōtēr* and *sōtēria* (savior, salvation), and *eirēnē* (peace)—and makes them central in his own gospel, thus presenting it as an alternative to the imperial gospel.[18] Indeed, the very heart of Paul's preaching, his focus on the cross of Christ (cf. 1 Cor 1:18–25; 2:1–5), suggests a challenge to the Roman imperial order. For it was the Roman rulers who had crucified the "Lord" *(kyrios,* a term often reserved for the emperor). God, however, had vindicated Jesus in resurrection. Not only that, ultimately all believers would be vindicated with the coming (Parousia) of the Lord in glory (cf. Phil 2:9–11), and "the rulers of this age" will perish (cf. 1 Cor 2:6–8).[19] Such preaching most certainly challenged the

---

16. Ibid., 108.

17. See the various essays in *Paul and Empire* (ed. Horsley); and also in Richard A. Horsley, ed., *Paul and Politics: Ekklesia, Israel, Imperium, Interpretation* (Harrisburg, Pa.: Trinity Press International, 2000).

18. For an extensive discussion of these and other terms, see Dieter Georgi, "God Turned Upside Down; Romans: Missionary Theology and Roman Political Ideology," in *Paul and Empire* (ed. Horsley), 148–57.

19. See Neil Elliott, "The Anti-imperial Message of the Cross" in *Paul and Empire* (ed. Horsley), 167–83.

power of the Empire and may have been directly responsible for Paul's various imprisonments and ultimate execution.[20] Thus, it seems that Paul understood his gospel, and perhaps his entire mission, as anti-imperial.

Yet Paul also appears to have borrowed one of the principal instruments of imperial dominance and patronage, the practice of commendation. He wrote commendations within the body of his seven extant uncontested letters. In fact, his letter to Philemon, in which he commends Onesimus, includes various components of a complete commendation letter. Also, the subject of letters of recommendation is a recurring issue in 2 Corinthians (cf. 3:1–3; 10:18). Moreover, Paul's passages of commendation share similar components with Greco-Roman commendations even though Paul's commendations were only parts of letters intended for other purposes. In his commendations, Paul generally identified by name those whom he commended, explained the basis for commendation, and requested some recognition or assistance from the letter recipients on their behalf.

Paul's use of commendation raises a whole series of questions. Did Paul borrow the standard cultural form of commendation, which served patronage so effectively? How closely did he follow it? How did his own and his assemblies' social location influence his use of the form? Commendations depended heavily on the relationship between the writer and the commended. What was the pattern of relationship between writer and commended in the respective cases of the Roman elite and Paul? And, finally, how did Paul's commendations function within his communities as compared with their function among the imperial elite? In the analysis that follows, I concentrate on commendation in four of Paul's Letters in order to address these questions.

First Thessalonians 5:12–13

In his earliest extant letter, Paul's concern about the survival of the young congregation in Thessalonica includes an endorsement of local leaders who have carried on the work of Paul and his associates during his absence. In large measure, the persecution suffered by this congregation (cf. 1 Thess 1:6; 2:14, 3:1–5) was probably due to the anxious religio-political climate of this Rome-oriented town. Paul and his associates offered an alternative *ekklēsia* (assembly) to that of the citizens' assembly of Thessalonica and an

---

20. On the reasons for Paul's various imprisonments, including his final one, see Richard Cassidy, *Paul in Chains: Roman Imprisonment and the Letters of Paul* (New York: Crossroad, 2001), especially 55–67 for a discussion of the "probable" charge against Paul: *maiestas* (treason). According to Cassidy, Paul's preaching was interpreted as detrimental to the stability of the Empire and, therefore, treasonous, a crime punishable by death.

alternative *kyrios* (Lord or emperor) to the Roman imperial cult there. They thus incurred for themselves, and those who joined the new community, persecution by the "city authorities" (Acts 17:6), who were eager to demonstrate their support of Rome by establishing a strong imperial cult as the official religious expression of the city.[21] Paul and his colleagues escaped with their lives (17:10), but they left behind a persecuted church (1 Thess 1:6). Only Timothy could return, console, and bring back good news to Paul (1 Thess 3:1–10).

Among Paul's admonitions to the Thessalonians was this word of commendation for the community's emerging local leadership:

> But we appeal to you, brothers and sisters, to respect those who labor *(kopiōntas)* among you, and have charge *(proïstamenous)* of you in the Lord and admonish *(nouthetountas)* you; esteem them very highly in love because of their work. (1 Thess 5:12–13a)

In contrast to letters in which a Cicero, a Pliny, or a Fronto recommended one of their protégés to the emperor or other high-ranking imperial figure for a position of power and status among the imperial or provincial elite, Paul here commends the assembly's own leaders to the group he had helped start a few months earlier. In his commendation, as throughout the letter, he addresses the community as "brothers (and sisters)," a practice common among popular resistance movements, such as the civil rights movement in the United States. The assembly consists of people who work with their hands (1 Thess 4:11), that is, at the very opposite end of the imperial social structure from the aristocrats and magnates involved in the imperial and provincial patronage network. In this sense, the audience for Paul's commendation reflects a similar audience for many of the Greek papyri letters studied by Chan-Hie Kim: writers and recipients who operated at ordinary people's level of life, non-elites dispatching messengers, envoys, freedmen and slaves; letters written for the purposes of small-scale business transactions, introductions, safe travel, and hospitality.[22] Stanley Stowers suggests that the "stereotyped and formulaic" nature of the

---

21. Karl P. Donfried, "The Imperial Cults of Thessalonica and Political Conflict in 1 Thessalonians," in *Paul and Empire* (ed. Horsley), 215–23; Robert Jewett, *The Thessalonian Correspondence: Pauline Rhetoric and Millenarian Piety* (Philadelphia: Fortress, 1986), 91–132; and Craig de Vos, *Church and Community Conflicts: The Relationships of the Thessalonian, Corinthian and Philippians Churches with Their Wider Civic Communities* (Atlanta: Scholars, 1999), 123–77.

22. See Kim, *Familiar Greek Letter,* 150–238, for copies of the letters, and 9–97 for discussion of their structure and contents, including the apparent social status of writers and recipients.

papyri letters "probably reflects the standard practice of professional letter-writers who tended to set the local standards for writers with little education."[23] While he himself was certainly not an uneducated letter-writer, Paul's constituents seem to be more identified as non-elites than as the elite of the imperial order.

The contents of Paul's commendation to the Thessalonians also differ dramatically from the typical letter of recommendation among the imperial elite. First, Paul does not identify the leaders by name or mention any distinguished family ties, as the Roman commendations do. Second, instead of focusing on social prestige, financial status, and political connections, Paul focuses on the leaders' role and functions in the community. The most striking contrast with the qualities or functions for which elite protégés would be recommended is Paul's designation of the leaders commended as "those who labor among you," *kopiaō* being a term for tiring manual labor and physical struggle, in which no respectable member of the elite would ever engage. Third, instead of recommending them for personal advancement in the ruling elite, Paul commends them to their community in their already-established function as leaders.

Paul's purpose in this commendation of community leaders is one component among many in his urging the solidarity of the assembly in its struggle against its hostile political environment in Thessalonica.

In this commendation, the closest Paul seems to come to standard letters of commendation among the elite is the term *proïstamenous,* which can mean either "be set over," "lead" (the sense in NRSV) or "help," "care for," and, therefore, "protect."[24] The more developed, institutionalized structure of the later churches, where bishops and elders "managed," "presided," or "governed" (1 Tim 3:4–5, 12; and 5:17, where the author uses *proïstamenous* and related forms), of course, should not be projected back into the first years of Paul's mission in Macedonia. The immediate context in 1 Thessalonians requires "helping" rather than "leading" or "presiding" because Paul praises the persons "on account of their work," which includes hard labor *(kopiōntas),* help, and admonishment.[25] In Rom 12:8, the participle appears again, with the adverb "earnestly," this time in one of Paul's lists of gifts, standing between "the one who contributes" and "the one who does acts of mercy." Again, contrary to NRSV's "the leader," the context requires the more general meaning, "helping."

---

23. Stanley Stowers, *Letter Writing in Greco-Roman Antiquity* (Philadelphia: Westminster, 1986), 153.

24. See the various definitions and ancient examples in Bo Reicke, *"proistemi" TDNT,* 6:700–703.

25. Ibid., 701–2. Similarly, Ernest Best, *The First and Second Epistle to the Thessalonians* (HNTC; repr., Peabody, Mass.: Hendrickson, 1988), 225.

Wayne Meeks opts for the translation "act as patron or protector" in 1 Thess 5:12–13, by analogy with the Corinthian community in which, he believes, "a position of authority grows out of benefits that persons of relatively higher wealth and status could confer on the community."[26] Meeks and others who generously estimate the relative wealth of some figures in the Corinthian assembly, however, have been challenged in recent studies. "The Pauline Christians en masse shared fully the bleak material existence which was the lot of more than 99 percent of the inhabitants of the Empire." Not enough evidence exists in the Pauline corpus to believe otherwise.[27]

"Helping" members of the community was a function of the leadership Paul expected of those whom he commended, not an act of patronage in terms of the exchange of benefits between patron and clients. As one who helps, the leaders would not be concerned with personal power, advancement, or riches, as in Roman letters of commendation.

Patronage entailed the exchange of benefits between those of unequal status, where the lower-status individual stands in debt to a higher-status individual because of a benefit bestowed.[28] Paul's commendation in 1 Thess 5:12–13 calls for a very different pattern of relationship. He calls for the Thessalonians to "esteem [the leaders] very highly in love because of their work," not because of their status and the ability to dispense favors of power and status. The next part of the exhortation following the commendation continues in the same vein. "Be at peace among yourselves. And we urge you, beloved, to admonish the idlers, encourage the fainthearted, help the weak, be patient with all of them" (1 Thess 5:13b–14). Such encouragement and help consisted of caring concern for those in need, in opposition to the typical patronage practiced by the elite.

First Corinthians 16:15–18

Toward the end of 1 Corinthians, Paul again commends leaders who served the community. First, he commends "the household of Stephanas" (16:15–16); second, "Stephanas and Fortunatas and Achaicus" (16:17–18), the latter two most likely members of the household in some capacity.

---

26. Wayne Meeks, *First Urban Christians: The Social World of the Apostle Paul* (New Haven, Conn.: Yale University Press, 1983), 134.

27. Justin J. Meggitt, *Paul, Poverty and Survival* (Edinburgh: T & T Clark, 1998), 75–154 (quote from 99). See also Steve Friesen, "Poor Paul," paper presented at SBL Annual Meeting, Toronto, 2002, which argues that not enough attention has been paid to issues of imperial economics and poverty in determining the social level of Paul and his communities.

28. See Saller, *Personal Patronage,* 1, for this emphasis on the "asymmetrical" relationship of "unequal status" in patronal relations. See also Andrew Wallace-Hadrill, ed., *Patronage in Ancient Society* (London and New York: Routledge, 1989), 3, for a similar description.

Now, brothers and sisters, you know that members of the household of Stephanas were the first converts *(aparchē)* in Achaia, and
they have devoted *(etaxan)* themselves to the service *(diakonian)*
of the saints; I urge you to put yourselves at the service
(hypotassēsthe) of such people, and of everyone who works and
toils with them. I rejoice at the coming of Stephanas and
Fortunatus and Achaicus, because they have made up for your
absence; for they refreshed my spirit as well as yours. So give recognition to such persons. (16:15–18)

This commendation incorporates elements of identification, credentials, and request. However, differing from a patron who recommends a
protégé to a higher-status patron in order to secure a position of power,
Paul commends leaders to their own community, apparently to reinforce
their authority. Paul here commends a whole "household," including two
who may well have been slaves or freedmen, judging from their names
("Lucky" and "the Greek"). That hardly fits the pattern of patronage
among the imperial elite. Also, in contrast to elite circles, Paul again commends the members of the household because they have "devoted themselves to the service *(diakonian)*" of the community or movement.
Diakonia, which often has connotations of menial service, is a key term
Paul uses for service or ministry in the communities of the movement he
is building, as in the reference to "everyone who labors together and toils
with them." Paul requests not advancement or positions of power for
Stephanas and company, but asks the community to subordinate themselves to and recognize such "workers."

Paul's purpose in this commendation at the end of 1 Corinthians is
clearly to reinforce the standing and authority of Stephanas and household, who had been the "firstfruits" *(aparchē)* of the movement in the
whole area of Achaia. He seems to be siding with, and depending on, his
special friends and allies in the Corinthian community in his attempt to
suppress conflict and restore unity in the assembly. While minimizing the
importance of who baptized whom, which was apparently causing controversy over apostleship in the Corinthian community (1:12–17), Paul
admits that he had indeed baptized the household of Stephanas, along with
Gaius and Crispus (1:14–16). It cannot be coincidental that he later mentions Gaius, as "host to me and to the whole assembly" (Rom 16:23,
author). One suspects a similar relationship with Crispus, (supposedly) a
"synagogue leader" who became "a believer in the Lord together with all his
household" through the ministry of Paul in Corinth (according to Acts
18:8). Stephanas, his household, and the others constitute Paul's "network

of friends" that help him "mediate" conflict with other leaders in Corinth.[29] Paul urges the Corinthians to respond to the *diakonia* (service, ministry) of Stephanas and company with a corresponding devotion and service: *hypotassēsthe* should probably be translated "be subject to such people," as in the RSV, but is seemingly softened to "put yourselves at the service of such people" in the NRSV. With this play on words with the verb *tassō*, Paul urges the community to reciprocate in service by being subject to Stephanas and his household.[30]

Paul's commendations of the household of Stephanas served his purpose of lending support to those who could help him best to resolve discord in Corinth. Paul benefited, like patrons in Roman commendations. Is Paul, therefore, practicing patronage in his commendation of Stephanas or in accepting hospitality from Gaius? If anything, Paul's Corinthian correspondence in general seems to have an anti-patronage tone to it. He seems to be at pains to avoid being drawn into a relationship resembling that of patron-client in his relations with the Corinthians. In 1 Cor 9, for example, he seems to reject the patronage of certain figures in Corinth who may have wanted Paul to become, in effect, their "house apostle."[31] Paul insists that he would rather do manual labor for some part of his financial support (2 Cor 11:7) than depend on those who interpreted Paul's apostleship of the Corinthian congregation as an opportunity to enhance their status by patronizing his ministry. To have Paul work for his keep was not only demeaning for Paul, in their estimation, but especially for them as "proud, potential patrons" of a movement founder like Paul.[32] Further, by refusing their financial support and working in manual labor to support his ministry,

---

29. As suggested by Richard Horsley, "1 Corinthians: A Case Study of Paul's Assembly as an Alternative Society," in *Paul and Empire* (ed. Horsley), 250.

30. The verb *tassō* carries the idea of placing or appointing someone to a fixed spot or an assigned position. The reflexive form, as here, has a sense of self-appointment, usually by means of active demonstration, through work or service. "To assign oneself," is to "devote oneself to service." See BAGD, "*tassō*" 805. Similarly, *hypotassō*, usually meaning "submit" or "subject oneself to," as in several Pauline texts (1 Cor 14:32; 15:27–28; Rom 8:7; 10:3; 13:1), here coupled with its root word *tassō* and the *diakonia* of Stephanas and others, probably also requests *diakonia* toward them from the rest of the community, as suggested by the NRSV: "Put yourselves at the service of such people." However, such service by both parties implies a mutual submission.

31. Horsley, "1 Corinthians," 250; and for more detail, Richard A. Horsley, *1 Corinthians* (ANTC; Nashville: Abingdon, 1998), 124–33, 147–48.

32. See Horsley, "1 Corinthians," 250. See also John Kingman Chow, *Patronage and Power: A Study in Social Networks* (Sheffield: Sheffield Academic, 1992), for an extensive argument of how the search for patronage by certain leaders may lie behind some of the conflicts Paul encounters in Corinth.

Paul created a situation of "enmity" with at least some of the leaders in the Corinthian community.[33] Instead, Paul commends those leaders whom he feels are genuinely serving the community, and not their own status enhancement. In doing so, of course, they also serve Paul and his concern for the unity of the Corinthian community. This emphasis on the solidarity of the community as a separate community (1 Cor 6:1–11; 10:14–22), however, was diametrically opposed to "replicating the controlling and exploitative power relations of the dominant society."[34] Such a system did not correspond to the empowering and liberating message of the gospel, which has as its motivating force a Messiah/Lord crucified on an imperial cross, "a foolish proclamation" for most people (cf. 1 Cor 1:18–25).

Philippians 2:25–30 and 4:2–3

In Philippians, Paul commends his close associate Timothy (Phil 2.19–24); an envoy from the Philippians, Epaphroditus (Phil 2:25–30); and his "co-workers" Euodia and Syntyche (Phil 4:2–3).[35]

Paul's comments come in passages that resemble not patronage recommendations but Greco-Roman diplomatic correspondence regarding envoys, including the four steps of "name, relationship (to sender and addressees), qualifications, and assignment."[36] The commendation of Timothy and Epaphroditus in that context, nonetheless, presents another striking contrast with patronage recommendations. Paul characterizes the singular relationship he has with Timothy, apparently his closest co-worker, as "like a son with a father" (Phil 2:22). For a comparison, in a letter to the emperor Trajan, Pliny praised the son of a longtime associate as "an honest, hard-working, young man *(iuvenem probum industrium),*" whose "industry" demonstrates that he is "well-worthy of his excellent father *(egregio patre dignissimum)*" (*Ep.* 10.87). That is, Pliny emphasizes how the youth's hard work in imperial positions had served to enhance his father's reputation. Paul highlighted his and Timothy's work together on behalf of the gospel's advancement, not personal reputation, achievement, or status. Their relationship was perhaps paternal, but not patronal.

Similarly in contrast to elite recommendations, Paul praises Epaphroditus because he was willing to confront even death for the cause

---

33. As argued by Marshall, *Enmity in Corinth*, especially 165–257.

34. Horsley, "1 Corinthians," 250.

35. I assume the integrity of Philippians, following, among others, the argument of Duane Watson, "A Rhetorical Analysis of Philippians and Its Implications for the Unity Question," *NovT* 30 (1987): 57–88.

36. Margaret Mitchell, "New Testament Envoys in the Context of Greco-Roman Diplomatic and Epistolary Conventions: The Example of Timothy and Titus," *JBL* 111 (1992): 641–62, quote from 651.

of the gospel (Phil 2:29–30). Paul often commended himself for endurance of hardship:

> But as servants of God we have commended ourselves in every way: through great endurance, in afflictions, hardships, calamities, beatings, imprisonments, riots, labors, sleepless nights, hunger. (2 Cor 6:4–5; cf. 1 Cor 4:9–13; 2 Cor 4:7–12, 6:3–10, 11:23–30)[37]

Except for extolling the valor of military officials, Roman commendations rarely cited risk-taking and selfless sacrifice as important credentials for the support. In fact, writers often took into consideration the risk of offering a commendation.

> My friend Sextus Erucius is standing for office, and this is worrying me very much; in fact, I feel far more anxious and apprehensive for my "second self" than I ever did on my own account. Besides my own honor, my reputation, and my position are all at stake. (Pliny, *Ep.* 2.9.1)

Pliny risks "imposing upon the Emperor" his preference in an election by commending someone who might lose and therefore sully Pliny's reputation. Such risk-taking in commendation differs from the risks taken by Paul and his associates in the gospel mission.

Closely related is Paul's commendation of Epaphroditus as a *leitourgos* (servant) of the Philippians on behalf of Paul (Phil 2:25); he renders a *leitourgia* (service) to Paul (2:30). In Greco-Roman contexts, *leitourgia* often referred to public works projects that Roman and provincial elites customarily undertook at their own expense, as a means of enhancing their status in the eyes of the people and the imperial hierarchy. Indeed, as I discussed above, the singular focus on the imperial cult in the Greek settings of the Roman Empire, including temple-building projects, served as a means of exercising power and control over those newly conquered territories in the East.[38] Paul, however, had a different notion of *leitourgia* in mind:

> But even if I am being poured out as a libation over the sacrifice and the offering *(leitourgia)* of your faith, I am glad and rejoice with all of you. (Phil 2:17)

---

37. For an extensive discussion of "hardship lists" in Paul, see John T. Fitzgerald, *Cracks in an Earthen Vessel: An Examination of the Catalogues of Hardships in the Corinthian Correspondence* (SBLDS 99; Atlanta: Scholars, 1988).

38. See Price, *Rituals and Power,* 133–69, on "the transformation of civic space" and architecture during the Roman imperial period in Greece and Asia Minor.

Paul faced possible execution in an imperial prison for his service to the gospel. Epaphroditus's service had been offered in a similar vein. His *leitourgia* included delivering a monetary offering from the Philippians to Paul, which Paul describes as "a fragrant offering, a sacrifice acceptable and pleasing to God" (4:18). Paul praises Epaphroditus for his visit to Paul's prison cell on behalf of the Philippians, even though he became ill in doing so. Thus, in stark contrast to the elites' *euergetism* (doing good services), Paul commended *leitourgia* in the sense of (self-) "sacrificial service" to God on behalf of the gospel community.

Just before Paul's final exhortations toward joy and unity (4:4–9), in the course of urging the unity of mind on two female leaders of the Philippian assembly, Euodia and Syntyche, Paul commends them (4:2–3). This passage incorporates the patterns of recommendation letters, including identification ("I urge Euodia and I urge Syntyche"), credentials ("for they have struggled beside me in the work of the gospel, together with Clement and the rest of my co-workers"), and request ("I ask you also, my loyal companion, to help these women").[39]

Paul may have geared his whole argument in Philippians toward addressing these two local "co-workers" in Philippi whose disagreement may have been with Paul himself.

> Rhetorical analysis and attention to the use of obedience language in Philippians supports the argument that these verses are very significant in the letter and suggests that Euodia and Syntyche should be considered central to the rhetorical problem.[40]

In commending these two co-workers, Paul again emphasizes themes diametrically opposed to typical Greco-Roman commendations. First, this is one of two of his five letters in which he commends women. In the extensive collection of Roman commendation letters by Cicero and Fronto, *none* commends women. Pliny recommends women in a few of his letters (e.g., *Ep.* 10.5, the freedwomen of a prominent doctor), as do a few of the Greek papyri letters collected by Chan Hie-Kim (e.g., Dionysius' sister in Oxyrhynchus Papyrus 293, from 27 C.E.[41]). Second, Paul commends Euodia

---

39. Kim, *Familiar Greek Letter*, 128–29.

40. Cynthia Briggs Kittredge, *Community and Authority: The Rhetoric of Obedience in the Pauline Tradition* (Harrisburg, Pa.: Trinity Press International, 1998), 93.

41. Reproduced in Kim, *Familiar Greek Letter*, 203. For a discussion of women in Greco-Roman commendations, including examples, see Efrain Agosto, "Paul's Use of Greco-Roman Conventions of Commendation" (Ph.D. diss., Boston University, 1996), 106–8.

and Syntyche on the same basis that he commends male leaders: "They have struggled beside me in the work of the gospel," invoking an athletic imagery of "joint struggle" *(synathleō)*. Like Paul and Epaphroditus, Euodia and Syntyche had taken on the risks of life and ministry for the gospel.[42]

In his commendations in Philippians, as in those in 1 Thessalonians and 1 Corinthians, Paul reminds his readers of the reality of conflict, opposition, and suffering as part and parcel of the gospel mission, over against the Roman order's triumphalism. With his gospel and gospel communities *(ekklēsiai,* assemblies), Paul "stands over against Roman imperial ideology," and not against "Judaism."

> Both Paul and the Philippians struggle against persecution by official and/or local opponents, but will attain martyrlike vindication, and whose real citizenship is in heaven, from which they expect the true "Savior" (Phil 1:15–30; 2:14–18; 3:20–21).[43]

Paul and his colleagues, Timothy, Epaphroditus, Euodia, and Syntyche, have demonstrated their willingness to suffer persecution and to struggle on behalf of the *euangelion* about Jesus Christ, the crucified *Sōtēr.* This commends them in ways that no typical Roman patron would find acceptable, and no Roman letter of commendation would seek to highlight.

Romans 16:1–2

Finally, we come to the Pauline commendation where he makes explicit reference to a "patroness." It comes, moreover, in Romans, the letter with the closest relationship to the center of the Empire. Paul commends Phoebe because, among other things, she has been a *prostatis.* Earlier translations, such as the RSV, translated this term "helper." However, the context and the lexical evidence points to the more specific term "patroness" or "benefactor," as in the NRSV.

The following translation lays out the various elements of commendation:

---

42. But see Kittredge, *Community and Authority,* 105–10, who argues the case differently. The language of "struggling together with Paul" indicates that Euodia and Syntyche were missionary partners, who remained of "one mind" with each other, but not with Paul. Thus Paul, in the Letter to the Philippians, has to construct "a rhetoric of obedience," with imitation of himself and others like him (Timothy, Epaphroditus) as the "authoritative model" of behavior for co-workers. A strong argument—but how does one explain Paul's praise of their prior "struggle" with him for the gospel and the friendly tone of the letter as a whole?

43. Horsley, "General Introduction," in *Paul and Empire* (ed. Horsley), 6.

a. Identification: I commend to you Phoebe,

b. Credentials: our sister, who has been a minister *(diakonos)* of
                   the church at Cenchreae,

c. Request: so that *(hina)* you may receive her in the Lord, in a
                   manner worthy of the saints, and assist her in
                   whatever matter *(pragmati)* she has need from you.

b'. Credentials: for she has been a benefactor *(prostatis)* of many
                   and of me also.[44]

By mentioning that she had been a *prostatis* last, Paul clearly wants to emphasize to his Roman readers that Phoebe is worthy of their hospitality and of whatever support she needs from them because she has been hospitable to other believers, including Paul himself.

While the components of Paul's commendation of Phoebe (identification, credentials, and request) seem similar to that of Roman letters of recommendation, the substance and use of the term *prostatis* does not fit the patronage system at the top of the Roman imperial order at all.[45] First, it is unusual to find a woman recommended.[46] Second, in Roman letters of recommendation, a social superior or patron (as recommender) would recommend a protégé (recommendee) to his patron (for a position of power, thus advancing a personal career). In Rom 16:1–2, however, Paul, as a leading apostle in the developing movement of Jesus-believers, refers to Phoebe, who is a local *diakonos* from Cenchreae, as his own "patroness." Hence, the "client" is recommending the "patron." Third, as noted earlier, it would be unusual in a Roman letter of recommendation for a member of the imperial elite to refer to another member of the aristocracy explicitly as a "patron" or a "client." Out of consideration for the other person and appropriate "decorum," he would be referred to as a "friend."[47] Fourth, that Paul asks the Jesus-believers at Rome to provide material support to Phoebe the patroness is the opposite of the typical Roman patronage relation, in which the patron provides material support to the clients, who reciprocate with social-political loyalty to the patron. For the patron to

---

44. Format adapted and translated from Kim, *Familiar Greek Letter*, 132.

45. On the following see Meggitt, *Paul, Poverty and Survival*, 146–49.

46. Although some cite the parallel case of Junia Theodora, a benefactor of Corinth at about the same time Phoebe was a benefactor of the Pauline movement from her base in nearby Cenchreae. However, Junia Theodora was clearly an elite patroness, while Phoebe's service was to an anti-imperial movement. For discussion of the Junia Theodora evidence, see James Walters, "'Phoebe' and 'Junia(s)'-Rom. 16:1–2, 7," in Carroll D. Osburn, ed., *Essays on Women in Earliest Christianity*, vol. 1 (Joplin, Mo.: College Press, 1993), 167–90.

47. Saller, *Personal Patronage*, 1, 10, and note 9, above.

accept any kind of financial support from potential clients would lower his or her status in the eyes of peers. Finally, the purpose of Paul's commendation is not to advance Phoebe's personal career into a position of power. As a *diakonos,* her role is that of a minister serving a community.

In short, Paul's description of Phoebe as a *prostatis* does not reflect typical elite patronage.

> Because Paul recommends her, and she appears to be dependent on him for access to the Roman community, there is a sense in which Paul acts as Phoebe's benefactor. But she also is a benefactor in her own right, and Paul acknowledges that she has also been his benefactor. The relationship between Phoebe and Paul has been described as one of mutual patronage.[48]

Such "mutual patronage" is not elite patronage, which depended on the asymmetrical exchange of benefits between unequal parties, to echo Saller's definition once again.

Why did Paul send Phoebe to Rome and commend her as a "sister," a *diakonos,* and a *prostatis?* Most likely, Phoebe carried this important letter to the various Roman house assemblies, a letter in which Paul introduced himself and his gospel to an audience of believers that did not know him personally (except for the litany of persons Paul greeted in the astounding catalogue of names in Rom 16:3–16, including several housechurch leaders). Perhaps he calls her a *prostatis* to indicate her prominence in the movement of Jesus-believers in Greece, using language that residents of Rome itself would readily understand. Moreover, that Paul asked them to provide Phoebe personal support indicates that he was using the term figuratively.

Paul's "letter of introduction" further proposes to seek missionary support from the Roman house assemblies for his own mission to Spain (Rom 15:22–24).[49] As with the Jerusalem collection, which he describes in the next passage (Rom 15:25–27), Paul expected a network of support for his gospel mission:

> So, when I have completed this [the collection for Jerusalem], and have delivered to them what has been collected, I will set out by

---

48. Margaret MacDonald, "Reading Real Women through the Undisputed Letters of Paul," in *Women in Christian Origins* (ed. Ross Shepard Kraemer and Mary Rose D'Angelo; New York, Oxford: Oxford University Press, 1999), 208–9.

49. See the series of articles on the "purpose of Romans" in Karl Donfried, ed., *The Romans Debate* (2d ed.; Peabody, Mass.: Hendrickson, 1991), 3–242.

way of you to Spain; and I know that when I come to you, I will come in the fullness of the blessing of Christ. (Rom 15:28–29)

Shortly after this passage and a prayer request for a safe trip to Jerusalem (15:30–32), Paul commends Phoebe to his Roman readers.

It is becoming increasingly clear that Paul's collection "for the poor among the saints at Jerusalem" constituted a kind of underground economy in the international anti-imperial movement that Paul was building:

> The network of assemblies had an "international" political economic dimension diametrically opposed to the tributary political economy of the empire. . . . The movement had developed its distinctive way of practicing international economic solidarity and (horizontal) reciprocity, the (relative) "haves" sharing with the "have-nots." . . . By contrast with the vertical and centripetal movement of resources in the . . . economy of the Empire, Paul organized a horizontal movement of resources from one subject people to another.[50]

Paul's Letter to the Romans invites the house assemblies there to join this "horizontal movement of resources," in this case from Rome to Spain, by supporting the missionary efforts of Paul and his associates. Paul has asked Phoebe, an experienced *diakonos* of the Pauline mission and leader of the movement in Cenchreae, not only to deliver the letter that makes this request, but perhaps even to explain it further and begin to organize the support in anticipation of Paul's arrival.[51] In Phoebe, Paul has a loyal co-worker who has presumably aided him in certain ways (hence a "patron"), loyal to and trusted by him, but more important, committed to spreading the gospel and the movement. She is commended not to a patron but as a "patron" whose patronage has served the cause of a gospel in a movement that stands over against the Roman Empire.

Conclusions

Commendation letters were an integral vehicle for promoting patron-client relations, which held together the Roman imperial order. In key passages

---

50. Horsley, "1 Corinthians," 251. See also Dieter Georgi, *Remembering the Poor* (Nashville: Abingdon, 1992); and Sze-kar Wan, "Collection for the Saints as an Anticolonial Act," in *Paul and Politics* (ed. Horsley), 191–215.

51. Suggested previously by Robert Jewett, "Paul, Phoebe and the Spanish Mission," in Jacob Neusner et al., eds., *The Social World of Formative Christianity and Judaism: Essays in Tribute to Howard Clark Kee* (Philadelphia: Fortress, 1988), 142–61.

of his letters, Paul employs the convention of commendation, raising the question of the degree to which he reinscribes the kind of patronage relations that held the Empire together. Close analysis of Paul's commendations, however, indicates that the use of the form does not imply ready compliance with the Roman imperial order. When he identifies co-workers or leaders of his assemblies for commendation, he does not dwell on their distinguished families, since they did not have any, but on their role in the movement. Whereas Roman patrons emphasized their protégés' high social status and great wealth—in the elite world far removed from Paul's people—Paul praised the labor and sacrifice of his co-workers on behalf of the communities of the movement. Pliny the Younger requested positions of power in the imperial system, in letters to the great patron at the top of the imperial patronage pyramid; but Paul urged his assemblies to value and imitate the hard work of his co-workers and/or their local leaders for the welfare and survival of their communities.

Whereas Paul reconfigured the terms of Roman political ideology (e.g., *euangelion, kyrios, sōtēr, pistis,* and so on) into the center of his anti-imperial gospel, he does not appear to have infused the language, much less the relationships of patronage, into either his letters or his relations with his communities. Paul's driving concern is for the spread of his gospel message and the well-being and solidarity of his communities. Paul commended co-workers and local leaders who had worked hard in service of the community in sacrificial ways, even to the point of hardship, risk, injury, persecution, and death. Exalted social status and the enhancement of personal political careers, typical in Roman commendations and patronage relations, did not figure in Paul's commendations.

Commendations in Paul's Letters do indeed serve a function somewhat parallel to that of commendation letters in the imperial system. However, that function is almost diametrically opposite to its function in the patronage system. In the latter, patrons recommended their protégés to higher-level patrons who had power to dispense benefits that would both advance their protégés' social status and their political career in the patronage system by which the Empire was controlled. Paul commends co-workers and local leaders to his communities in order to enhance their authority in the community. However, the relations are not parallel to those in the patronage system and are located at the opposite end of the political-economic spectrum; also, Paul's broader purpose is to strengthen the cohesion of his communities so that they are better able to survive repression and persecution by local and imperial rulers. In this way, Paul was actually undermining the traditions of Roman patronage, power, and the imperial order.

– 6 –

PHIL 2:6–11 AND RESISTANCE TO LOCAL TIMOCRATIC RULE

Isa theō and the Cult of the Emperor in the East

Erik M. Heen

Forty years ago Per Beskow observed that it is only with the book of Revelation that an explicit critique of Rome emerges in the New Testament. Resistance against Roman rule may exist elsewhere in the NT, Beskow noted, but its recovery always would be tentative and rely on methods not acceptable to all researchers.[1] Such a view articulates the traditional suspicion of NT exegetical projects that recover resistance against the hegemony of imperial Rome. This reserve about anti-Roman views in NT texts is especially pronounced in Pauline studies.[2] The liturgical fragment in Phil 2:6–11 may serve as an example. The terminology *isa theō* (godlike/equal), used in this panegyric of Christ in 2:6b, has a long history in the Greek ruler cult and in the first century C.E. was applied to the Roman emperor. But studies of Phil 2:6–11 have not explored the possibility that *isa theō* should be read against this background, much less that it articulates a criticism of the emperor. Two factors have contributed to this. First, the imperial cult was understood by many scholars to be an institution of empty ceremonial that was of little importance to the majority of the residents of Greek cities. Second, specific methods designed to recover an implicit critique of imperial politics in the NT were slow to develop.[3]

---

1. Per Beskow, *Rex Gloriae: The Kingship of Christ in the Early Church* (Stockholm: Almquist & Wiksell, 1962), 72.

2. Rom 13:1–7 has often been interpreted as revealing Paul's normative stance to Rome to be one that accepted the power dynamics as well as the legitimacy of Rome's governing authority. See discussion in Neil Elliott, *Liberating Paul: The Justice of God and the Politics of the Apostle* (Maryknoll, N.Y.: Orbis Books, 1994), 214–26.

3. For a selection of essays that reassess the imperial context of Paul's mission and his relations to it, see Richard A. Horsley, ed., *Paul and Empire: Religion and Power in*

Developments in scholarship, both on the imperial cult and in methods, provide the tools necessary to restate the issue. Recent investigations of the imperial cult have reassessed its importance in the construction and maintenance of political hegemony in the cities of the Greek East.[4] Today the imperial cult is understood to be a medium through which the web of power and influence was constructed and maintained on the city, provincial, and imperial level. Also, a way of discerning the resistance to Roman imperial rule in NT texts is now available in the work of anthropologists and postcolonial scholars who analyze the social dynamics of subaltern groups and their interaction with dominant cultural formations.[5] The work of James C. Scott on the hidden and disguised modes of resistance among subjugated groups may be particularly helpful in discerning previously unnoticed aspects of NT texts.

In this investigation of *isa theō* in Phil 2:6–11, I explore how Scott's discussion of the interaction between *public* discourse controlled by the elite and the *hidden* and disguised discourses of the subordinate illuminates the social function of the Roman imperial cult in the Greek cities of the eastern Empire. Against this background of the Eastern civic tradition of assigning "divine honors" *(isotheoi timai)* to Roman imperial rulers, the attribution of the term *isa theō* to Jesus Christ in a "hymn" sung by Pauline communities can be seen as a particular mode of resistance to the local urban elite's articulation of imperial rule.

To identify the subtler modes of popular resistance to domination, James C. Scott argues that the public interaction between the elite and

---

Roman Imperial Society (Harrisburg, Pa.: Trinity Press International, 1997). For a more in-depth presentation of the ideas and evidence of this article, see Erik M. Heen, "Saturnalicius Princeps: The Enthronement of Jesus in Early Christian Discourse" (Ph.D. diss., Columbia University, 1997).

4. S. R. F. Price, *Rituals and Power: The Roman Imperial Cult in Asia Minor* (Cambridge: Cambridge University Press, 1984) holds a central place in the revision of the academic attitude concerning the imperial cult. For a succinct description of the new understanding of the role of the imperial cult in the East, see Allen Brent, *The Imperial Cult and the Development of Church Order: Concepts and Images of Authority in Paganism and Early Christianity before the Age of Cyprian* (Leiden: Brill, 1999), xix–xx.

5. On recent anthropological literature see Sherry B. Ortner, "Resistance and the Problem of Ethnographic Refusal," *Comparative Studies in Society and History* 37 (1995): 173–93. The term "subaltern," which means "subordinate or inferior," was used by Antonio Gramsci (1891–1937) in Prison Notebooks to refer to the proletariat. The term is now used more broadly in many disciplines to cover investigations into the relationships between dominant groups and those subject to them, see, e.g., John Beverley, *Subalternity and Representation: Arguments in Cultural Theory* (Durham, N.C.: Duke University Press, 1999).

those subject to them tells only part of the story. Scott uses the term *public transcript* to get at the nature of the interaction between subordinates and those who dominate. *Public* here refers to action that is openly displayed to the other party in the power relationship. *Transcript* is used to indicate Scott's interest in a complete "record" of what was said and done.[6] The ongoing public transcript, controlled by the elite for their own benefit, provides a detailed map of the behavior required of subordinates when they encounter their superiors, and vice versa.

The public discourse, however, is not the only transcript produced where there is a strong bifurcation between those who have power and those who do not. There are also hidden discourses that are spoken "off stage" in response to the social dynamics encoded in the public transcript. The private discourse of the subordinate "spoken behind the backs of the dominant" is, predictably, highly critical of the public transcript. In this private discourse subordinates experience a "realm of relative discursive freedom, in a privileged site for nonhegemonic, contrapuntal, dissident, subversive discourse."[7]

Although most "hidden transcripts" have perished with the groups who produced them, not all traces of these discourses have been lost to historical inquiry. This is because, as Scott explains, certain aspects of the concealed private transcripts of subordinates emerge onto the public stage in a veiled form. Scott explores rumor, gossip, folktales, jokes, and trickster tales as mediums through which the private discourse of subject peoples appear in the public realm. Others observe that subaltern religion provides another platform for the private discourse, however veiled and "sanitized," to emerge into public view.[8] Given that the nature of the historical sources generally preclude access to the private discourse of subordinate groups, we must give attention to a third realm, somehow between public and private, to tease out a fuller picture of how subordinate groups viewed their relationship to those who dominated them. The Greek hymns preserved in the New Testament may provide such a middle term between the hegemonic and public transcript of the cities of the East and the potentially subversive deconstruction of it that took place among some of the early followers of Christ out of earshot of the local authorities.

---

6. James C. Scott, *Domination and the Arts of Resistance: Hidden Transcripts* (New Haven, Conn.: Yale University Press, 1990), 2.

7. Scott, *Domination*, 25.

8. See Bruce Lincoln, "Notes toward a Theory of Religion and Revolution," in *Religion, Rebellion, Revolution: An Interdisciplianry and Cross-cultural Collection of Essays* (ed. Bruce Lincoln; Hampshire, U.K.: MacMillan, 1985), 266–92.

The Greek Urban Elite's Honoring the Emperor as *Iso theōs*

It has long been recognized that ancient society was timocratic and that the high elite, in particular, were obsessed by the love of honor *(philotimia)*.[9] Patronage was, therefore, a central theme of the public transcript of the ancient city. A wide range of honors *(timai)* awarded for a multitude of benefactions that the wealthy received from the city were inscribed and prominently displayed in public places. At the lower end of the range was a simple acclamation granted by the assembly. At the top of the scale were those that identified the patron with the gods *(isotheoi timai)*.[10]

Even though it was *philotimia* and not a concern for the welfare of the city that motivated the largess of the elite, the picture of elite rule that the rhetoric of *euergetism* (doing good services) projected was that of a happy exchange—the enthusiastic awarding of honors by loyal and grateful clients for the benevolence of the high elite. The "mutual benefit" language of euergetism pertained to the sharp division between two classes in the ancient Greek city.[11] These classes exhibited an inverse ratio of power to size. Although the high elite controlled most of the property (and hence the power) in antiquity, they represented only a half percent to 5 percent of the total population.[12] Scott's analysis of public transcripts suggests that this flattering picture of hegemonic rule (a) was a self-portrait constructed by the high elite themselves, and (b) helped legitimate the exalted position the elite maintained over all other residents of the city. One of the more important functions of the culture of euergetism in antiquity, therefore,

---

9. Bibliography on *philotimia* may be found in Price, *Rituals and Power,* 123 n. 131. See also discussion in Robin Lane Fox, *Pagans and Christians* (New York: Alfred A. Knopf, 1987), 53. Stephen Mitchell, "Festivals, Games, and Civic Life in Roman Asia Minor," *JRS* 80 (1990): 183, translates *philotimia* as "patriotic zeal." On *philodoxia,* a term related to *philotimia,* see Klaus Bringmann, "The King as Benefactor: Some Remarks on Ideal Kingship in the Age of Hellenism," in *Images and Ideologies: Self-Definition in the Hellenistic World* (ed. Anthony Bulloch et al.; Berkeley: University of California Press, 1993), 16.

10. Some of the inscriptional evidence has been collected in Frederick W. Danker, *Benefactor: Epigraphic Study of a Graeco-Roman and New Testament Semantic Field* (St. Louis: Clayton Publishing House, 1982). See also C. P. Jones, *The Roman World of Dio Chrysostom* (Cambridge, Mass.: Harvard University Press, 1978), 104–14. Examples found in Holland Hendrix, "Benefactor/Patronage Networks in the Urban Environment: Evidence from Thessalonica," *Semeia* 56 (1990): 39–50.

11. The understanding of ancient society in terms of a two-class system is discussed in Bengt Holmberg, *Sociology and the New Testament: An Appraisal* (Minneapolis: Fortress, 1990), 23–24.

12. This figure of half a percent is discussed in Holmberg, *Sociology,* 22. Ramsay MacMullen, *Paganism in the Roman Empire* (New Haven, Conn.: Yale University Press, 1981), 7, gives a figure of 1 percent. R. L. Fox, *Pagans and Christians,* 57, puts the upper limit at 5 percent.

was to provide a rationale that justified the domination of the elite: it operated to mutual benefit.

The public honors awarded to the elite preserved in the epigraphic evidence represent only the most concrete acknowledgment of the hierarchical relationship that existed between the city's elite benefactors and its other residents. The gulf between the elite and their subordinates was also articulated in many subtle and not so subtle ways in the daily life of the city. The elite were distinctly marked by differences in dress, education, and speech; the means of their travel; and even their diet. The homes and public buildings they built in the city, their villas in the countryside, set them apart. So also did their aristocratic mores, which required a display of contempt for those below their own station. It was, however, not simply that the elites of antiquity exhibited markers of high status and were confident of their own superiority. Their dominance also required the ritualized performance of others' submission on a day-to-day basis. The complementary differentiation that existed between the elite and the non-elite was displayed in "ceremonies" both large and small, in quite different social contexts ranging from the mundane to the festive.[13]

While they were in public—in whatever context—the elite expected ritualized deference from their inferiors. This script was basic to the public discourse of antiquity, and it did not allow much room for critical revision. "Submission and dignity were, at every stage, the most important lessons to be learned."[14] For the subordinate—and again in antiquity this class could include almost everyone—it was wiser and safer to defer to the high elite according to the well-worn script rather than to risk the consequences of insubordination. Often such submission masked the true feelings of the subordinate. In the Latin context the word that best captures this kind of deference is *dissimulatio,* "the concealment of one's true feelings by a display of feigned sentiments."[15]

---

13. Ramsay MacMullen has collected many different examples of these public displays of dominance/submission in antiquity. See MacMullen, *Roman Social Relations: 50 B.C. to A.D. 284* (New Haven, Conn.: Yale University Press, 1974), 8–12; R. MacMullen, "Personal Power in the Roman Empire," *AJP* 107 (1986): 512–24; and "Power Effective," in MacMullen, *Corruption and the Decline of Rome* (New Haven, Conn.: Yale University Press, 1988), 58–121.

14. Wayne A. Meeks, *The Origins of Christian Morality* (New Haven, Conn.: Yale University Press, 1993), 39. On the demand for public submission of the non-elite, see also MacMullen, "Personal Power," 513–14. Real or imagined public slights to the dignity of a notable could bring violent retaliations. See MacMullen, *Corruption and the Decline of Rome,* 69–71, for more violent examples; on the lighter side, Apuleius, *Metamorphoses* (trans. J. Lindsay; Bloomington: Indiana University Press, 1960), 47–48.

15. V. Rudich, *Political Dissidence under Nero: The Price of Dissimulation* (London: Routledge, 1993), xxii.

The rhetoric of patronage claimed that elite rule was not only benevo-lent, but also divinely ordained. Even in ancient times shrewd observers noted the role of religion in maintaining the distance between the few *(hoi oligoi)* and the many *(hoi polloi)*. They observed, for instance, that since both the elite and the gods were patrons of a city, a similar loyalty *(pistis)* was appropriate.

Religion permeated the public discourse of antiquity.[16] It provided the context for the larger-scale public gatherings and festivals *(panēgyreis)*. Theaters were often structurally integrated to temple complexes in order to allow large numbers of people access to the drama of sacral rites. Conversely, freestanding theaters had altars incorporated into their design, and the performances that occurred in them were opened by religious rit-uals. Theaters were, therefore, to some extent temples, as the temples were theaters. The great agonistic festivals (financed by the elite) that trans-formed the city were also tied to religious concerns. They were not so dif-ferent in ethos from their offspring, the medieval religious fairs. They blended formal religious ceremonies with pilgrimage, trade, recreation, entertainment and spectacles, special foods, and the exchange of different forms of information. Even the gladiatorial contests, the most expensive of gifts offered to the city, were tied to celebrations of the imperial cult.

While religion was integral to the way the city publicly organized its internal social relations—on all levels—it also provided an important

---

16. Religion played an integral part in the drama that constructed and legitimated the power of the elite in antiquity. The classic statement of this position is found in Numa Denis Fustel de Coulanges, *The Ancient City: A Study on the Religion, Laws, and Institutions of Greece and Rome* (Baltimore: Johns Hopkins University Press, 1980). See also L. Zaidman and P. Pantel, *Religion in the Ancient Greek City* (Cambridge: Cambridge University Press, 1992). References for the following topics: On festivals, see L. de Ligt and P. W. de Neeve, "Ancient Periodic Markets, Festivals and Fairs," *Athenaeum* 56 (1988): 391–416; Steven Mitchell, "Festivals," 183–93; S. Mitchell, *Anatolia: Land, Men, and Gods in Asia Minor*, vol. 1 (Oxford: Clarendon, 1993), 217–25; Steven Friesen, *Twice Neokoros: Ephesus, Asia and the Cult of the Flavian Imperial Family* (Leiden: Brill, 1993), 114–41; MacMullen, *Paganism in the Roman Empire*, 26; and Dio Chrysostom, *De Virtute/Or.* 8.9.; *De compotatione/Or.* 27.5. On theaters, see John Arthur Hanson, *Roman Theater-Temples* (Princeton, N.J.: Princeton University Press, 1959); MacMullen, *Paganism and the Roman Empire*, 20–21; and Ramsay MacMullen, *Enemies of the Roman Order: Treason, Unrest, and Alienation in the Empire* (London: Routledge, 1992), 171–72. On gladiatorial con-tests, see Keith Hopkins, "Murderous Games," in *Death and Renewal: Sociological Studies in Roman History*, vol. 2 (Cambridge: Cambridge University Press, 1983), 13; and L. Robert, *Les Gladiators dans l'orient grec* (Amsterdam: Adolf M. Hakkert, 1971), 264–65.

medium through which a city related to the most important outside power that determined its civic life, that of imperial Rome. The imperial cult, which emerged in the cities of the East during the late Republic and early Principate, was taken up in ongoing competition between cities for honor among themselves. It became, therefore, an important element in the complex "etiquette" that ordered this wider world of privilege and power. The notables of the city were the primary actors in this appropriation of cult to articulate their city's relationship to rival cities (and Rome itself), a process that served to elevate their status while it helped construct an ideology of empire.[17]

The imperial cult in the East is an outgrowth of the ruler cult that preceded it during the period of the Hellenistic kingdoms.[18] A king or ruler who had demonstrated characteristics that were traditionally attributed to civic gods (such as founder *[ktistēs]*, benefactor *[euergetēs]*, or savior *[sōtēr]*),[19] could be awarded the highest distinction possible, *isotheoi timai*—honors equal to those paid the gods.[20] Since civic deities were construed as the archetypal benefactors of the city, the assignment of a cult to a ruler who had used his power to benefit the city was a logical development of the culture of euergetism.[21]

---

17. The imperial cult served not only to formalize and maintain good relations between the cities and Rome. It also provided the high elites of the *poleis* with an institution through which they could assert their own rule over the city. See, in particular, Price, *Rituals and Power,* 247–48.

18. Divine honors were assigned to Greek rulers in the East beginning with Alexander the Great. The literature on Hellenistic ruler cults is vast. Two classic works are Arthur Darby Nock, "*Synnaos Theos,*" in *Essays on Religion and the Ancient World,* ed. Zeph Stewart (Cambridge, Mass.: Harvard University Press, 1972), 202–51; and E. R. Goodenough, "The Political Philosophy of Hellenistic Kingship," *YCS* 1 (1928): 55–102.

19. An annotated bibliography on the terms *euergetēs* and *sōtēr* may be found in H. S. Versnel, *Ter Unus: Isis, Dionysos, Hermes* (Leiden: Brill, 1990), 70 n. 108. See also A. D. Nock, "Soter and Euergetes," in *Essays on Religion and the Ancient World* (ed. Stewart), 720–35.

20. See discussion in Duncan Fishwick, "Isotheoi Timai," in *The Imperial Cult in the Latin West: Studies in the Ruler Cult of the Western Provinces of the Roman Empire,* vol. 1 (Leiden: Brill, 1987), 21–31; A. D. Nock, "Notes on Ruler-Cult I–IV," *Essays on Religion and the Ancient World* (ed. Stewart), 135; Saul Lieberman, "Metatron, the Meaning of His Name and His Functions," in Ithamar Gruenwald, *Apocalyptic and Merkavah Mysticism* (Leiden: Brill, 1980), 235–44; H. Mason, *Greek Terms for Roman Institutions: A Lexicon and Analysis* (Toronto: A. M. Hakkert, 1974), 124; S. R. F. Price, "Between Man and God," *JRS* 70 (1980): 28, 30.

21. See Fishwick, *The Imperial Cult,* 6.

One of the more prominent schools of interpretation of the Greek ruler cult has thought of it as essentially a "political" rather than a "religious" institution.[22] In this view, founding a cult was a shrewd political calculation in that the city could anticipate benefactions from the one honored. Scholars who have seen in the Roman imperial cult a calculated maneuvering for political advantage by individual cities in the East have recognized a critical dynamic of the Greek honorific tradition. That is, the imperial cult represents an evolution of timocratic traditions native to the East that contain no little measure of civic self-interest.

The proliferation of the Roman imperial cult during the reign of Augustus is evidence of its importance for the high elite in the East.[23] Its centrality to the public discourse of the city is indicated by the fact that the temples and altars of the cult moved into the very center of urban public space.[24] As the cult came to enjoy a high profile in the religious life of the city, its priesthoods also became a principal source of prestige for the elite. In the large-scale religious gatherings in the East, the public roles of the elites were conspicuous. Thus, not only did the elite provide the funds for the celebrations, they also as priests presided over the sacrifices that accompanied them. In the course of their lifetime, the same individuals, the *archontes* (rulers) of the city, were both its magistrates and its high priests.[25]

The highest status one could attain in Asia Minor came to rest in the

---

22. See, for example, the discussions in Fishwick, *The Imperial Cult*, 11; and K. Bringmann, "The King as Benefactor." A trajectory of scholarship has opposed the "politics" or "pseudoreligion" of the imperial cult to the true "religion" of Christianity. See discussions in Price, *Rituals and Power*, 15–16, 234–35; and Price, "Between Man and God," 28; Holland Hendrix, "Beyond 'Imperial Cult' and 'Cults of the Magistrates,'" *SBLSP* 25 (1986): 301.

23. The expansion of the imperial cult under Augustus was rapid. See Price, *Rituals and Powers*, 57. Price includes maps of the distribution of the cult in Asia Minor (xvii–xxvi) and discusses the data (78–100). See also, Steven Mitchell, "The Imperial Cult," in *Anatolia: Land, Men, and Gods in Asia Minor*, vol. 1 (Oxford: Clarendon Press, 1993), 100–17.

24. Price, *Rituals and Power*, 109, 136–46; Mitchell, *Anatolia*, 107, 117; Paul Zanker, *The Power of Images in the Age of Augustus* (Ann Arbor: University of Michigan Press, 1988), 298; Donald Engels, *Roman Corinth: An Alternative Model for the Classical City* (Chicago: The University of Chicago Press, 1990), 13, 101, 227 n. 33.

25. Although religious offices were to some extent distinguished from other civic offices, the borders between the two were fluid. In the performance of their regular magisterial duties the high elite could also function as priests. See Friesen, *Twice Neokoros*, 95; Price, "Between Man and God," 31; Zaidman and Pantel, *Religion in the Ancient Greek City*, 9; MacMullen, *Paganism in the Roman Empire*, 24–43, 105–6.

position of provincial high priest of the imperial cult.[26] As this position evolved into the ultimate prize for those who displayed *philotimia*, the imperial cult also increasingly became the institution through which the most extravagant displays of euergetism were funneled.[27] In order to become a high patron of the city or province, one needed to finance the foundations and festivals of the imperial cult. The imperial cult, then, came to epitomize the public discourse of the cities of the East in a unique way. While it was controlled by the local elite and advanced their own prestige, it also helped construct an ideology of empire, an ideology that was anchored in the depiction of the emperor as a god, that is, the high patron of the Empire and the source of grace *(charis)* for the city.[28]

By the end of Augustus' reign, the divine honors *(isotheoi timai)* given by the cities of the East had become restricted to the emperor and his family.[29] Thus, whatever official reserve the early emperors may have publicly expressed in Rome concerning divine honors,[30] in the East such honors were not only enthusiastically given, but had become exclusively reserved for the emperor. It had been perceived in the East that further formation of divine honors to individuals other than the emperor, "would certainly have

---

26. A. D. Nock, "A Feature of Roman Religion," 485; Price, *Rituals and Power,* 62–64, 122–23; Mitchell, *Anatolia,* 107, 116–17; Friesen, *Twice Neokoros,* 76–113; and H. Hendrix, "Benefactor/Patron Networks in the Urban Environment," *Semeia* 56 (1992): 50–51.

27. Mitchell, *Anatolia,* 108, 112. See also Mitchell, "Festivals," 189–90; Price, *Rituals and Power,* 62–64.

28. On "grace" and the imperial cult, see Friesen, *Twice Neokoros,* 158–60, 166.

29. See discussion in Price, *Rituals and Power,* 49–50; Jones, *The Roman World of Dio Chrysostom,* 104–5.

30. There was a discrepancy between the Greek and Roman understanding of the divinity of the emperor. In Rome itself, the official position was clear: the apotheosis of the emperor took place only after his death. In the Greek world, on the other hand, the reigning emperor could be called *theos,* god, in his lifetime. Friesen discusses the Greek application of honorific traditions to the Roman emperor under the rubric "Divine or Human?" in *Twice Neokoros,* 146–52. See also, Adela Yarbro Collins, "The Worship of Jesus and the Imperial Cult," in *The Jewish Roots of Christological Monotheism* (ed. Carey C. Newman et al.; Leiden: Brill, 1999), 249. Even though the imperial cult was not originally a part of Roman ideology, it soon became a tool both of provincial administration and one of the more prominent features of Roman imperial propaganda. Regarding its propagandistic value, see H. S. Versnel, *Transition and Reversal in Myth and Ritual* (Leiden: Brill, 1993), 196–205; Price, *Rituals and Power,* 64, 122–23; P. Zanker, *The Power of Images,* 304–5; A. N. Sherwin-White, *The Letters of Pliny: A Historical and Social Commentary* (Oxford: Clarendon, 1985), 526–27; and Friesen, *Twice Neokoros,* 156.

been politically undesirable."[31] In the new political reality that came with Augustus, it was clear—at least to the elite in the East—that only the emperor was deserving of *isotheoi timai*.[32] From this perspective, it is important to note that if indeed the hymn in Phil 2 assigns such honors to the crucified Jesus, this constitutes a clear breach of the etiquette that informed the public displays of the imperial cult.

It seems likely that Paul found a developed pattern of honors to the Roman emperor in most of the Greek cities in which he worked. Yet since the imperial cult was apparently particularly well developed in Philippi, it may not be by accident that he cites the "Christ hymn" in his letter to the assembly he had founded at Philippi. A brief review will suggest the ways in which Philippi in Macedonia resembles the general picture of the imperial cult in the East and how it might differ from it.

During the period that stretched from the mid-second century to the mid-first century B.C.E., the city of Philippi served as a provincial outpost for Rome on the Via Egnatia, the main overland link between Rome and the East.[33] In 42 B.C.E., following intra-Roman power struggles, Philippi became a Roman colony, and discharged veterans received land allotments to settle there. Following the battle of Actium in 31 B.C.E., more Roman settlers were accommodated, and the city's relationship with Octavian (Augustus) was reestablished and deepened.[34] The colony was renamed *Colonia Iulia Augusta Philippensis* (after the Julian family) and granted the highest privilege possible for provincial municipality, the *ius italicum*. The colonists who qualified enjoyed Roman citizenship and extensive property and legal rights. A new Roman aristocracy was established, new buildings constructed, and the colony flourished.[35]

The archaeological evidence for the mid-first-century Philippi is thin. Still, some consensus exists among researchers as to the demographic,

---

31. Price, *Rituals and Power*, 49.

32. As Friesen, *Twice Neokoros*, 156, notes, such identifications occurred more at the local than on the provincial level.

33. On the various forms of the Roman rule in Macedonia, see J. A. O. Larsen, "Roman Greece," in *An Economic Survey of Ancient Rome: Africa, Syria, Greece, Asia Minor* (ed. Tenney Frank et al.; Baltimore: Johns Hopkins University Press, 1938), 437–41, and F. F. Bruce, "Macedonia," *ABD* 4:455. On the strategic importance of Philippi, see Holland Hendrix, "Philippi," *ABD* 5:314.

34. On the city's relationship with Augustus, see Lukas Bormann, *Philippi: Stadt und Christengemeinde zur Zeit des Paulus* (Leiden: Brill, 1995), 46; Valerie A. Abrahamsen, *Women and Worship at Philippi: Diana/Artemis and Other Cults in the Early Christian Era* (Portland, Maine: Astarte Shell Press, 1995), 11.

35. C. Koukouli-Chrysantaki, "Colonia Iulia Augusta Philippensis," in *Philippi at the Time of Paul and after His Death* (ed. C. Bakritzis and H. Koester; Harrisburg, Pa.: Trinity Press International, 1998), 8, 14.

physical, and religious makeup of the city.[36] While the town displayed an elitist and oligarchic social structure typical of Eastern municipalities, its colonial status necessarily meant its ties with Rome were more substantial than the norm elsewhere. The form of the local government, for example, was patterned after that of Rome, with two chief magistrates. At the time of Paul's visit, the population of the colony would have included a privileged core of descendants from the original Roman settlers, Greeks descended from the inhabitants of earlier Hellenistic cities and from other Greek settlements in the area, Greeks involved in commerce who had migrated from Asia Minor, and native Thracians. Latin was the official language of the colony, in use among the ruling class of the colony while always coexisting with Greek. Thus, although Latin was the dominant *public* frame of reference in the mid-first century C.E. (and had been for over a century), the extent to which the presence of Latin ever represented more than a cultural veneer in the colony is difficult to determine.

Most researchers are confident, on the basis of epigraphic and archaeological evidence and cautious inference, in claiming that the imperial cult was an important part of public cultic life during the time of Paul's mission.[37] The available evidence suggests that by the time of Paul's stay in Philippi, cultic honors were paid to Augustus and Livia, to Augustus' adopted sons Gaius and Lucius Caesar, and probably to Claudius. The temple at the

---

36. See C. Koukouli-Chrysantaki, "Colonia," 14, 23; Craig de Vos, *Church and Community Conflicts* (Atlanta: Scholars, 1999), 234, 246–47. On the history of archaeology in Philippi, see L. Michael White, "Visualizing the 'Real World' of Acts 16: Toward Construction of a Social Index," in *The Social World of the First Christians* (ed. L. Michael White and O. L. Yarbrough; Minneapolis: Augsburg Fortress, 1995), 235, 241–42. On ruling structure, see Markus N. A. Bockmuehl, *A Commentary on the Epistle to the Philippians* (London: A & C Black, 1997), 4–5. On language and demographics, see H. Hendrix, "Philippi," *ABD* 5:315; and Abrahamsen, *Women and Worship*, 11.

37. The recent exception is Peter Pilhofer, *Philippi: Die erste christliche Gemeinde Europas*, vol. 1 (Tübingen: J. C. B. Mohr [Paul Siebeck], 1995); on 93 Pilhofer points out that it is difficult to establish the dating of many of the inscriptions that deal with the cultic institutions in Philippi. In particular, he is concerned about the lack of attested imperial priests in the first half of the first century C.E. Because of his reluctance to use uncertain evidence, Pilhofer declines to pursue an analysis of the imperial cult in his study. C. Koukouli-Chrysantaki, "Colonia," 15–16, 25, suggests the temple at the northeastern corner of the forum was dedicated to the emperor. De Vos, *Church and Community Conflicts*, 249, citing inscriptional evidence, claims both temples for the emperor. See discussion in Bormann, *Philippi*, 41. On Silvanus, see L. M. White, "Visualizing," 251 n. 51. On Apollo, Cybele, Isis, and the priestly administration, see Mikael Tellbe, "The Sociological Factors behind Philippians 3:1–11 and the Conflict at Philippi," *JSNT* 55 (1994): 109 n. 49. On the assimilation of cults to the imperial cult, see Bormann, *Philippi*, 33, 55–60.

east end of the forum was probably devoted to the emperor's cult, and perhaps the temple on the western edge as well. Statues of the emperor and his family also stood in the forum. Other cults also were brought into the sphere of emperor worship (e.g., Isis, Mercury, Silvanus, Jupiter, Apollo, Cybele, and Isis). Inscriptions mentioning "official priests" of the imperial cult, an augur, two "high priests" and a number of other priests of Divus Julius, Divus Augustus, and Divus Claudius, indicate that the imperial cult was prominent in the city. In addition, the city was managed in the name of *Imperator Divus,* and the head of the administration was a high priest of the cult of the Augusti.

The special status of Philippi as a colony of Rome means that it was not embedded in the provincial network of Macedonia in the same way as were other cities. It would not have participated, for example, in the imperial cult at the provincial level in the same manner. Its competition with other cities in the province, therefore, would have been played out somewhat differently than in other municipalities. Given its status as a colony, one also assumes that the rituals of the cult would have followed Roman and Italian etiquette, expressing a reserve to assign divine honors to a living emperor in ways noncolonial Greek cities did not. One can also assume, however, that a certain amount of assimilation from the Greek environment had taken place with regard to the details of the cult practice in Philippi.[38] Given the thinness of the evidence, however, it is difficult to judge just what were (a) the actual parameters of the cult, and (b) the balance between Roman and Greek styles of its liturgical observance.

The details of the imperial cult in Philippi are difficult to reconstruct, as well as the precise manner in which it differed from expressions originating in noncolonial cities and those occurring at the provincial level. Nevertheless, it seems reasonable to assume that in Philippi at the mid-first century C.E., there was a flourishing imperial cult and that it had moved to the center of public discourse of the city.

Resistance to the Imperial Cult in the Christ Hymn of Phil 2:6–11

Phil 2:6–11 (RSV)

⁶ who, though he was in the form of God *(en morphe theou),*
   did not count equality with God *(isa theō)*
   a thing to be grasped *(harpagmon)*
⁷ but emptied himself, taking the form of a servant *(morphēn doulou,*
   being born in the likeness of men.

---

38. On differences, see Larsen, "Roman Greece," 452; and Bormann, *Philippi,* 36–37. On competition among cities in Macedonia played out in terms of the imperial cult, see L. M. White, "Visualizing," 242.

[8] And being found in human form he humbled himself and
   became obedient unto death, even death on a cross.
[9] Therefore God highly exalted him *(hyperypsōsen)* and
   bestowed on him the name which is above every *(pan)* name,
[10] that at the name of Jesus every *(pan)* knee should bow,
   in heaven and on earth *(epigeiōn)* and under the earth,
[11] and every tongue confess that Jesus Christ is Lord,
   to the glory of God the Father.

The "Christ hymn" in Phil 2:6-11 is usually understood as the earliest articulation of the preexistence of Christ. When set against the background of the use of *isa theō* in the contemporary civic and imperial cult in the Greek cities where Paul conducted his mission, however, it may be more appropriately understood as an expression of a hidden transcript that sets Christ over against the Roman emperor. A reexamination of the term *isa theō*, which occurs in the NT in this inflected form only at Phil 2:6,[39] suggests precisely such a reading.

The majority position of scholarship considers Phil 2:6–11 to be an early pre-Pauline hymn[40] composed in Greek but influenced by the Semitic poetic device of *parallelismus membrorum*.[41] Recently, scholars have turned to rhetorical studies in search of new insights into this pericope. This rhetorical turn is partially in response to a certain unease in calling Phil 2:6–11 a "hymn," which has surfaced in NT scholarship,[42] and partially

---

39. A related formulation, *ison theōn*, is found at John 5:18. The exact form *isa theō* is, actually, exceedingly rare in Greek literature. Previous to the secondary references to the term found in patristic exegesis of the term, I am aware of only one other example in all of Greek literature. See note 71, below.

40. For opposing views see Gordon Fee, "Philippians 2:5–11: Hymn or Exalted Pauline Prose?" *BBR* 2 (1992): 29–46; and Samuel Vollenweider, "Der 'Raub' der Gottgleichheit: Ein religionsgeschichtlicher Vorschlag zu Phil 2.6(–11)," *NTS* 45 (1999): 414–15.

41. See discussion in Stephen E. Fowl, *The Story of Christ in the Ethics of Paul: An Analysis of the Function of the Hymnic Material in the Pauline Corpus* (Sheffield: JSOT Press, 1990), 23–24. Fowl accepts J. Kugel's view of parallelism defined in terms of "seconding": "The sentence 'A is so, and what's more, B is so' provides a model for this seconding process. That is, clause B is a continuation of clause A, or a going beyond clause A in force or specificity. The virtue of Kugel's description of parallelism is that it accounts for numerous, different ways that B can second A." Critique of "the alleged Semitic parallelism" in this hymn can be found in Fee, "Philippians 2:5–11," 31–32.

42. See, e.g., discussion in R. P. Martin, "Preface to the 1997 Edition," in *A Hymn of Christ: Philippians 2:5–11 in Recent Interpretation in the Setting of Early Christian Worship* (Downers Grove, Ill.: InterVarsity Press, 1997), xliv.

because of the recognition that "Greek rhetoricians define the hymn as a subcategory of the *enkomion,* itself a form of epideiktik rhetoric."[43] I retain the traditional description of Phil 2:6–11 as a "Christ hymn" but appreciate the extent to which the recovery of the rhetorical aspects of the pericope push the discussion forward.

The traditional interpretation of Phil 2:6–11 understands the passage in terms of the incarnation of the preexistent Christ, since the hymn begins in the heavenly realm where Jesus has the "form of God." According to this majority position, the hymn moves in a three-step process from Jesus' state of preexistence (v. 6) through his incarnation (vv. 6–7) to his enthronement (vv. 9–11). A minority believe v. 6 refers not to Jesus' preexistence but to his "humanity," understood in contrast to that of Adam. The minority position has the hymn advancing only a two-act drama, which moves from Jesus' life as a human servant/slave *(doulos)* to his exaltation.[44]

Placing the hymn against the background of the imperial cult, however, opens up another avenue of interpretation, one that sees in *isa theō* a reference to the Greek civic tradition of awarding divine honors *(isotheoi timai)*. In addition to challenging the interpretations that recover either the preexistence of Jesus or a comparison with Adam, reading *isa theō* as an honorific term may also illuminate the meaning of the difficult term *harpagmos* at Phil 2:6b.[45] If one reads the term *isa theō* against its use in the imperial cult, it may be most natural to take *harpagmos* in the *res rapienda*[46] sense of "something to be grasped *de novo,* that is, not already possessed."[47] If this reading is justified, the meaning of the first lines of the Philippians hymn might be paraphrased by saying that in contradistinction to the emperor, Jesus did not think *divine honors* a thing to be "grasped" after.[48]

---

43. Edgar Krentz, "Epideiktik and Hymnody: The New Testament and Its World," *BR* 40 (1995): 55.

44. See Collins, "The Worship of Jesus and the Imperial Cult," 243.

45. On the history of interpretation of this *hapax legomenon* in the NT, see Martin, *A Hymn of Christ*; Roy W. Hoover, "The Harpagmos Enigma: A Philological Solution," *HTR* 64 (1971): 95–119; and N. T. Wright, "*Harpagmos* and the Meaning of Philippians 2:5–11," *JTS* 37:2 (1986): 321–52.

46. The debate over the meaning of *harpagmos* has been carried out with reference to two Latin terms: (a) *res rapta*, which is usually taken to mean "something already in the possession of the owner and held on to," and (b) *res rapienda*, which is taken to mean "something which is not in one's possession and is grasped after."

47. N. T. Wright, "*Harpagmos*," 324. This interpretation is favored among those who have discerned an Adamic typology behind v. 6 and do not, therefore, presuppose that the phrase refers to Jesus' "preexistence."

48. Alexander the Great set the precedent for a ruler to aggressively seek divine honors. See the discussion in *The Oxford Classical Dictionary,* 2d ed. (1971), 40.

The text does suggest that such a divine status *(to einai isa theō)* was granted to Jesus *in response to* his life of service and obedience (vv. 7–8).[49] This pattern of a divine reward given for humble service is a common topos of the panegyrics of rulers and emperors.[50] One possible reason for the thematic similarities evidenced in pagan panegyrics and hymns addressed to Christ is suggested by the work of Scott. Seen from within the community that honored Christ, the appropriation of this topos by the emperor (or for the emperor by the local high elite) may have been dismissed as typical of the self-aggrandizement of the dominant class. Its application to Jesus in the private discourse of the house churches, on the other hand, may have been construed as providing a proper reflection over Jesus' life of hidden service. That is to say, in their assemblies, the followers of Christ may have sung that it was Jesus *rather than* the emperor who was deserving of the honorific *isa theō*. Such a reading strengthens the comparison with the emperor some exegetes see surfacing first at verses 10 and 11.

In the traditional minority reading of Phil 2:6, *morphē* is taken as a synonym for *eikōn* in an allusion to Gen 1:26–27 (LXX), where Adam was created *kat' eikona theou*. This (image) reading of *morphē* does not require a reference to Christ's preexistence,[51] since Jesus in this interpretation is construed as a second Adam. Other interpreters have noted, however, that an antithetical parallelism exists between *morphē theou* of v. 6a and *morphēn doulou* of v. 7b. Whatever meaning one assigns to *morphē* in v. 6a, therefore, must also function in v. 7b, an observation that is problematic for the Adamic reading.[52]

Those who perceive an Adamic typology in these verses, however, do recognize something that other commentators often gloss over: vv. 6–7 seem to draw a comparison between two figures, an observation strengthened by the recent work that classifies Phil 2:6–11 as an encomium.[53] If the distinction being made is *not* between the first Adam (the one who sought to be *isa theō*) and the second Adam *(ouch harpagmon hēgēsato to einai isa*

---

49. See Krentz, "Epideiktik and Hymnody," 91.

50. Wilfred L. Knox, "The 'Divine Hero' Christology in the New Testament," *HTR* 41 (1948): 233. See also the discussion on the desired characteristics of Hellenistic rulership in Andrew Wallace-Hadrill, "Civilis Princeps: Between Citizen and King," *JRS* 72 (1982): 33–34.

51. C. A. Wanamaker, "Philippians 2:6–11: Son of God or Adamic Christology?" *NTS* 33 (1987): 180, with 191 n. 4 listing adherents of this position.

52. Jean-François Collange, *The Epistle of Saint Paul to the Philippians* (London: Epworth, 1979), 82–83.

53. One category of the encomium was *synkrisis*, through which two people were compared. See Bruce J. Malina and Jerome H. Neyrey, *Portraits of Paul: An Archaeology of Ancient Personality* (Louisville, Ky.: Westminster John Knox, 1996), 33.

theō), to whom is Jesus being compared in vv. 6–7? One possibility that has been generally overlooked in NT scholarship is that of the Roman emperor.[54]

The major challenge to the notion that Phil 2:6a refers to the "preexistence" of Jesus has come from those who see the Adamic typology behind *morphē*.[55] Although this particular reading of the text may be problematic in its own right, it has managed to highlight the difficulties with the traditional interpretation that posits the "preexistence" of Jesus. In addition to noting the comparison being drawn in vv. 6–7, another problem observed in the traditional interpretation is that Jesus' exalted status as sovereign lord, with which the hymn ends, seems to be of a higher order than his status at the beginning of the hymn. This reading is strengthened by the use of *hyperypsoō* (superexalts) in v. 9.[56] If one does posit a "preexistent" status to Jesus in v. 6a, then it seems natural to rank his initial status (in the hymn) among the lower divinities in the hierarchy of heaven.[57]

It is, of course, possible that *en morphē theou* in v. 6a refers neither to a second Adam nor to a preexistent Christ.[58] The antithetical use of *morphē* in vv. 6a and 7b may be a way of saying that although the "nature" of Jesus was of God (i.e., of divine origin), he assumed the "character" of a servant.[59]

---

54. There are exceptions to this rule. See K. Bornhäuser, *Jesus Imperator Mundi (Phil 3:17–21 u. 2:5–12)* (Gütersloh: Verlag C. Bertelsmann, 1938), 15–19; A. A. T. Ehrhardt, "Jesus Christ and Alexander the Great," *JTS* 46 (1945): 45–51; Knox, "The 'Divine Hero' Christology," 233, 236, 240; N. T. Wright, "The New Testament and the 'State,'" *Themelios* 16 (1990): 14; D. Georgi, *Theocracy in Paul's Praxis and Theology* (Minneapolis: Fortress, 1993), 73; Norman A. Beck, *Anti-Roman Cryptograms in the New Testament: Symbolic Messages of Hope and Liberation* (New York: Peter Lang, 1997), 61–68; David Seeley, "The Background of the Philippians Hymn (2:6–11)," *Journal of Higher Criticism* 1 (1994): 49–72; Vollenweider, "Der 'Raub' der Gottgleichheit," *NTS* 45 (1999): 413–33; Collins, "The Worship of Jesus and the Imperial Cult," 240–51; Mikael Tellbe, *Paul Between Synagogue and State: Christians, Jews, and Civic Authorities in 1 Thessalonians, Romans, and Philippians* (Stockholm: Almqvist & Wiksell, 2001), 253–59.

55. Jerome Murphy-O'Connor, "Christological Anthropology in Phil 2:6–11," *RB* (1976): 25–50, also disputes the "preexistent" reading. He sees, however, "the Righteous Man of Wisdom" rather than Adam in the text.

56. Reading *hyperypsoo* as "superexalts" is disputed by some exegetes. See the discussion in Murphy-O'Connor, "Christological Anthropology," 46–47.

57. See A. Segal, *Two Powers in Heaven: Early Rabbinic Reports about Christianity and Gnosticism* (Leiden: Brill, 1977), 210.

58. One alternative that I do not discuss in this paper involves the discussion of God's *kābôd* (doxa). See, e.g., *TDNT*, 4:751; and Collins, "The Worship of Jesus," 243.

59. This possibility plays off the definition of *morphē* found in Johannes P. Louw and Eugene A. Nida, eds., *Greek-English Lexicon of the New Testament Based on Semantic Domains* (2 vols.; New York: UBS, 1988–89): "The nature or character of something, with emphasis upon both the internal and external form—'nature, character.'"

The story line of the hymn seen from this perspective would be: (1) Jesus, sharing (in some hidden manner) the glory/honor of God (2) in return for his paradigmatic service to humankind, (3) was rewarded with an "apotheosis." This is a common Greek notion—an immortal (i.e., one who is destined to enjoy everlasting fame), because of his/her service to humanity, receives veneration upon death. One finds this pattern, for example, in both the cult legends of heroes (e.g., Heracles)[60] and in the panegyrics of deified rulers and emperors.[61] This topos—immortality won by valor—is also recognized as one of the basic concerns of the encomium.[62]

There may not be much difference, however, between positing the preexistence of Jesus as a "lesser deity" and claiming that he is a "divine man" or one destined to become "immortal,"[63] or a godlike individual[64] whose service on earth is rewarded by receiving divine honors. The boundaries between divinity and humanity blurred in antiquity in a way that causes more problems for modern exegetes than it did for people in the first century. Thus v. 6 can be taken as referring neither to the ontological status of a "preexistent" Christ nor to a second Adam. *En morphē theou* can be understood to mean that Jesus was destined to acquire "godlike authority," according to Greek conceptions of divinity, that is, upon ascension. Given the parallel construction of v. 6, the formulation *isa theō* in v. 6b has also been assumed, by most scholars, to refer to Jesus' preexistent state as a doubling of *en morphē theou* in v. 6a. If, however, preexistence is not necessarily referenced by *morphē theou*, the phrase *to einai isa theō* in Phil 2:6 may point more in the direction of the Greek tradition of divine honors (i.e., *isotheoi timai*) than the traditional scholarly interpretation has acknowledged.

---

60. See, e.g., Diodorus of Sicily, 1.2.4.

61. See Knox, "The 'Divine Hero' Christology," 231–32. Knox's New Testament text base is Rom 1:3–4; Phil 2:6–11; Col 1:15–20; and Heb 2:10, 18. For a reading of Jesus' exaltation against the background of the apotheosis of the emperor, see Dominique Cuss, *Imperial Cult and Honorary Terms in the New Testament* (Fribourg: The University Press, 1974), 113–34.

62. See Krentz, "Epideiktik and Hymnody," 89–90.

63. Charles Talbert, "The Concept of the Immortals in Mediterranean Antiquity," *JBL* 94 (1975): 421, makes a distinction (based on an ancient typology) between "eternals" and "immortals." An "eternal" is without beginning. By contrast, an "immortal" had originally been mortal, and at the end of his career experienced a transformation to obtain the same honors as the eternals.

64. See Dieter Georgi, "Social Aspects of the Phenomenon of the Divine Man," epilogue in *The Opponents of Paul in Second Corinthians* (Philadelphia: Fortress, 1986), 390–422; Helmut Koester, "The Divine Human Being," *HTR* 78 (1985): 243–52; David L. Tiede, "Aretalogy," *ABD* 1:372–73; C. Talbert, "Concept of the Immortals," 419–36.

The term *isotheoi timai* was virtually a *terminus technicus* for the highest honors a city might bestow on an individual. As noted above, beginning with the reign of Augustus such honors were restricted to the emperor and his family. Previous to the first century C.E., however, these honorific terms were applied to a wide range of figures such as heroes (as evidenced as early as Homer),[65] Apollonius of Tyana, and the divine *anthrōpos* of the Hermetic literature.[66] The figure could also be applied to gods,[67] Hellenistic rulers,[68] provincial governors, and (in Egypt) even animals.[69] It was also open to a variety of metaphorical applications.[70] The actual terms used to describe these honors occur in a variety of syntactic combinations. In addition to the adjectival compound *isotheos*, for example, both the dative construction with the adjectival form *(isos theō/theois)* and the adverbial form *(isa theō/theois)* appear in such honorific formulas. As the technical term for divine honors suggests (i.e., *isotheoi timai*), some form of the verb *timaō* or the noun *timē* is common in these texts, although *timaō/timē* is not always present.[71] Texts that use these expressions tend to fall naturally into two groups. One stems directly from the civic tradition of *isotheoi timai*. The other group consists of responses, including Jewish texts, that are variously critical of the civic usage.

In discussing those who had received *isotheoi timai*, the first-century B.C.E. historian Diodorus Siculus (of Sicily) notes, in particular, the importance of heroes, demigods, and "good men":

---

65. See especially section 5, "Equality by Nature and Equality with God outside the New Testament," of Gustav Stählin's article on *"isos" TDNT* 3:351–52, citing examples.

66. G. Stählin, *"isos, isotes, isotimos," TDNT* 3:352. This article gives numerous citations of the ancient literature.

67. Wayne A. Meeks, "Equal to God," in *The Conversation Continues: Studies in Paul and John in Honor of J. Louis Martyn* (ed. Robert T. Fortna and Beverly R. Gaventa; Nashville: Abingdon, 1990), 312.

68. C. Spicq, *"isos, isotes, isotimos"* in *Theological Lexicon of the New Testament* (Peabody, Mass.: Hendrickson, 1994), 229. In the article, Spicq provides numerous citations from ancient sources.

69. In this category would be, for example, the Egyptian Osiris and its Greek equivalent (i.e., according to Diodorus Sic. 4.1.6) and Daedalus. Diodorus speaks of Osiris/Dionysus in 1.22. In 1.22.6–7 he recounts why the phallus is accorded particular respect in the Dionysian rites. On the divine honors offered to Dionysus, see also 3.64.2. For those offered to Daedalus, see 1.97.6.

70. Meeks, "Equal to God," 312.

71. In the heroic tradition, the only example of *isa* plus the dative singular is found in Homer, *Odyssey* 15.520. The verb or substantive of *timaō* does not occur in this example. More common in the material relating to heroes is the combination of *isa* with the dative plural of *theos*. For example, see the description of Kastor/Castor and Polydeukes/Polydeuces in *Odyssey* 11.301–4. Compare also the description of Achilles in *Odyssey* 11.482–86; Homer, *Iliad* 1.494; 21.315; 21.518; and Plato, *Phaedrus* 255a.

For very great and most numerous deeds have been performed by
the heroes and demi-gods and by good men, who, because of the
benefits they conferred which have been shared by all men, have
been honored *(etimēsan)* by succeeding generations with sacrifices which in some cases are like those offered to the gods
(isotheois), in other cases like such as are paid to heroes, and of
one and all the appropriate praises have been sung by the voice of
history for all time. (4.1.4)

Among the "good men" of whom Diodorus writes was Philopoemen, who
died c. 182 B.C.E.:

Philopoemen, the general of the Achaean League, was a man of
outstanding attainments, intellectual, military, and moral alike,
and his life-long political career was irreproachable throughout.
Time and again he was preferred to the office of general, and for
forty years he guided the affairs of state. More than anyone else he
advanced the general welfare of the Achaean confederacy, for he
not only made it his policy to treat the common man kindly, but
also by force of character won the esteem of the Romans. Yet in the
final scene of life he found Fortune unkind. After his death, however, as if by some divine Providence he obtained honors equal to
those paid the gods *(tas isotheous timas)*, in compensation for the
misfortunes that attended his demise. In addition to the decrees in
his honor voted by the Achaeans jointly, his native city set up an
altar, (instituted) an annual sacrifice to him, and appointed hymns
and praises of his exploits to be sung by the young men of the
city.[72] (29.17.18)

Lamenting the decay of old Roman values, Diodorus focuses on men
who might serve as countermodels,[73] such as Quintus Scaevola, proconsul
in Asia in 97 B.C.E.:

Mucius Scaevola, by maintaining the administration of justice
incorruptible and exact, not only relieved the provincials from all
legal chicanery, but in addition redressed the unjust exactions of

---

72. Another passage from Diodorus (20.102.3), describing the liberation of the
city of Sicyon by Demetrius (ca. 303/2 B.C.E.), indicates that divine honors could be
given to leaders. For a text that criticizes the use of this tradition, see Isocrates, *Ad
Nicoclem/Or.* 2.5.
73. See Diodorus, 37.3.1–37.4.1.

the publicans. He assigned scrupulously fair tribunals to hear all
who had been wronged, and in every case found the publicans
guilty; he forced them to reimburse the plaintiffs for financial
losses they had suffered, while he required those who were accused
of having put men to death to stand trial on capital charges. . . .
The governor's wisdom and virtue, together with the assistance he
was enabled to render, served as a corrective to the hatred that had
previously arisen against the ruling power. He himself was
accorded . . . divine honors *(timōn isotheōn etyche)* among those he
had benefited, and from his fellow citizens he received many trib-
utes in recognition of his achievements. (37.5.1–37.6.1)

Nicolaus of Damascus' *Life of Augustus* provides two examples of the
adverbial usage of *isa* in reference to the deification of Julius Caesar. Just
after the death of Caesar, as spectators viewed his body carried through the
forum on a litter, it was noted that:

no one refrained from tears, seeing him who had lately been honored like a god *(horōn ton palai isa kai theon timōmenon).*[74]

Then in the conflict between Anthony and Octavian, a soldier from a
"crowd" shouted his support of Octavian

and bade him be of good cheer and be assured that he had inherited
all their support, for they thought of his late father as of a god
(memnēsthai gar tou kata gēs patros isa kai theou), and would do
and suffer anything for his successors.[75]

The singular form of the adverbial construct *(ison)* appears in an
aphorism recorded by Menander with no apparent change in meaning
from the plural form *(isa):*

---

74. C. Hall, "Nicolaus of Damascus' *Life of Augustus:* A Historical Commentary
Embodying a Translation," *Smith College Classical Studies* 4 (1923): 51. Note that in
the participial construction (again the verb is *timaō*), *theos* is in the accusative case
and not the dative.

75. Here the verb *timaō* is lacking and *theou* is in the genitive. Felix Jacoby, *Die
Fragmente der griechischen Historiker* (Berlin: Weidmann, 1923), on Nikolaos von
Damaskos, Fragment 130.117; translation from C. M. Hall, "Nicolaus of Damascus'
Life of Augustus," 62.

> Be willing to honor your friends like you would honor a god *(Ison theo sou tous philous timan thele).*[76]

An interesting use of *isotheos* (without *timaō*) is found in an edict of Germanicus of 19 C.E.; in accordance with good Roman reserve, he shuns the divine honors awarded to him in the East:

> Proclamation of Germanicus Caesar, son of Augustus [i.e., Tiberius] and grandson of the deified Augustus, proconsul. Your goodwill, which you display on all occasions when you see me, I welcome, but your acclamations, which for me are invidious and such as are addressed to gods *(isotheous)*, I altogether deprecate. For they are appropriate only to him who is actually the saviour and benefactor of the whole human race, my father.[77]

Isotheoi are to be reserved for the reigning emperor (his father).

Texts that are critical of the civic tradition of divine honors incorporate some form of *isos* and *theos,* often without a substantive or verbal form of *timaō.* Plato (d. 347 B.C.E.) gives voice to a tradition that perceived how the *isotheoi timai* could be used to legitmate an abuse of power, a common trait of tyrants.[78] In a discussion of justice and injustice in connection with two rings that have the power to make one invisible, Plato says:

> If now there should be two such rings, and the just man should put on one and the unjust the other, no one could be found, it would seem, of such adamantine temper as to persevere in justice and endure to refrain his hands from the possessions of others and not touch them, though he might with impunity take what he wished even from the marketplace, and enter into houses and lie with whom he pleased, and slay and loose from bonds whomsoever he

---

76. This aphorism is found in two different collections. Menandri, *ΓΝΩΜΑΙ ΜΟΝΟΣΤΙΧΟΙ,* in *Fragmenta Comicorum Graecorum,* vol. 4 (ed. Augustus Meineke; Berlin: G. Reimeri, 1841), 347, line 269; and in Siegfried Jaekel, ed., *Menandri Sententiae: Comparatio Menandri et Philistionis* (Leipzig: Teubner, 1964), 53, line 357.

77. Text and translation may be found at item no. 211 in *Select Papyri,* vol. 2 (ed. A. S. Hunt and C. C. Edgar; LCL; Cambridge, Mass.: Harvard University Press, 1937).

78. An ad loc. editorial comment in the LCL edition notes that *isotheos* is "a *leitmotif* anticipating Plato's rebuke of the tragedians for their praises of the tyrant." The rebuke occurs in Book 7 of the *Republic* (568c).

would, and in all other things conduct himself among mankind as
the equal of a god *(kai talla prattein en tois anthrōpois isotheon
onta)*. And in so acting he would do no differently from the other
man, but both would pursue the same course. And yet this is a
great proof, one might argue, that no one is just of his own will but
only from constraint. (*Republic* 360c)

Among Jewish sources 2 Macc 9:12 relates Antiochus IV's confession
of hubris on his deathbed:

And when he could not endure his own stench, he uttered these
words, "It is right to be subject to God; mortals should not think
that they are equal to God *(onta isothea phronein)*."

In Philo a representative text uses *isotheos* to characterize idolatry:

Pride also brings divine things into utter contempt, even though
they are supposed to receive the highest honors. But what honor
can there be if truth be not there as well, truth honorable both in
name and function, just as falsehood is naturally dishonorable?
This contempt for things divine is manifest to those of keener
vision. For men have employed sculpture and painting to fashion
innumerable forms which they have enclosed in shrines and temples and after building altars have assigned celestial and divine
honors *(timas isolympious kai isotheous)* to idols of stone and
wood and suchlike images, all of them lifeless things. Such persons
are happily compared in the sacred Scriptures to the children of a
harlot; for as they in their ignorance of their one natural father
ascribe their paternity to all their mother's lovers, so too throughout the cities those who do not know the true, the really existent
God have deified hosts of others who are falsely so called. Then as
some honor one, some another god, diversity of opinion as to
which was best waxed strong and engendered disputes in every
other matter also. (*On the Decalogue* 8–9)

A second text from Philo warns "the mind" not to desire the status of
God:[79]

---

79. On Philo's notion of a second god *(deuteros theos)*, see A. Segal, *Two Powers*,
159–81.

The mind shows itself to be without God and full of self-love, when it deems itself as on a par with God *(oiomenos isos einai theō)*. *(Legum allegoriae* 1.149)

Only one other NT passage, in addition to Phil 2:6, uses the *isotheos* group:

This was why the Jews sought all the more to kill him, because he not only broke the sabbath but also called God his own Father, making himself equal to God *(ison heauton poiōn tō theō)*. (John 5:18, RSV)

Finally, two passages from the *Sibylline Oracles* that use the construction *isazō*[80] are of interest in this context. Both occurrences are in reference to the self-proclaimed status of Nero *redivivus:*

Then he will return declaring himself equal to God *(isazōn theō)*. *(Sib. Or.* 5.34)

Making himself equal to God *(isazōn theō auton)*, he will convince a willing people. *(Sib. Or.* 12.86)

This brief review indicates that there were many different ways to express the notion of "godlike" or "godequal."[81] The syntactic boundaries between the expressions *isotheos, isos theō, ison theō,* and *isa theō/theois* blurred in actual usage. All the examples reflect the honorific tradition of the Greek cities, which granted heroes and rulers *isotheoi timai* ("honors like those awarded the gods"), although some are critical of it or make a metaphorical application. The majority of these texts include a verbal or substantive use of *timaō.*

As noted above, the texts which fall within the "critical" tradition do not as often include *timaō* (Plato, *Republic* 360c; 2 Macc 9:12; Philo, *Legum allegoriae* 1.49; John 5:18; *Sib. Or.* 5.34; 12.86). Also, the second group's use

---

80. *Isazō theō* seems to be synonymous with the construction found at John 5:18, *ison heauton poiōn tō theō.*

81. This review focuses on syntactic constructions most closely related to the expression *isa theō* found in Phil 2:6. The impropriety of human appropriation of divine status is, of course, a theme explored in depth in the biblical corpus in a variety of grammatical expressions. See, for example, Gen 3:5; Isa 14:14; Ezek 28:1–10; Dan 11:36–39; Acts 12:22; 2 Thess 2:4; Rev 13.

of *isos* + *theos* criticizes various forms of ideology and lampoons the presumption of various individuals for usurping the status of God. Plato identifies tyrants. Among the Jewish texts, two of the human objects of this critique are notoriously wicked rulers (Antiochus IV and Nero). A third recipient of this charge is Jesus, but the usage is, on its surface, similarly accusatory.[82]

The two traditions (one positive, one negative) of using *isotheos* are related to each other. The critical tradition responds to abuses it perceives in the civic usage. In the case of the Jewish texts, the Greek civic tradition of awarding divine honors and the traditional Jewish concern for the exclusive sovereignty of God are antithetical.

The observation that the Jewish usage of *isa theō* represents a critique of its "positive" use in the public discourse may help determine the intended audience of the term at Phil 2:6b. A question will further clarify the issue: Does the *isa theō* of v. 6 positively value the civic honorific tradition of *isotheoi timai;* or does it reflect the Judaic usage in which *isa theō* functions rhetorically to critique one who usurps the unique status of God (i.e., Antiochus, "the mind," Jesus, Nero)?

As noted above, *isa theō* is used *positively* in v. 6 of the hymn. It is not the status of *isotheos* that is being critiqued, but the "grasping" after it.[83] While Jesus himself does not grasp after divine honors, it is, in the end, exactly the status he receives from God. That is, Phil 2:6–11 is similar to the narrative found in Diodorus (29.17.18) regarding Philopoemen who "made it his policy to treat the common man kindly, . . . but in the final scene of life he found Fortune unkind. After his death, however, as if by some divine Providence, he obtained honors equal to those paid the gods." This is a different application of *isa theō* from what one would expect in "Jewish" usage.[84] It suggests that the hymn was written for or by Gentile followers of Christ.[85] If Jews sang the hymn, their acknowledgment

---

82. Meeks, "Equal to God," 315.

83. From the perspective of the hymn, Jesus did not *make himself* "godequal," since it was God's doing. See Meeks, "Equal to God," 311.

84. E.g., Philo, *De confusione linguarum* 168–69, deals with statements in Genesis in which the first person plural pronoun is used of God. In doing so, he makes the claim that "no existing thing is of equal honor to God *(hoi ouden tōn ontōn isotimon hyphestēke theō).*"

85. See the discussion by J. Reumann, "Contribution of the Philippian Community to Paul and to Earliest Christianity," *NTS* 39 (1993): 442–46. That the hymn was written for/by Gentiles is strengthened by the lack of evidence for a Jewish presence in Philippi in the mid-first century C.E. See Bockmuehl, *Epistle to the Philippians,* 8–10.

that Jesus was worthy of divine honors transgressed what appears to be a traditional interdiction. That is, the assignment of the status of *isa theō* to Jesus would have functioned in the church in Philippi as it did in the later Johannine community. The award of "godequal" honors to Jesus would have necessarily subverted both "the classical Scriptures and traditions" of Judaism.[86]

Does this mean, then, that the use of *isa theō* in Phil 2:6 reflects the positive evaluation of the term evidenced in the public discourse of the cities? I believe it does. In a lecture given in 1938, K. Bornhäuser made the suggestion that Gaius's claims of divinity as well as his attack on the temple in Jerusalem in 39–40 C.E. provided the specific background against which one should read the hymn now found at Phil 2:6–11. Phil 2:6 is making a comparison between Caligula and Jesus.[87] To argue that Gaius's cultic claims were *the* impetus for the composition of the hymn may go beyond the evidence. Yet Phil 2:6–11 does appropriate for Jesus the honorific tradition of the ruler cult. The status claimed for the emperor *(to einai isa theō)* in the civic religions of the Greek cities of the East has been reassigned to Jesus in the early Christian hymn. The honor associated with the term in the public discourse is retained but redirected to one who is, from the perspective of the Pauline subaltern community, legitimately worthy of its claims.

One historical factor in particular, however, further illuminates how just how sharp the comparison *(synkrisis)* being made in the Philippian hymn is, sharper than perceived by Bornhäuser. As noted above, by the early first century of the common era, the award of *isotheo timai* had been reserved exclusively for honors to the imperial family. That the hymn of Phil 2:6–11 assigns a comparable status to Jesus (i.e., a nonenfranchised Jewish provincial of lower status, who had been executed by Rome) would be a particularly outrageous transgression of the interdict that divine honors were to be restricted to the emperor.[88] Various NT scholars read the unspecified conflict with the outside community evident in Phil 1:27–30 (and Acts 16:20–24) as stemming from members of the Pauline community's withdrawal from cultic associations in Philippi, including those dedicated

---

86. Meeks, "Equal to God," 319.

87. Bornhäuser, *Jesus Imperator Mundi,* 17–19.

88. From this perspective, one is led to speculate that the hymn's description of Jesus as *morphē theou* may be a way of camouflaging the extremely radical claim that the church was, in effect, awarding divine honors to an enemy of Rome of recent historical memory.

to the emperor.[89] The disunity in the new sect evident from Paul's letter reflects, according to this view, differing opinions about how to deal with the ongoing conflict with other cultic assemblies in the colony.[90] Perhaps the conflict was due, in part, to the claim that the group had appropriated for Jesus an honor reserved for the emperor. If so, the subaltern criticism of the emperor and the local elite was not concealed well enough to protect the Pauline community from the hostility of those more favorably disposed to the social relations the imperial order assumed.

W. Knox speculated that the closest Greco-Roman parallels to the hymn of Phil 2:6–11 could be found in the panegyrics for rulers given in the context of the pagan public festivals.[91] It is interesting to contemplate that hymns sung about Jesus in the worship life of the early followers of Christ may have shown many superficial similarities to those sung about emperors who were proclaimed to be *isa theō* within the context of euergetistic festivals of the imperial cult.[92] If so, the similarities would be those of a mirror image—a reflection of reality turned upside down.

Conclusion

In Phil 2:6–11, the exaltation of Jesus comes as a result of his choosing to live a life of submission (for others) and not one of dominance (over others). Hidden here, I believe, is a pointed critique of those who chose the opposite, i.e., those who grasped after honors on both the civic and imperial level. In the first place, this critique points a finger at the emperor. It was, after all, only the emperor who was awarded the status of being *isa theō* in the early Empire. In the enthronement picture Phil 2:6–11 draws, it is Jesus *rather than* the Princeps who is depicted as the true cosmocrator. From the perspective of the hymn, the claims made on behalf of the emperor in the public discourse—that the emperor is *isa theō*—are false. In other words, v. 6 of the hymn characterizes the emperor as a pretender to a throne that rightfully belongs to Jesus.

Another social function of the imperial cult in the cities of the East, in addition to constructing the power of the emperor, was to elevate and

---

89. See, for example, de Vox, *Church and Community Conflicts,* 262–65; Bockmeuhl, *Epistle to the Philippians,* 100–1, 148, 190.

90. The interest in Phil 3:2–11 in circumcision, for example, may reflect the belief that adopting Jewish identity markers might provide the appropriate cultic means to negotiate the conflict with wider Philippian society.

91. Knox, "The 'Divine Hero' Christology," 249.

92. Such hymns were sung to the glory of the emperors, but the evidence for the hymns themselves is thin. See Krentz, "Epideiktik and Hymnody," 54; and Price, *Rituals and Powers,* 37–38.

legitimate the status of the high elite of those cities. The imperial cult bene-fited the local urban magnates as well as the emperor. The prestige of the local elites was tied structurally to their functions within the civic imperial cults. When the early clients of Christ criticized the cult of the emperor, they included the pretensions of the local elite in their line of sight. A cri-tique of the emperor implied a critique of his local clients. In addition, therefore, to the comparison being made between Jesus and the emperor in v. 6 of the Philippian hymn, the hymn may also be seen to resist the claims made by the local high elite upon the underclass. For some early clients of Christ, the earthly powers over which Jesus is enthroned in Phil 2:l0b surely included those high elites who were the *archai kai exousiai* in the cities of the East. Jesus, in replacing the emperor as cosmocrator in the hymn, also assumes his lordship over the *archontes* of the city (Acts 16:19). Again, from the perspective of the hymn, the exaltation of Jesus means that the *decuri-ons* of the city find themselves subordinate to Jesus rather than the Princeps. Scott's analysis of the public discourse suggests that the high elites of the cities of the East, including those in Philippi, had the most invested in the public rituals of the imperial cult. One suspects that they would not have taken kindly to the notion that the emperor (whom they dressed with an impressive and expensive cult) was being stripped of his finery in the liturgy of a new cult in which an executed criminal was being proclaimed *isa theō*. It is also safe to assume that the high elites would not have appreciated the fact that, in the hymns of the sectarians, they too paid obeisance to *kyrios* Jesus.

The elites, however, were not the intended audience of the hymn found at Phil 2:6–11. The audience of the hymn was the house church itself. With the knowledge that it was Jesus (and not the emperor) who was now the cosmocrator, came the power to turn the world of the public discourse on its heels. It was a power that, specifically, reversed the polarities of the com-plementary differentiation (i.e., domination/subordination) that scripted the culture of euergetism on the civic level. That is, the liturgy of the *ekklēsia* of Christ provided a vision of Jesus enthroned in heaven through which, as Luke put it in another hymn, God had "put down the mighty *(dynastēs)* from their thrones, and exalted those of low degree" (Luke 1:52, RSV). This aspect of the liturgical tradition of the early church, it seems, represented a major reevaluation—by the large underclass of the cities—of the power relations projected by the public discourses of the *poleis.*

Two points should be emphasized in conclusion. First of all, it simply needs to be noted that in the encomium of Phil 2:6–11, terminology *(isa theō)* that long legitimated elitist rule has been reappropriated in the hymn to sanction an alternative *ekklēsia.* The *gravitas* of the ruler cult maintained at great expense by the local elite is appropriated for a different *kyrios*. Such a shift in metaphorical reference, scholars of the subaltern might suggest, represents a critical resymbolization of a term central to the dominant discourse in the religion of the subordinate.

In addition to the hymn's cultural-critical role, Scott's work suggests an equally important social function of the symbolic reversal (subordinate/dominant) effected by the Christ hymn:

> Inversions . . . play an important imaginative function. . . . They do, at least at the level of thought, create an imaginative breathing space in which the normal categories of order and hierarchy are less than completely inevitable. . . . When we manipulate any social classification imaginatively—turning it inside out and upside down—we are forcibly reminded that it is to some degree an arbitrary human creation.

Symbolic inversions can provide the impetus to construct social classifications that are alternatives to those offered in the public discourse. The private and hidden discourses of the subordinate not only provide a range of *negative* responses to the public discourse, but also are places where *positive* social experimentation may occur. That is, these subaltern discourses are not only products of culture, but also produce culture:

> The dialectical relationship between the public and hidden transcripts is obvious. By definition, the hidden transcript represents discourse—gesture, speech, practices—that is ordinarily excluded from the public transcript of subordinates by the exercise of power. The practice of domination, then, *creates* the hidden transcript. If the domination is particularly severe, it is likely to produce a hidden transcript of corresponding richness. The hidden transcript of subordinate groups, in turn, reacts back on the public transcript by engendering a subculture and by opposing its own variant form of social domination against that of the dominant elite. Both are realms of power and interests.[93]

In addition to criticizing the imperial cult and appropriating its sophisticated rhetorical tradition to legitimate their claims of Christ's lordship, the Jesus-believers may also have used *isa theō* in Phil 2:6 to leverage a

---

93. Scott, *Domination*, 27.

conceptual "breathing space" that allowed the early followers of Paul in Phillipi—and elsewhere—to imagine a different social world from the one structured in the public discourse.

The encomium at Phil 2:6–11 applied *isa theō* to one crucified by Roman power. If Scott's analysis is correct, and Plato's *Republic* and the Jewish reserve regarding the civic cults give voice to sentiments that were often thought but little expressed among the non-elite, then the followers of Paul—while singing hymns that claimed Jesus was *isa theō*—were protesting their daily experience of the abuse of patronal power. Jesus' exaltation helped them see through the splendor of the emperor's new clothes given to him by the cult and rhetoric of the local imperial cult. What they saw was not the foolishness of a naked god, but an oppressive system that constructed the prestige and power of the few at the expense of the many.

– 7 –

PAUL AND THE POLITICS OF VIRTUE AND VICE

Jennifer Wright Knust

In his letters, Paul argued that the brothers and sisters in Christ have made a decisive break with the depravity of the world. According to Paul, Gentiles *(ta ethnē)* are characterized by fornication *(porneia)* and the passion of lust *(pathei epithymias)*, but the brothers and sisters in Christ avoid sexual misbehavior. As he put it in his letter to the Thessalonians:

> For this is the will of God, your sanctification: that you abstain from fornication; that each of you know to possess his own wife (lit., "vessel") in holiness and honor, not with lustful passion like the Gentiles who do not know God; that no one transgress and defraud his brother in the matter, because the Lord is an avenger in all these things, just as we told you before, and we solemnly warned you. For God did not call us for impurity, but in holiness. (1 Thess 4:3–7, trans. author)[1]

Insiders—brothers and sisters in Christ—practice self-control *(enkrateia)*, since they have "crucified the flesh with its passions and desires" (Gal 5:24). Outsiders—Gentiles and others—have been "given up in the lusts of their hearts to impurity, to the degrading of their bodies among themselves" (Rom 1:24). Outsiders are "enslaved to lust," but insiders are "slaves of

---

1. O. Larry Yarbrough suggests that here "wife" is the best translation of "vessel" *(skeuos)*. Defrauding one's brother can then be understood to refer to a man committing adultery with the wife of a "brother." See his *Not Like the Gentiles: Marriage Rules in the Letters of Paul* (SBLDS 80; Atlanta: Scholars, 1985), 68–76.

God" (Rom 6:13–23). Gentiles fornicate (1 Thess 4:5; Gal 5:16–26, Rom 1:18–32); the faithful glorify God in their bodies (1 Cor 6:15–20). Outsiders join their bodies to prostitutes (1 Cor 6:15); insiders exercise self-control, or they marry and thereby channel their desire appropriately (1 Cor 7:1–40). Paul consistently contrasts the self-control of the brothers and sisters in Christ with the depravity of Gentiles and other outsiders, condemning this "crooked and perverse generation" for sexual corruption (Phil 2:15), while setting the "saints" apart on the basis of their strict self-control. Given the repeated insistence among ancient Greek and Latin authors that good emperors and kings are characterized by their exceptional virtue, such an argument can be read as a further indication of Paul's disdain for empire and emperor alike.

I am not the first to notice that, when read carefully, Paul is decidedly critical of his rulers. As Horsley, Georgi, Wengst, Elliott, and others have noted, Christianity in general and Pauline Christianity in particular emerged in the context of the reconfiguration of piety and power under the figure of the emperor.[2] During this period, Augustus and later emperors were represented as universal benefactors, saviors, the sons of a god, fulfilling divinely ordained providence, and guaranteeing both peace and piety.[3] Reading early Christian texts in light of imperial rhetorics of power, these scholars argue that Paul and other early Christian authors cannot be read as recommending accommodation to the Empire. Indeed, the gospel of the crucified Messiah stands in direct contrast to the "gospel according to Augustus."[4] Paul's injunctions to "distinguish what really matters" and to "resist conformity to this world" directly opposed Roman rule.[5] Paul explicitly denied the claim that the emperor had instituted "peace and security":

---

2. See the collection of essays in Richard A. Horsley, ed., *Paul and Empire: Religion and Power in Roman Imperial Society* (Harrisburg, Pa.: Trinity Press International, 1997); Richard A. Horsley, *1 Corinthians* (ANTC; Nashville: Abingdon, 1998), esp. 22–38; Dieter Georgi, "Who Is the True Prophet?" in *Paul and Empire: Religion and Power in Roman Imperial Society* (ed. Richard A. Horsley; Harrisburg, Pa.: Trinity Press International, 1997), 36–46; Klaus Wengst, *Pax Romana* (trans. John Bowden; Philadelphia: Fortress, 1987); Neil Elliott, *Liberating Paul: The Justice of God and the Politics of the Apostle* (Maryknoll, N.Y.: Orbis Books, 1994). See also Walter E. Pilgrim, *Uneasy Neighbors: Church and State in the New Testament* (OBT; Minneapolis: Fortress, 1999). For important background, see Simon Price, *Rituals and Power: The Roman Imperial Cult in Asia Minor* (Cambridge: Cambridge University Press, 1984), esp. 2–5, 49–51, 53–62, 243–46.

3. Price, *Rituals and Power*, 51, 54; John K. Chow, "Patronage in Roman Corinth," in *Paul and Empire* (ed. Horsley), 104–25.

4. Georgi, "Who Is the True Prophet?" 36.

5. Elliott, *Liberating Paul*, 189; citing Phil 1:10 and Rom 12:2.

"just as people are saying 'peace and security,' sudden destruction will come upon them."[6] Pauline "faith" or "loyalty" *(fides, pistis)* can be compared to the Augustan claim that the whole Roman realm is distinguished by *fides* and *iustitia (dikaiosynē)*.[7] Paul offered a critique of empire and did not support conformity to imperial or other governmental authority.

Paul's claim that outsiders are inevitably tainted with sexual vice while "the saints" preserve sexual purity offers further support for the thesis that Paul was critical of Roman imperial pretensions and propaganda. Still, however pointed Paul's critique may have been, when he adopted sexual virtue and vice as his anti-imperial code language, he reconfirmed a gendered hierarchy that assumes woman is derived from man and identifies desire with "slavishness." Though Paul may have opposed the broader Roman political, economic, and cultural order, he reproduced cultural presuppositions more commonly employed to support empire. He employed the widespread rhetorical strategy of associating one's enemies with sexual misconduct, he described this misconduct in terms of the violation of "natural" gender, and he associated desire with "slavishness" even as he undermined traditional status distinctions.

Paul and Rhetorical Invective

By claiming that the followers of Christ are sexually pure and implying that outsiders are sexually depraved, Paul participated in a common argumentative strategy: defining one's opponent in sexual terms. The vilification of enemies or outsiders on the basis of (alleged) sexual vice can be found in numerous ancient contexts—from Athenian and Roman lawcourts to ancient biography, history, and works of moral philosophy. For example, in his famous speech "On the Crown" *(De corona)*, the Athenian orator Demosthenes attacked the origin, occupation, and character of his target Aeschines by suggesting that Aeschines' mother engaged in indiscriminate intercourse in a public latrine; Aeschines (allegedly) imitated her example by involving himself in suspect religious rituals, wearing exotic apparel, and associating with old women (129, 260).[8] Cicero followed Demosthenes' example, accusing opponents of family scandals, indiscriminate lust, and other "shameful deeds" (e.g., *In Catalinam*

---

6. Wengst, *Pax Romana*, 11–19; citing 1 Thess 5:3.

7. Georgi, "Who Is the True Prophet?" 36–46.

8. Similarly, Aeschines attacked the target of one of his forensic speeches by claiming that he had prostituted himself in his youth and squandered his inheritance; *In Timarchum* 40–42. This speech is thoroughly discussed by Kenneth J. Dover, *Greek Homosexuality* (Cambridge, Mass.: Harvard University Press, 1978).

1.13–16).[9] Ad hominem attacks were not reserved for forensic oratory, however. The Greek moralist and biographer Plutarch evaluated the subjects of his *Parallel Lives* entirely in terms of their relative virtues or vices.[10] Roman historiographers excoriated "bad" emperors for extravagant excess, outrageous sexual exploits, and even incest.[11] The Stoic philosopher Musonius Rufus observed that sexual vice always brings disgrace; those trained in philosophy would never visit prostitutes or engage in relations with their female slaves (4.20; echoed by pseudo-Plutarch, *Moralia* 5b–c).

Given this discursive context, charges of sexual licentiousness against target outsiders should be expected. With at least some training in Greek oratory, Paul was likely to have been aware of the standard topics of blame.[12] Greek and Latin rhetorical training included an introduction to appropriate categories of praise and blame, categories outlined in Greek rhetorical handbooks *(progymnasmata)* and in Latin discussions of rhetoric. Speeches of praise closely paralleled speeches of blame, with the standard topics assigned to each serving as mirror opposites. Noble birth, association with a noble city, education in philosophy and rhetoric, self-control, beauty, courage, and vitality were to be praised. Slave or non-Greek origin, degrading occupation, reprehensible sexual behavior,

---

9. R. M. Nisbet offers a thorough survey of the sorts of charges commonly employed by Cicero: "The *In Pisonem* as an Invective," Appendix 6, in *Cicero: In L. Campurnium Pisonem* (Oxford: Clarendon, 1961), 192–97. Cicero specifically commended the rhetorical methods of his Athenian predecessors in *De oratore* 22.94; 23.94–95. Plutarch compared Cicero to Demosthenes in his *Parallel Lives,* noting that they share much in common. See his *Demosthenes* 2.3–4 and *Comparatio Demosthenis et Ciceronis.*

10. See Alan Wardman, *Plutarch's Lives* (Berkeley: University of California Press, 1974).

11. See, for example, the descriptions of Nero found in Suetonius, Tacitus, and Dio, and discussed in Jás Elsner and Jamie Masters, ed., *Reflections of Nero: Culture, History, and Representation* (Chapel Hill: University of North Carolina Press, 1994).

12. William V. Harris has demonstrated that only a very small minority of the Greco-Roman world could have achieved anything like functional literacy; *Ancient Literacy* (Cambridge, Mass.: Harvard University Press, 1989), 3–25, 139–46, 248–84. As a member of the educated few, Paul would have received at least some training in the techniques of rhetoric, though he should not be counted among the most highly educated of his day. On rhetorical education, see Robert Kaster, *Guardians of Language: The Grammarian and Society in Late Antiquity* (Berkeley: University of California Press, 1987). On the importance of Greek intellectual culture to early Christians, see especially the now classic study by Werner Jaeger, *Early Christianity and Greek Paideia* (Cambridge, Mass.: Harvard University Press, 1961). On Paul and rhetoric, see, for example, Hans Dieter Betz, *Galatians: A Commentary on Paul's Letter to the Churches of Galatia* (Hermeneia; Philadelphia: Fortress, 1979); Stanley Stowers, *The Diatribe and Paul's Letter to the Romans* (SBLDS 57; Atlanta: Scholars, 1981).

improper appearance and dress, military desertion, misanthropy, and gloominess were to be censured.[13] Standard topics of praise and blame were learned by every Greek- or Latin-speaking schoolboy. Orators were expected to evaluate their subjects in terms of their (real or alleged) virtue or vice. Thus, Paul's decision to represent Gentiles as ridden with vice was, perhaps, entirely predictable. Moreover, as a Hellenistic Jew well versed in Torah, Paul was no doubt familiar with the biblical association of Gentiles and fornication (Exod 34:15–16; Deut 31:16; Judg 2:17; 8:27; 1 Chr 5:25; 2 Kgs 9:22; Ezek 6:9; 16:15; 20:30). Still, by adopting this particular argumentative strategy, Paul's own rhetoric of virtue and vice can be read not only as stereotypical polemic but also as a pointed attack. Since status was frequently justified in terms of virtue, the association of outsiders with sexual vice can be interpreted as an attempt to undermine the pretensions of those who linked their authority to their (supposedly) superior morals, including the emperor.

The Virtue (or Vice) of Emperors and Kings

As early as Plato, Greek writers had asserted that only good men could truly be kings (*Republic* 427c–434d, 543c–580a). Dio Chrysostom attributed this view to Homer:

> Homer, in the same manner as other wise and truthful men, says that no wicked or licentious or avaricious person can ever be a ruler or master either of himself or of anybody else, nor will such a man ever be a king even though all the world, both Greeks and barbarians, men and women, affirm the contrary. (*De regno i/Or.* 1.14)

Following Plato's lead, Greek historians evaluated kings by their relative virtues. For example, Diodorus Siculus describes the exceptional self-control (*enkrateia*), justice (*dikaiosynē*), and magnanimity (*megalopsychos*) of the

---

13. In his handbook, Aphthonius recommended that the following topics be addressed: family, nation, ancestors, livelihood, customs, prudence, beauty, manliness, and bodily strength, among other features; *Progymnasmata* 8. The topics of praise and blame are summarized by Severin Koster, *Die Invektive in der griechischen und römishen Literatur* (Beiträge zur Klassischen Philologie 99; Meisenheim am Glan: Verlag Anton Hain, 1980), 16–17. A survey of Latin invective terminology yielded the familiar categories, with lowly origin, degrading occupation, improper appearance, criminality, sexual vice, and gluttony emerging as central topics. Ilona Opelt, *Die lateinischen Schimpfwörter und verwandte sprachliche Erscheinungen: Eine Typologie* (Heidelberg: Carl Winter Universitätsverlag, 1965), 125–89. See also Jacqueline Flint Long, *Claudian's "In Eutropium": Or, How, When, and Why to Slander a Eunuch* (Chapel Hill: University of North Carolina Press, 1996), 66–67.

Egyptian kings of old (1.70.6–12). Elsewhere, Diodorus records with approval their exceedingly strict laws regarding women (1.78.4–5). Arrian relates the superb self-control *(sōphrosynē)* of Alexander, who chose neither to violate the beautiful wife or daughters of Oxyartes, nor the wife of king Darius of Persia, though as the victor he had the opportunity to do so *(Anabasis* 4.19.4–6; 20.1–3.). Dionysius of Halicarnassus records a speech attributed to Romulus, the mythical founder of Rome, in which Romulus exhorts the citizens of the new city to embrace virtue. Romulus/Dionysius asserts that men who are brave in battle and at the same time masters of their desires *(epithymiai)* "are the greatest ornaments to their country." In turn, a government founded wisely produces men of bravery, justice, and the other virtues *(Antiquitates romanae* 2.3.5). Romulus, in a demonstration of this wisdom, appointed slaves and foreigners to serve in trades that promote shameful passions. Freemen, on the other hand, were allowed only two professions, agriculture and warfare, "for he observed that men so employed became masters of their appetite [and] are less entangled in illicit love affairs" *(Antiquitates romanae* 2.28.1–2). Slaves and foreigners were thereby associated with "shameful passion" and freemen with self-control.

The theory that a king's virtue legitimates his rule appears in a Roman context as well. Following Actium, Octavian Augustus[14] fashioned himself as the restorer of Roman mores, instituting a moral reform through legislation, building projects, and a revival of Roman religion at the expense of "foreign" cults.[15] In 27 B.C.E., the Senate recognized Augustus' exceptional political achievements by praising his *virtus, clementia, iustitia,* and *pietas,* commemorating his restoration of the *res publica* on a golden shield (*Res gestae divi Augusti [RG]* 34.1–3).[16] The court poet Horace celebrated the return to morality heralded by the rise of Augustus. Prior to Augustus, Horace claimed, Rome was overrun with immorality: "O most immoral age! First you tainted marriage, the house, and the family. Now from the same source flows pollution over fatherland and people!" (*Carmina* 3.6). The Augustan moral revival restored the city to its proper virtue; thanks to Augustus, "the pure house is no longer sullied by adultery. Law and custom

---

14. On the significance of the title "Augustus," see Mary Beard, John North, and Simon Price, *Religions of Rome,* vol. 1: *A History* (Cambridge: Cambridge University Press, 1998), 182–84.

15. Paul Zanker, *The Power of Images in the Age of Augustus* (trans. Alan Shapiro; Ann Arbor: University of Michigan Press, 1988), 101–39; Ronald Syme, *The Roman Revolution* (Oxford: Oxford University Press, 1939), 150. On the religious reforms of Augustus, see Beard, North, and Price, *Religions of Rome,* 1:186–210; on actions against foreign cults, see 1:228–35.

16. For discussion, see J. Rufus Fears, "The Cult of the Virtues and Roman Imperial Ideology," *ANRW* 2.17.2 (1981): 885–86.

have tamed unclean lust. Mothers are proud of legitimate children. Punishment follows on the heels of guilt" (*Carm.* 4.5).[17]

Augustus came to set the standard for the "good emperor," a man in control of his passions who rules both himself and the empire well.[18] Stories of his life and conduct were offered as moral *exempla* in all sorts of discourse.[19] Even the Alexandrian Jew Philo asserted that Augustus' "every virtue outshone human nature" since "he alone was able to quiet the storms of civil war, set every city at liberty, bring order to disorder and civilization to barbarians" (*Legatio ad Gaium* 143–51).[20] Later emperors were also evaluated according to their (relative) virtues or vices, with "good" emperors praised for magnanimity, clemency, piety, and self-control. For example, the younger Pliny asserted that Trajan's deeds and person exemplified *pudor, moderatio, temperantia, concordia,* and *pietas* (*Panegyricus* 22–25). Thanks to Trajan, all the subjects of the Empire, even the poorest, are exceptionally fertile; proud parents raise legitimate children who will grow to adulthood (*Pan.* 26–28); slaves obey their masters and masters care for their slaves (*Pan.* 42).[21] The emperor had come to embody "the divine blessings of justice, peace, concord, abundance, and prosperity," guaranteeing the well-being of the entire Empire.[22] By the second century, the association of the emperor with the virtues had become a cliché.[23] Indeed, a

---

17. For discussion of Horace's presentation of Augustus as savior, see V. G. Kiernan, *Horace: Poetics and Politics* (New York: St. Martin's Press, 1999), 74–78; but also see R. O. A. M. Lyne, *Horace: Behind the Public Poetry* (New Haven, Conn.: Yale University Press, 1995), 193–214.

18. Helen North, "Canons and Hierarchies of the Cardinal Virtues in Greek and Latin Literature," in *The Classical Tradition: Literary and Historical Studies in Honor of Harry Caplan* (ed. Luitpold Wallach; Ithaca, N.Y.: Cornell University Press, 1966), 177–78.

19. For example, Seneca recommends that his readers emulate Augustus' moderate response to excessive anger. Seneca tells us that Augustus, when confronted with the intemperate anger of Vedius Pollio toward a slave, interceded on the slave's behalf. Thus, the slave escaped a most horrid punishment—being eaten by huge lampreys kept in a fish pond (Seneca, *De ira* 3.40.2–5). The *exempla* were anecdotes telling the exceptional deeds of great men. These *exempla* were memorized by students during their rhetorical training and regularly appear in forensic oratory, historiography, biography, and even philosophical works. See Richard Saller, "Anecdotes as Historical Evidence for the Principate," *Greece and Rome* 27 (1980): 71–83.

20. E. Mary Smallwood, trans., *Philonis Alexandrini: Legatio ad Gaium* (Leiden: Brill, 1961), 91.

21. See the extensive discussion of Trajan's virtues, according to Pliny, and on coins, inscriptions, and reliefs, in Fears, "The Cult of the Virtues," 913–24.

22. Ibid., 938.

23. Andrew Wallace-Hadrill, *Suetonius: The Scholar and His Caesars* (London:

third-century treatise on epideictic oratory explicitly recommended what was already in practice: emperors are be praised for their bravery *(andreia)*, justice *(dikaiosynē)*, moderation *(sōphrosynē)*, and wisdom *(phronēsis)* (Menander [of Laodicea] Rhetor 367.5–8),[24] a moderation further demonstrated by the propriety of their subjects:

> Because of the emperor, marriages are chaste, fathers have legitimate offspring, spectacles, festivals, and competitions are conducted with proper splendor and due moderation. (Menander Rhetor 367.8)[25]

The prevailing cultural logic during Paul's day presupposed that the good ruler was firmly in control of himself and responsible for a moral climate in which the virtues flourish and vices are punished.[26] Augustus claimed that he had accomplished this very goal. In a record of his achievements designed to be erected at his death, Augustus noted that "the senate and the people of Rome agreed that I should be appointed supervisor of laws and morals" (RG 6.1).[27] Moreover, "I had brought back into use many exemplary practices of our ancestors which were disappearing in our time, and in many ways I myself transmitted exemplary practices to posterity for their imitation" (RG 8.5). Though intended for a Roman audience, Augustus' *Achievements* (RG) were published across the Empire in the form of bilingual Greek/Latin inscriptions. Indeed, the principal surviving source of the *Achievements,* as known to us today, is an inscription from Galatia, not Rome.[28]

In such a context, Paul's claim that those who do not accept Christ are characterized by fornication, "unnatural" intercourse, and out-of-control passion can be read as a critique of both emperor and the Empire. In a world where legitimacy rested on claims about virtue and piety, Paul's argument that outsiders are, by definition, sexually licentious, "slaves to sin" and "slaves to lust," undermines the proposition that the emperor and

---

24. See further C. E. V. Nixon and Barbara Saylor Rodgers, *In Praise of Later Roman Emperors: The Panegyrici Latini* (Berkeley: University of California Press, 1994), 22–23. On the four cardinal virtues, see North, "Canons and Hierarchies," 177–80.

25. D. A. Russell and N. G. Wilson, trans., *Menander Rhetor* (Oxford: Clarendon, 1981).

26. For further examples, see G. Maslakov, "Valerius Maximus and Roman Historiography. A Study of the *Exempla* Tradition," *ANRW* 2.23.1 (1984): 451–53.

27. P. A. Brunt and J. M. Moore, trans., *Res Gestae Divi Augusti: The Achievements of the Divine Augustus* (Oxford: Oxford University Press, 1967).

28. See discussion in Brunt and Moore, *Res Gestae*, 1–6.

other rulers deserve the honor and authority granted to them. According to the logic of Paul's argument, without Christ such persons can only be degenerates. Early in his letter to the Romans, Paul describes the punishment reserved for those who reject God: lust. Three times Paul states that they have been "given up" to lust of one form or another: "God gave them up in the lusts of their hearts to impurity" (Rom 1:24), "gave them up to dishonorable passions" (1:26), and "gave them up to a base mind and to do the things that are improper" (1:28, RSV/author). Thus, they "deserve to die" since they violated God's decree by engaging in "unnatural" intercourse and "shameless acts" (Rom 1:27–28, 32).[29] Later in Romans, Paul argues that Jesus Christ is the best available cure for the problem of sin, a problem that ought to trouble the faithful no longer (Rom 3:21–26). A primary attribute of sin here is lack of control of one's body. In baptism, "the sinful body" *(to sōma tēs hamartias)* is destroyed so that "we might no longer be enslaved to sin" (Rom 6:6). Sin causes the sinner to "obey the appetites" and to yield his "members" *(ta melē,* bodily parts)[30] to impurity (Rom 6:19). Sin is linked to death, just as those guilty of idolatry, "unnatural" sex, dishonorable passions, and other offenses were said by Paul to "deserve to die" earlier in the letter.[31] Sin, therefore, is a bodily condition, as is righteousness, with sin resulting in death and righteousness in life.[32] Sin "reigns in your mortal bodies so that you obey its desires" (Rom 6:12, author). Righteousness involves yielding your "members" to God. In this way, the Christian's body becomes an obedient instrument of God as opposed to an obedient instrument of desire. Paul suggests that two types of slavery are possible: slavery to desire and impurity, or slavery to God and righteousness. Believers who do not control desire join outsiders in a dishonorable, debased sort of "slavery."

Since virtue is a litmus test of fitness for leadership, Pauline assertions about the moral superiority of the brothers and sisters in Christ, read

---

29. For further discussion of the implications of Paul's arguments here, see Kathy L. Gaca, "Paul's Uncommon Declaration in Romans 1:18–32 and Its Problematic Legacy for Pagan and Christian Relations," *HTR* 92 (1999): 165–98.

30. Ernest Käsemann, *Commentary on Romans* (trans. Geoffrey W. Bromily; Grand Rapids: Eerdmans, 1980), rejects the view that *ta melē* refers to bodily parts here, preferring the interpretation "our capabilities" on the basis of 1 Cor 12:12–25. But see Dale B. Martin, *The Corinthian Body* (New Haven, Conn.: Yale University Press, 1995), 92–96.

31. Stanley Stowers, *A Rereading of Romans: Justice, Jews and Gentiles* (New Haven, Conn.: Yale University Press, 1994), 255–58, sees the language and argumentation of Rom 6 as intentionally linked to the language and imagery of Rom 1:18–32.

32. Daniel Boyarin, *A Radical Jew: Paul and the Politics of Identity* (Berkeley: University of California Press, 1994), 158–70, suggests that, in Rom 5–8, "sin" is "sex."

together with his arguments about the moral corruption of Gentiles in Romans and elsewhere (Gal 5:16–26; 1 Thess 4:3–7; 1 Cor 6:15–20), suggest a decided anti-imperialist stance. Outsiders, incapable of virtue, can only be wicked, licentious, and avaricious tyrants, incapable of ruling themselves, let alone others. Yet, by employing these charges, Paul demonstrates that, however critical he may have been of "the world," he remained dependent upon many of the same assumptions and rhetorical strategies employed by that world, including the assumption that women are "naturally" passive and that desire can lead to "slavery."

Paul, Gender, and Status

Recent studies have proposed that sex and gender in the ancient Mediterranean world were configured according to a strict hierarchy, with "male" understood to be more perfect and "female" deficient. Sex and gender conformed to a matrix of active/passive, superordinate/subordinate, and dominant/submissive, with the elite male expected to assume the active, superordinate, dominant role; and women or persons of lesser status, especially slaves, expected to be passive, subordinate, and submissive.[33] As Aristotle put it, slaves are different from their masters "by nature." They have no faculty of deliberation but require masters, those who are capable of moral goodness and reason, to rule over them (*Politicus* 1260a4–1260b8). Freeborn women were likewise thought to be incapacitated "by nature," weaker and colder than men, less capable of virtue and therefore in need of special protection and surveillance (*Pol.* 1260a4; see also Plato, *Timaeus* 50d; Aristotle, *Metaphysica* 1.6.998a).[34] Though

---

33. The bibliography on this topic is enormous. Examples include Michel Foucault, *The Care of the Self. The History of Sexuality,* vol. 3 (trans. Robert Hurley; New York: Pantheon, 1986); Aline Rouselle, *Porneia: On Desire and the Body in Antiquity* (trans. Felicia Pheasant; Cambridge: Blackwell, 1988); David M. Halperin, John J. Winkler, and Froma I. Zeitlin, eds., *Before Sexuality: The Construction of Erotic Experience in the Ancient Greek World* (Princeton, N.J.: Princeton University Press, 1990); Maude Gleason, *Making Men: Sophists and Self-Presentation in Ancient Rome* (Princeton, N.J.: Princeton University Press, 1995); Bernadette J. Brooten, *Love between Women: Early Christian Responses to Female Homoeroticism* (Chicago: University of Chicago Press, 1996); Craig Williams, *Roman Homosexuality: Ideologies of Masculinity in Classical Antiquity* (Oxford: Oxford University Press, 1999). See also the responses to Foucault found in David H. J. Larmour, Paul Allen Miller, and Charles Platter, eds., *Rethinking Sexuality: Foucault and Classical Antiquity* (Princeton, N.J.: Princeton University Press, 1998); and responses to Brooten in Elizabeth A. Castelli, ed., "Lesbian Historiography before the Name?" *GLQ* 4 (1998).

34. On this view in classical Greek sources, see Kenneth J. Dover, *Greek Popular Morality in the Time of Plato and Aristotle* (Oxford: Blackwell, 1974), 96–102; in Hellenistic Greek sources, see Eva Cantarella, *Pandora's Daughters* (trans. Maureen

Aristotle should not be viewed as representative of the entire ancient world, he is far from alone in his insistence that slaves, women, and, to a lesser extent, freedmen and laborers, are deficient in virtue.[35] The freeborn, elite, citizen male, on the other hand, is the opposite of the deficient female or slave. He is dominant. He controls himself. He embodies *virtus (aretē)*. In sexual acts, he penetrates; he pursues. As Halperin put it, sex in Greek society "is conceived to center on, and to define itself around, an asymmetrical gesture, that of the penetration of one person by the body—and, specifically, by the phallus—of another."[36] Gender was delineated on the basis of status: "What counted, then, was not the anatomical 'sex' of the sexual partners but their social genders—the degree, that is, to which their sexual roles did or did not correspond to their respective positions in a rigid social hierarchy."[37]

With gender and status so defined, Greek and Roman men could lose their reputations or even their citizenship if their enemies succeeded in demonstrating that they had violated cultural norms. In both the Greek and the Roman case, an adult citizen male who sought penetration by another could be accused of violating both his status and his gender. He was "like a woman," "like a slave," or even worse, "like a prostitute." There was a whole complex of charges—effeminate, weak, soft, womanish (*malakos, trypheros, thēlytes,* and related terms)[38]—available to accuse a

---

B. Fant; Baltimore: Johns Hopkins University Press, 1987), 92–97; in Roman sources, see Susan Treggiari, *Roman Marriage* (Oxford: Clarendon, 1991), 205–28; in late antiquity, see Joëlle Beaucamp, *Le Statut de la Femme à Byzance (4e–7e siècle),* vol. 1 (Paris: De Boccard, 1990), 26–27.

35. On this view as expressed by Aristotle's contemporaries, see Dover, *Greek Popular Morality,* 114–15. Some Stoic philosophers argued that slaves could achieve wisdom and cultivate virtue. See, for example, Seneca, *Epistulae morales* 47. For discussion, see Keith Bradley, *Slave and Society at Rome* (Cambridge: Cambridge University Press, 1994), 135–45. The fact that the questions "Are slaves fully human?" and "Can slaves cultivate virtue and wisdom?" were raised at all emphasizes that slaves were commonly assumed to be deficient in virtue, wisdom, and humanity. On the supposed moral deficiencies of freedmen, see Petronius's satirical portrait of the vulgar freedman Trimalchio, who "would wish as a matter of course to ape the lifestyles of the rich and famous. . . . A former slave like Trimalchio would show no hesitation at all in submitting a host of underlings to the sorts of indignities of which he had firsthand experience himself" (Bradley, *Slave and Society,* 64, on Petronius, *Satira* 26).

36. David Halperin, *One Hundred Years of Homosexuality and Other Essays on Greek Love* (New York: Routledge, 1990), 30.

37. Ann Pellegrini, "Lesbian Historiography before the Name?," 580.

38. The second-century Greek lexicographer Pollux mentions the several terms to be used to accuse someone of being loathsome, licentious, or reprehensible, and other terms to refer to softness and effeminacy. Passive homosexuality is referred to by calling a man a "catamite," a "vendor of his youthful beauty," and a "prostitute's

man of being "feminine," preference for the passive role in sexual acts being the most disturbing. Describing the situation in fifth-century Athens, Winkler concludes, "The *kinaidos* [defined here as a man who seeks anal or oral penetration of himself] is a scare-image standing behind the more concrete charges of shaming one's integrity as a male citizen by hiring out one's body to another man's use."[39] In the case of Rome, accusations of *mollitia* (softness, effeminacy) were made in lawcourts, emperors were evaluated in terms of their relative effeminacy, and satirists described the outrageous "feminine" exploits of their (male) targets. Other potent charges included corrupting freeborn youths or women; squandering one's inheritance on pleasures, especially of the sexual or gastronomical type; engaging in incestuous relations with one's mother or sisters; and participating in religious rituals where orgies, cannibalism, or other horrific rites were presumed to occur.[40] Freeborn women could also be accused of sexual crimes: among the most common charges were adultery, behaving like a prostitute, joining in orgiastic foreign cults, and excessive indulgence in luxuries.[41] These women brought shame not only upon themselves but upon their families. Actually, the state of an entire city could be measured on the basis of the behavior of its women. A good Rome, indeed, any harmonious city, is exemplified by the chastity of its women.[42]

Greeks turned accusations of sexual licentiousness against Rome, Romans turned them against Greeks, and both associated "barbarians"

---

colleague." See Gleason, *Making Men*, 65. For a discussion of the Latin vocabulary, see Williams, 142–59 and J. N. Adams, *The Latin Sexual Vocabulary* (Baltimore: Johns Hopkins University Press, 1982).

39. John Winkler, *The Constraints of Desire* (New York: Routledge, 1990), 46.

40. Plutarch, *Comparatio Cimonis et Luculli* 1.5-6; *Lysander* 2; *Mor.* 145B; *Cato Major* 20.8; Nepos, *Dion* 4.3–4; Polybius 21.25.5; Sallust, *Bellum Catalinae* 11.5; Suetonius, *Gaius Caligula* 36–37, 40, 41; Cicero, *De or.* 2.283; *Epistulae ad familiares* 97; Pliny the Elder, *Naturalis historia* 18.32; Lucian, *Nigrinus* 15–16; Musonius Rufus 5.10, among other examples.

41. See esp. Cassius Dio 55.12–16; Plutarch, *Lucullus* 6.2–4; *Solon* 23; Cicero, *Pro Caelio* 49; Horace, *Carm.* 3.6.17–32; Livy 39.15.9; Seneca, *De beneficiis* 6.32.1; Suetonius, *Divus Augustus* 65.1–2; Juvenal, *Satirae* 6; *Anthologia Palatina* 31. On the stereotype of the "hysterical" woman, see further Margaret MacDonald, *Early Christian Women and Pagan Opinion: The Power of the Hysterical Woman* (Cambridge: Cambridge University Press, 1996).

42. Juvenal's satiric portrait of Rome offers an excellent example of this logic. There, Juvenal suggests that *pudicitia* has fled and all the elite women of the city (empresses, the wives of senators and equestrians) commit adultery with impunity, especially with men of lesser status than they (*Sat.* 6.285–290). For discussion, see Edward Courtney, *A Commentary on the Satires of Juvenal* (London: Althone Press, 1980).

with insatiable lust. For example, the Syrian Greek satirist Lucian described Rome as a cesspool of sexual vice. In Rome "every place and every agora is full of the things they love most, and they admit pleasure at every gate— this one by the eyes, that one by the ears or the nostrils, yet another by the throat and by sexual intercourse" (lit., "by means of Aphrodite"; *Nigr.* 15–16, trans. author). Roman authors often represented the Greeks as slaves to pleasure and extravagance, with "Greek leisure" serving as a stereotypical accusation (e.g., Sallust, *Bellum Catalinae* 11.5),[43] and Persia or "the East" could stand for sexual and sumptuary excess to both Greeks and Romans (e.g., Aeschylus, *Persae* 1.230–45; Cassius Dio 48.301). Barbarians were said to be soft *(malakos)* and slavish *(douleia)*. Even Jews were said to be "prone to lust" by Tacitus (*Historiae* 5.5). In this way, invective categories were extended to indict entire nations and peoples. At the same time, these categories reinforced a definition of gender and status that favored freeborn citizen men by associating women, slaves, foreigners, and barbarians with weakness in the face of desire.

Jews from the Hebrew Bible onward also defined themselves against "the peoples" *(ta ethnē)* in sexual terms. Leviticus prefaces prohibitions about incest, intercourse with a menstruating woman, child sacrifice, "lying with a man as with a woman," and bestiality with the warning that Israel is not to "do as they do in the land of Egypt" or "as they do in the land of Canaan" (Lev 18:2–3).[44] Throughout much of the Hebrew Bible, idolatry (i.e., false religiosity) is described in sexual terms as "fornication" or "prostitution."[45] The third *Sibylline Oracle* juxtaposed Jews who are "mindful of pure wedlock" with Phoenicians, Egyptians, Romans, and Greeks who commit adultery and pederasty (*Sib. Or.* 3.590–600; cf. 3.762–65).[46] Similarly, according to Josephus, "the [Jewish] law recognizes no sexual intercourse except the natural union of man and wife, and that only for the procreation of children. And it abhors that of men towards men" (*Contra Apionem* 2.198). By contrast, the Greeks engage in "unnatural" pleasures such as incest, adultery, and male homoerotic sex (*C. Ap.* 2.275). Such an

---

43. See Catharine Edwards, *The Politics of Immorality in Ancient Rome* (Cambridge: Cambridge University Press, 1993), 93.

44. See Brooten's excellent discussion of the influence of Leviticus on Paul; *Love between Women*, 288–94.

45. See discussion in Phyllis A. Bird, "'To Play the Harlot': An Inquiry into an Old Testament Metaphor," in *Gender Difference in Ancient Israel* (ed. P. Day; Minneapolis: Fortress, 1989), 75–94.

46. See discussion in Erich S. Gruen, "Jews, Greeks, and Romans in the Third Sibylline Oracle," in *Jews in a Graeco-Roman World* (ed. Martin Goodman; Oxford: Clarendon, 1998), 15–36.

argument continued in rabbinic literature, with homoerotic sex, adultery, promiscuity, pimping, and bestiality described as a Gentile problem, not a Jewish one.[47]

To what extent did Paul accept and depend upon a hierarchical configuration of sex, gender, and status? Some recent considerations of Paul have convincingly argued that he adopted much of this sex-gender system as his own, despite his claim that "there is neither Jew nor Greek, neither slave nor free, not male and female, for you all are one in Christ Jesus" (Gal 3:28, author). In 1 Corinthians, Paul affirms the view that woman is second to man: "The head of every man is Christ, the head of a woman is her husband, and the head of Christ is God" and "Man was not made from woman, but woman from man. Neither was man created for woman, but woman for man" (11:3, 8–9, RSV).[48] In this same passage, Paul asserts that "nature itself" teaches woman that her hair is her pride; cutting her hair would be shameful (*aischros*, 11:6, 14–15). Likewise, long hair for men is equally shameful (*aischros*, 11:14). Though these statements may be interpreted in a variety of ways, when read in conjunction with other ancient arguments about "natural" gender, it seems difficult to deny that Paul presupposed that woman is naturally subordinate to man.[49] Hairstyles were

---

47. Sacha Stern, *Jewish Identity in Early Rabbinic Writings* (Leiden: Brill, 1994), 23–26. See also Michael Satlow, "Rhetoric and Assumptions: Romans and Rabbis on Sex," in *Jews in a Graeco-Roman World* (ed. Goodman), 137–44.

48. See discussion in Mary Rose D'Angelo, "Veils, Virgins and the Tongues of Men and Angels: Women's Heads in Early Christianity," in *Off with Her Head! The Denial of Women's Identity in Myth, Religion, and Culture* (ed. Howard Eilberg-Schwartz and Wendy Doniger; Berkeley: University of California Press, 1995), 131–64; Martin, *Corinthian Body*, esp. 229–49. Paul's discussion of veiling has been called chaotic, irrational, conflicted, and confusing. See, for example, Joette Bassler, "1 Corinthians," in *The Women's Bible Commentary* (ed. Carol A. Newsome and Sharon H. Ringe; London: SPCK, 1992), 327. Moreover, what, precisely, Paul was so exercised about when he composed this passage continues to be debated. Perhaps Paul was arguing against the practice, familiar in Greco-Roman mystery cults, of women wearing their hair unbound during worship; see Elisabeth Schüssler Fiorenza, *In Memory of Her: A Feminist Theological Reconstruction of Christian Origins* (New York: Crossroad, 1986), 226–27. Perhaps Paul sought to quiet and subordinate a group of pneumatic women by reasserting gender hierarchies by means of hairstyles and veiling; see Antionette Clark Wire, *Corinthian Women Prophets: A Historical Reconstruction through Paul's Rhetoric* (Minneapolis: Fortress, 1990), 116–34, 181–88. Alternatively, perhaps Paul's real concern was with men who prayed with their heads covered, an activity reserved for elite men alone (Elliott, *Liberating Paul*, 210–11). I have been most persuaded by those who argue that Paul seeks here to reassert gender hierarchies.

49. A few commentators have questioned whether or not Paul wrote 1 Cor 11:3–16; see discussion in Horsley, *1 Corinthians*, 152–57. Still, the vast majority of commentators have concluded that Paul did write this passage.

commonly believed to mark gender difference or gender deviance. According to Dio Chrysostom, men who violate "nature's laws" have a propensity for "feminine" glances, posture, and hairstyles (*Tarsica prior/Or.* 33.52). Seneca the Elder suggested that effeminate men commonly braid their hair and thin their voices to compete with women in softness and finery (*Controversiarum excerpta* 1.8–9; cf. Caesar, *Bellum gallicum* 5.14.3; Lucan, *Bellum civile* 1.443; Quintilian, *Institutio oratoria* 2.5.12).[50] A Hellenistic Jewish text, *The Sentences of Pseudo-Phokylides,* cautions against allowing young boys to wear their hair long and braided, for long hair is reserved for voluptuous women.[51] According to these authors, long, carefully coifed hair symbolized an abandonment of masculinity.[52] Similarly, women's short hair also indicated gender deviance (e.g., Lucian, *Dialogi meretricii* 5.3). Therefore, when Paul stated that men ought never to wear their hair long and women ought never to wear their hair short, the maintenance of gender difference was clearly a primary concern.

Paul's indictment of human sin at the opening of his letter to the Romans offers further evidence of his dependence upon hierarchical assumptions about gender. In that letter, Paul presents the violation of "natural" gender as the premier example of human sinfulness. Women who have "exchanged natural relations for unnatural" and men "committing shameless acts with men" expose their depraved, dishonorable lusts and deserve to die (1:26–32, RSV). These men no longer sought the "natural use" of women, having become "consumed with passion for one another" (1:27, RSV). According to Paul's logic here, "nature" requires women to be penetrated, and men to penetrate; men who seek penetration are "naturally" deviant. As Brooten put it, in Rom 1:18–32, Paul repeated "certain fundamental assumptions of his highly gendered culture" and

---

50. See discussion of Roman representations of the "womanish" long hair of the barbarians and *cinaedi (kinaidi)* in Amy Richlin, "Making Up a Woman: The Face of Roman Gender," in *Off with Her Head!* 201–4.

51. Cited and discussed by Brooten, *Love between Women,* 63.

52. Plucking the beard was thought to be an even clearer indication of gender deviance, but long hair also cast suspicion on a man's manliness, claimed Arrian, *Epicteti dissertationes* 1.16.9–14, discussed in Maud Gleason, "The Semiotics of Gender: Physiognomy and Self-Fashioning in the Second Century C.E.," in *Before Sexuality: The Construction of Erotic Experience in the Ancient Greek World* (ed. David Halperin, John J. Winkler, and Froma L. Zeitlin; Princeton, N.J.: Princeton University Press, 1990), 399–400. See also Dover, *Greek Homosexuality,* 74–77.

53. Brooten, *Love between Women,* 241–66, 298–99, quotation from 266. See further Elizabeth Castelli, "Paul on Women and Gender," in *Women and Christian Origins* (ed. Ross Shepard Kraemer and Mary Rose D'Angelo; New York and Oxford: Oxford University Press, 1999), 221–35.

"gave [them] a theological foundation."[53] Paul's condemnation of the sinful world in Rom 1 relied upon the gendered assumptions of his culture even though his goal was to depict his culture as entirely depraved.

Though Paul should not be read as a proponent of ancient slavery,[54] he did employ slavery metaphorically in a way that presupposes the association between slaves and sexual immorality.[55] In both Romans and Galatians, he juxtaposed "slaves to lust" and "slaves to sin" with those who are now "slaves of Christ" (Rom 6:15–23; 7:5; 8:15; Gal 3:25–29).[56] Paul was not the first ancient author to connect slavery and desire. Slaves in the ancient world were often thought to be morally suspect. Slaves were supposedly "unscrupulous, lazy, and criminous,"[57] different "by nature," and lacking the requisite faculty of deliberation (Aristotle, *Pol.* 1260a4–1260b8; Achilles Tatius, *Leucippe et Clitophon* 7.10; Pliny the Elder, *Nat.* 35). Tied to this negative evaluation of slaves was the accusation that a free citizen could become a "slave" to luxury and desire.[58] "Free" and "slave" were set apart from one another on the basis of self-control. Thus, Seneca (the Younger), recommending that Roman masters occasionally invite deserv-

---

54. See Richard A. Horsley, "Paul and Slavery: A Critical Alternative to Recent Readings," *Semeia* 83/84 (1998): 153–200. Yet Paul has often been read to support slavery, however inappropriately. See Allen Dwight Callahan, "'Brother Saul': An Ambivalent Witness to Freedom," *Semeia* 83/84 (1998): 235–50; and J. Albert Harrill, "The Use of the New Testament in the American Slave Controversy," *Religion and American Culture* 10.2 (2000): 149–86.

55. Moreover, Paul's emphasis on sexual self-control would have been difficult if not impossible for slaves to achieve. See Jennifer A. Glancy, "Obstacles to Slaves' Participation in the Corinthian Church," *JBL* 117.3 (1998): 481–501.

56. For discussion of Paul's metaphorical use of slavery, see Dale B. Martin, *Slavery as Salvation: The Metaphor of Slavery in Pauline Christianity* (New Haven: Yale University Press, 1990); on Rom 6:20–23, see esp. 60–68. Martin stresses the "status-improvement" aspect of these two "spheres of slavery" but his argument is called into question by Horsley, "Paul and Slavery," 173–76.

57. Bradley, *Slave and Society,* 66; Peter Garnsey, "Legal Privilege in the Roman Empire," in *Studies in Ancient Society* (ed. Moses I. Finley; London: Routledge & Kegan Paul, 1974), 141–65.

58. According to Paul, the Roman Christians, in their previous life, seem to have emulated the miseducated sons described here by non-Christian moralist pseudo-Plutarch: "[They] disdain the sane and orderly life, and throw themselves headlong into disorderly and slavish pleasures. . . . [They] buy the freedom of courtesans and prostitutes, proud and sumptuous in expense; . . . some finally engage in the wildest forms of vices, committing adultery and being decked with ivy, ready to pay with life itself for a single pleasure (*Mor.* 5B–C). Pseudo-Plutarch's solution to the problem— careful education and upbringing, training in philosophy—contrasts with Paul's "in Christ" teaching. According to pseudo-Plutarch, good training and a proper education will establish virtue and lead toward happiness, preventing sons from falling into licentious, "slavish" excess (*Mor.* 5D).

ing slaves to dine with them, notes that "if there is any slavish quality in them as a result of their low associations, it will be shaken off by keeping company with men of gentler breeding *(Ep.* 47.16)"[59] In other words, slavish slaves may be improved in the company of noble noblemen. This argument only becomes possible if slaves are assumed to be morally second-rate and masters are thought to be their obvious moral superiors. Seneca continues, however, by asserting that even masters can become "slaves," one to lust, another to greed, another to ambition, and all to fear. Seneca concludes, "No slavery is more disgraceful than that which is voluntary" *(Ep.* 47.17). In this moral epistle, Seneca sought to improve slavish slaves by recommending a closer relationship between slave and master. At the same time, he sought to shame citizen men into rejecting "slavishness," indulgence in lust, greed, and excessive ambition.[60]

Paul may have had this traditional association between "slavishness" and desire in mind when he composed Rom 6–8. The "sin" in which the "slaves to sin" partake is largely sexualized. Sin and the passions *(ta pathēmata)* are linked, and the body, prior to baptism, is said to be inherently sinful. Bodily parts, without faith in Christ, are obedient to impurity, lawlessness, and shame (Rom 6:6, 19, 21; 7:5). Like Seneca, Paul suggests that all are in danger of becoming "slaves" to the appetites[61] and warns against "yielding one's members" to sin, impurity, and lawlessness (Rom 6:13). Still, unlike Seneca, Paul suggests that the cure for slavery to lust is unity with Christ rather than moral improvement through the study of philosophy (Rom 7:5; compare Seneca, *Ep.* 16, 17; see also Plutarch, *Mor.* 76B–D, 78E–79, 83A–E; Musonius Rufus 6). All of the brothers and sisters in Christ must choose "slavery to sin" or "slavery to righteousness," whether they are slave or free.[62] All will yield their bodily members. The question is,

---

59. Richard Gummere, trans., *Seneca*, vol. 4 (LCL).

60. Epictetus (Arrian, *Epict. diss.* 2.1.28) made a similar point: "Have you no master? Have you not as your master money, or a girl, or a boy, or the tyrant or some friend of the tyrant?" To Epictetus, "slave" and "master" is, ultimately, an improper and unimportant distinction, since all are sons of Zeus, yet all can become enslaved by desire: "How can you be my master? Zeus has set me free. Or do you really think that he was likely to let his own son be made a slave? You are, however, master of my dead body; take it" (1.9.9). W. A. Oldfather, trans., *Epictetus*, vol. 1 (LCL).

61. Dale B. Martin, "Paul without Passion: On Paul's Rejection of Desire in Sex and Marriage," in *Constructing Early Christian Families* (ed. Halvor Moxnes; London: Routledge, 1997), 207–10.

62. See also 1 Cor 7:22: " For whoever was called in the Lord as a slave is a freedman of the Lord. Likewise, whoever was free when called is a slave of Christ" (author). Gal 3:28: "There is neither Jew nor Greek, there is neither slave nor free, there is not male or female; for you are all one in Christ Jesus" (author). Gal 4:7: "So through God you are no longer a slave but a son, and if a son then an heir" (RSV).

to what? To sanctification or to lust? Anyone who rejects Christ is essentially incapable of virtue, whether slave, freed, or free. One can sell oneself to impurity, lawlessness, and desire; or one can sell oneself to God.

Comparing slavery to sin with slavery to God in Rom 6–8, Paul emphasizes the significant break between the brothers and sisters in Christ and everyone else in bodily, sexual terms; the negative slavery conforms to the Greco-Roman topos of enslavement to lust, and the positive slavery— slavery to God—leads to a kind of bodily discipline in which one's body becomes an instrument of *dikaiosunē*. By placing these two slaveries in opposition to one another, making a very real institution—slavery—stand either for devotion to God or devotion to desire, Paul subverted traditional status conceptions to some degree, even as he built upon the association of slavery and desire. Instead of simply reinscribing the traditional relationship between enslavement, lust, and shame, Paul asserted that slavery to God is advantageous, demanding that all the believers become the right kind of "slave" and, ultimately, God's "child" (Rom 8:12–17).[63] Still, he continued to play upon ancient assumptions about "slavishness," even as he asserted that everyone, regardless of status, must become a slave of righteousness.[64] The link between slavery and sexual immorality is preserved, though contrasted with a positive, righteous slavery exhibited by sexual self-control.

To Paul, therefore, outsiders are idolaters; they have been given up to lust, impurity, the dishonoring of their bodies, their dishonorable passions, and homoerotic sex; they possess a base mind, exhibit improper conduct, are fornicators and slaves of sin, and deserve to die/will die. Living according to the flesh, they are lawless, hostile, and cannot please God (Rom 1:18–32; 2:8–9, 21–24; 6:12–13, 19; 7:14–15; 8:5–8, 12–13; 12:2; 13:12–14). By contrast, the brothers and sisters in Christ are united with Christ; they have destroyed their sinful bodies and gained bodies that are instruments of righteousness. They are "slaves of God" and sons of God, living according to the Spirit, whether they are slave or free. They have been sanctified, set free from sin, and bear the fruits of the Spirit, having "crucified the flesh with its passions and desires" (Rom 5:1–5, 18–19; 6:6–7, 11–14, 18, 22; 8:2–4, 9, 11, 14, 30; 10:11–12; 12:1, 6–13, 16–18; 13:9–10; Gal 5:24). The distinction between these two groups is plain. Outsiders can be

---

63. See discussion in Martin, *Slavery as Salvation*, 30–49; but also see Horsley, "Paul and Slavery," 174–76.

64. See further Elizabeth A. Castelli, "Romans," in *Searching the Scriptures*, vol. 2: *A Feminist Commentary* (ed. Elisabeth Schüssler Fiorenza; New York: Crossroad, 1994), 293–95.

expected to engage in reprehensible sexual conduct of every kind. Insiders must be virtuous. Paul has staked the claim of Christian purity and right-eousness on sexual self-mastery and indicted the world in sexual terms.

Conclusion

Though Paul may have rejected Rome and the prevailing imperial order, at the same time he adopted the hierarchical sex-gender-status cultural pre-suppositions that had previously served to uphold imperial, not Christian, claims to legitimacy. His critique of Roman imperial pretensions, framed, in part, in terms of sexual virtue and vice, depended upon and reinscribed hierarchical theories of sex and gender that, historically, had been used by Romans and Greeks to claim their own privileged status while undermin-ing the claims of their rivals. Jews, Greeks, and Romans all defined "the other" in sexual terms, with the good Jew, the true Greek, and the proper Roman represented as one who controls the passions and avoids sexual licentiousness. By utilizing sexual virtue and vice to delineate the brothers and sisters in Christ from everyone else, Paul participated in this well-worn strategy. In the process, he adopted sex-gender-status presuppositions that underpinned his hierarchical society, even if he called into question the validity of imperial claims about the virtue of the emperor and the purity of the empire he ruled. He assumed that women are "naturally" passive. He associated "slavishness" with an inability to control desire. He continued to argue that "good" men (in this case "good" believers) control desire. Thus, Paul's argument in Romans that those who have rejected God have been rejected by God and thereby left to their "unnatural," degrading passions, can be read as a condemnation of "the world," but also as a restatement of the assumptions of that world. Similarly, Paul's warnings that "the saints" are to avoid behaving "like the Gentiles" or "like the idolaters" by eschew-ing the "works of the flesh" in favor of the "fruits of the Spirit" (1 Thess 1:9; 4:5; 1 Cor 5:10–12; 6:9–11; 10:7–22; 2 Cor 6:14–18; Gal 5:16–26), while highly critical of the larger society, rearticulates the argument that the proof of the righteousness and piety of a person, a household, a city, or even an empire lies in sexual morality. Indeed, Horace's encomium to Augustus could be recast as Pauline paraenesis, however distant Paul and Horace may have been from one another, both in terms of language (Paul wrote in Greek, Horace in Latin) and social location (Paul was a Greek-speaking provincial Jew, Horace a poet who counted Augustus among his patrons). Thanks to Christ, adulteries have ceased, unclean lust has been overcome, and the wrath of God follows on the heels of guilt.

– 8 –

RESPONSE

Simon R. F. Price

These remarks draw upon those that I gave at the panel on "Paul and the Roman Imperial Order" sponsored by the Paul and Politics Group at the 2000 Annual Meeting of the Society of Biblical Literature. I was honored to be asked to comment on that occasion, and am pleased to make some further remarks on the revised versions of the papers given at the SBL meeting and on two new papers (by Professors Elliott and Jewett). I should say that I write not as an expert in Paul and politics, but as an ancient historian interested in the eastern Roman Empire and in the possible connections between Christian and Jewish material and their contemporary contexts.

The important intellectual issue in thinking about Paul and politics is to get two things straight: what "politics" are at issue, and how we are to consider the relationship between Paul and that context. The previous generation of New Testament scholars focused on the politics of Rome itself. More recently, scholars (including those represented in this volume) have begun to focus more on local situations. This is in accordance with the realization in Pauline studies more generally that each letter is a piece of ad hoc correspondence with a particular community in a distinctive local situation. The papers in this volume generally take "politics" to mean the politics of the Roman Empire (not just of Rome). They also argue that Paul takes a very critical, even subversive, line in relation to Rome. For example, Smith relates his reading of Paul to other work that reads him "against the Empire," in the context of contemporary resistance struggles.

I want to make some general remarks about these two points: the political context and Paul the subversive. It follows from all this that the context in which Paul should be set is not that of Rome, but (as the papers in the volume mostly argue) of local communities.

The Roman Context

How to understand the Roman Empire has undergone major changes in the last generation. For a long time, Roman historians were very Rome-centered, interested in the politics of the capital, and interested in seeing how Rome ran her Empire and what (beneficial) differences flowed from that administration. The publication of Fergus Millar's *The Emperor in the Roman World* in 1977 marked a turning point in the study of the Roman Empire. For the first time, we could see that the Empire was not simply a structure imposed by Rome, but resulted from a series of ongoing choices and negotiations between subjects and ruler. This book opened up the possibility of looking at the Empire from the outside and inward.[1] Since then, numerous studies have taken up that challenge.[2] In studies of cultural development in this period, it has now become standard to talk not of Romanization and Hellenization as top-down processes imposed by the center, but as processes in which inferiors negotiate new positions for themselves.[3] The fullest Anglophone synthesis of imperial history, the second edition of The Cambridge Ancient History, has responded in part to the new trends, and includes as much on the provinces as on Rome itself.[4]

---

1. Fergus Millar, *The Emperor in the Roman World, 31 B.C.–A.D. 337* (London: Duckworth, 1997; Ithaca, N.Y.: Cornell University Press, 1977; repr., 1992). A reaction to the current orthodoxy is represented by Clifford Ando, *Imperial Ideology and Provincial Loyalty in the Roman Empire* (Berkeley: University of California Press, 2000), which is a long and thorough study of the creation of consensus on the part of Rome, and its reception by provincials.

2. My *Rituals and Power: The Roman Imperial Cult in Asia Minor* (Cambridge: Cambridge University Press, 1984) was inspired by *The Emperor in the Roman World* and attempted to add a cognitive dimension to the picture.

3. For the West, see Greg Woolf, *Becoming Roman: The Origins of Provincial Civilization in Gaul* (Cambridge: Cambridge University Press, 1998). For the East, see Susan E. Alcock, ed., *The Early Roman Empire in the East* (Oxbow Monograph 95; Oxford: Oxbow, 1997; Guy Rogers, *The Sacred Identity of Ephesos: Foundation Myths of a Roman City* (London and New York: Routledge, 1991), presents a case study of the manipulations of local mythology to accommodate Rome; Simon Swain, *Hellenism and Empire: Language, Classicism and Power in the Greek World, A.D. 50–250* (Oxford: Oxford University Press, 1996), argues that Greek identity preceded loyalty to Rome (though it was also in part a reaction to Rome). See, in general, Susan E. Alcock et al., eds., *Empires: Perspectives from Archaeology and History* (Cambridge: Cambridge University Press, 2001).

4. See Alan K. Bowman, Peter Garnsey, et al., eds., *The Augustan Empire, 43 B.C.–A.D. 69* (CAH 10; 2d ed.; Cambridge: Cambridge University Press, 1996); and

Studies that seek to place provincial figures in relation to the Empire need to start from an understanding of how our picture of Rome and her Empire has changed and become more complex. In particular, the relationship between Rome and the provinces now is different. We cannot assume that it is right to move smoothly from analyses of Augustan Rome to analyses of provincial culture. Put bluntly, there is no necessary connection between the imagery of the Ara Pacis (a monumental altar in Rome in honor of Augustus) or the poetry of Horace and the thought world of the Greek East. The issue is whether the provinces took any notice of developments in Rome, and if so, how they did so, and what differences (if any) local reception made to the local context. In other words, understanding the Greek context on its own terms is crucial. This cannot be done without a proper sense of the chronological developments in that context. The relations between a Greek city and Rome in the second century B.C.E. and the first century C.E. are completely different. In the early part of the period, Roman rule was, of course, much more problematic: it did not look as though it was going to endure, and for locals to side with Rome was to make a sometimes unpopular political choice. By the first century C.E. the situation had changed. There were still recognizable groups of "resident Romans" (of Italian origin) in provincial cities, and members of local elites sought to serve the interests of Rome. There was by now no realistic alternative to Roman rule in the Greek world.

In order to understand an allegedly "subversive" provincial figure, it is necessary to set him against the background of "subversion" in the Roman Empire. The thrust of most modern scholarship on the period makes this quite difficult. Scholars have generally placed much emphasis on consensual happiness, without giving much attention to strains and tensions or the perspectives of complete outsiders.[5] There is a gap in scholarship here, partly because the primary data tends to emphasize successes and consent.[6]

Alan K. Bowman, Peter Garnsey, et al., eds., *The High Empire, A.D. 70–192* (CAH 11; 2d ed.; Cambridge: Cambridge University Press, 2000). These volumes, CAH 10–11, should be the primary points of reference for statements about the Empire. Biblical scholars seem hesitant to use them and instead cite less authoritative sources, works by ancient historians that have been excerpted in edited volumes, and derivative works by other biblical scholars.

5. Brent Shaw, in CAH 11 (2000): 361–403, brilliantly studies "rebels and outsiders," but mainly from the perspective of the center.

6. See, however, D. J. Mattingly, ed., *Dialogues in Roman Imperialism: Power, Discourse, and Discrepant Experience in the Roman Empire* (*Journal of Roman Archaeology*, Suppl. 23; Portsmouth, R.I.: JRA, 1997).

The Roman Empire was extremely complex and diverse. It was a "militarily created hegemony of immense land mass that harboured hundreds, if not thousands, of different societies."[7] It was a massive unity, with great diversity.

Cities formed the backbone of the Empire. It used to be held that in the Hellenistic and Roman periods, people were lost in great empires (and as a result needed new forms of identity, including religious identity). This old view is sometimes still found in the writings of nonspecialists, but the new consensus is quite different. Cities remained basic, both as administrative units that served the interests of Rome, and as entities to which individuals belonged. Cities were major bearers of local meanings: they embodied common values, expressed in rituals and in iconography. Because of the construction of local meanings and local societies, diversity was inevitable.

The extent of diversity was, however, affected by the impact of specifically Roman rules. The impact of those rules varies in different contexts and over time.

Some were uniform from the outset of the Empire (Rome reserved the death penalty for herself, and banned local gold and silver coinages). In the Roman *coloniae* of the early Empire, whose citizens were all Roman citizens at a time when Roman citizenship was rare in the provinces, the whole community followed specifically Roman rules. This accounts for the otherwise rather odd claim by locals of the *colonia* of Philippi that Paul and Silas were advocating customs which it is "not lawful for us as Romans to adopt or observe" (Acts 16:21).[8] As Roman citizenship spread in the second century C.E., and especially after the gift of citizenship to almost all the free population by Caracalla in 212 C.E., other Roman rules increased in their impact.

Many prospered under Roman rule and were at least content to acquiesce, but we should not forget Rome's regulatory procedures, which were widespread and as efficient as those of any premodern empire. Censuses were held under the Empire on a regular basis, so that there were comprehensive lists of people and property, which of course formed the basis of Roman taxation.[9] Luke (2:1–5) was wrong to claim that there was a universal census under Augustus, but the Gospel stories give a vivid impression of the local impact of census-taking, and it is no accident that, according to Josephus, it was this census that was the decisive event in the formation

---

7. Shaw, in CAH 11 (2000): 361.

8. Acts 16:19–24. Cf. M. Beard, J. North, and S. Price, *Religions of Rome*, vol. 1 (Cambridge: Cambridge University Press, 1998), 240, 328–34.

9. P. A. Brunt, *Roman Imperial Themes* (Oxford: Clarendon, 1990), 324–46.

of the "Fourth Philosophy."[10] On a day-to-day basis there were other regulatory procedures. According to Tertullian, low-level Roman officials kept detailed tabs on a variety of "low-life":

> I don't know whether it should be a matter of anger or shame when Christians are listed by the officers *(beneficiarii)* and their official spies *(curiosii)* in their registers, along with the bar hounds, bouncers, bath thieves, gamblers, and pimps, and are compelled to pay the same "taxes" as these other creatures. (*De fuga in persecutione* 13)

These and other Roman officials, of course, abused their positions of local power. Throughout the Empire, Roman governors repeatedly sought to prevent the illegal appropriation of local means of transport.[11] This is the background to the bizarre advice in the Sermon on the Mount that "if anyone orders you to go one mile, go two miles with him" (Matt 5:41, JB).[12]

Unsurprisingly, not all kept within Rome's rules. Bandits were endemic in the Roman Empire, and controls over them were local and their effectiveness highly spasmodic. These and other aspects of the under-side of the Empire are seen vividly in Apuleius's *Metamorphoses*.[13] Piracy too remained a problem, despite systematic suppression by Rome in the first century C.E.: For example, Syedra in southern Turkey consulted the oracle of Apollo at Claros as to what it should do about raids from pirates. The oracular advice was to set up a special statue group in the city, symbolizing the victory of Justice over Violence. The original consultation may have been made in the first century B.C.E., but it was inscribed under the Empire, when coins of the city depict this statuary group.[14]

The attitudes of those on the margins to Rome is difficult to determine, but it is clear that Jews (and Christians) were not the only people to be unhappy. In the Latin West it is remarkable that, despite uprisings in the first century C.E., not long after conquest, there seems to be a complete loss

---

10. *Jewish Antiquities* 18.1–10, 23–25.

11. S. Mitchell, "Requistioned Transport in the Roman Empire: A New Inscription from Pisidia," *JRS* 66 (1976): 106–31. Cf. S. R. Llewelyn, "Systems of Transport and Roman Administration," in *NewDocs* 7 (North Ryde, N.S.W.: Macquarie University, Ancient History Documentary Research Centre, 1994), 58–129.

12. The word "orders *(angareusei)*" is the technically correct term for pressing someone into service.

13. Fergus Millar, "The World of the *Golden Ass*," *JRS* 71 (1981): 63–75.

14. Simon Price, *Religions of the Ancient Greeks* (Cambridge: Cambridge University Press, 1999), 75, 179–80.

of cultural memory of the pre-Roman past. Histories written by Westerners were wholly Romanocentric: Vercingetorix (leader of the Gauls, executed by Julius Caesar in 46 B.C.E.), Arminius (Herman, Teutonic leader against the Romans to save Germania, first century C.E.), and Boudicca (Queen of the Celtic tribe Iceni, who led a revolt against the Romans, 60–61 C.E.) became heroes to Westerners only with the rise of nationalism in the nineteenth century. Apparently they were not employed as symbols of resistance by subjects of the Roman Empire. In the East, however, not only Jews but also Greeks, Phoenicians, and Egyptians recorded their own cultural pasts.

It is difficult to find articulate examples of "enemies of the Roman order," but local cultic traditions could become the rallying ground for opposition to Roman rule. The stories of Alexandrian Greeks protesting against the perceived tyranny of Rome include appeals to the Alexandrian god Sarapis. The account of a hearing before Trajan says that "they set sail from the city of Alexandria, each bearing their own gods, the Alexandrians [a bust of Sarapis, and the Jews their sacred books]." At Rome, the Alexandrian Greeks accused Trajan of having his council packed with impious Jews. While they were saying this, "the bust of Sarapis which the ambassadors were carrying suddenly broke into sweat. Trajan was amazed at the sight. And soon crowds gathered in Rome, numerous shouts rang forth, and everyone began to flee to the tops of the hills."[15] The so-called Potter's Oracle, an extraordinary piece of writing, was a form of prophecy, originating in the Hellenistic period but still circulating under the Roman Empire, which foretold the liberation of Egypt and her gods from the foreign oppressor.[16] In actual revolts, local religious figures are sometimes claimed to have stimulated or even led the rebels. In an Egyptian rebellion of 172–173 C.E., the leader was a priest.[17] An incursion into the Empire from Thrace was led by a priest of Dionysos, who gained a following by his performance of rites; he was probably acting to recover the sanctuary of Dionysos, which the Romans had earlier handed over to another tribe.[18] In

---

15. Beard, North, and Price, *Religions of Rome*, 2:327–328.

16. L. Koenen, "The Prophecies of a Potter: A Prophecy of World Renewal Becomes an Apocalypse," 249–54; in *Proceedings of the Twelfth International Congress of Papyrology, Ann Arbor, 13–17 August 1968* (ed. D. H. Samuel; American Studies in Papyrology 7; Toronto, 1970); L. Koenen, "A Supplementary Note on the Date of the Oracle of the Potter," *ZPE* 54 (1984): 9–13. Translation: Allen Kerkeslager, "The Apology of the Potter: A Translation of the Potter's Oracle," in *Jerusalem Studies in Egyptology* (ed. Irene Shirun-Grumach; Aegypten und Altes Testament 40; Wiesbaden: Harrassowitz, 1998), 67–79.

17. Cassius Dio 72.4.

18. Cassius Dio 51.25.5 (29 B.C.E.); 54.34.5–7 (11 B.C.E.).

Gaul, at a time of political chaos in Rome, the Druids allegedly prophesied that the (accidental) burning of the Capitoline temple in Rome signified the end of Roman rule over the Gauls. At around the same time, a revolt on the Rhine frontier started with a feast in a sacred grove and a religious vow and was strongly supported by a local prophetess.[19] The Jewish revolts against Rome, which were much more significant in military terms than any I have just mentioned, were also aided by the fact that the Jewish faith could be interpreted to offer a coherent religious basis for revolt. At least some of the rebels in Judea in 66–70 and 132–135 C.E. were inspired by the principle that their god alone should be master of Israel. In the revolt of 116–117 C.E.—which flared up in Egypt, North Africa, and Mesopotamia— the rebels in Cyrene seem to have damaged or destroyed temples of the pagan gods. The subsequent massacre of the Jews in Egypt was probably due in part to traditional enmity to the Jews as religious enemies of Egypt's gods and the "victory" was still celebrated in Egypt eighty years later by pagan civic festivals.[20]

Implications for Paul and Politics

It follows from all this that it is misguided to assume at the outset that the context (or even a context) in which Paul should be set is that of Rome. The world of Augustan court ideology is very remote from the world of the eastern cities of the Roman Empire. There is a large leap between Augustus' Saecular Games and Ara Pacis (as a way of thinking about Roman ideas of "nature," as in the article by Jewett) and the world of Paul. In fact, the gap could be made smaller with reference to ideas articulated by the Assembly *(koinon)* of the province of Asia and other bodies. For example, the *koinon* in 9 B.C.E., in creating a new calendar that would start on Augustus' birthday and again a little later, passed decrees that talked of the divine providence, which divinely orders "our" lives, producing Augustus for the benefit of the human race; eternal and immortal nature had devised this as the greatest possible benefaction.[21] These ideas were picked up by Philo in

19. Tacitus, *Historiae* 4.54, 61, 65; 5.22, 24.

20. D. Frankfurter, "Lest Egypt's City Be Deserted: Religion and Ideology in the Egyptian Response to the Jewish Revolt (116–117 C.E.)," *JJS* 43 (1992): 203–20.

21. The two *koinon* decrees are to be found most conveniently in V. Ehrenberg and A. H. M. Jones, *Documents Illustrating the Reigns of Augustus and Tiberius* (2d ed.; Oxford: Clarendon, 1955), 98 and 98a; with U. Laffi, "Le iscrizioni relative all'introduzione nel 9 a. C. del nuovo calendario della provincia d'Asia," *Studi Classici e Orientali* 16 (1967): 5–98, esp. 21–22, 55–59; translation of first decree in N. Lewis and M. Reinhold, *Roman Civilization*, vol. 1 (3d ed.; New York: Columbia University Press, 1990), 624–25. Cf. Price, *Rituals and Power*, 54–55. Long ago, Adolf Deissmann, *Licht vom Osten* (4th ed.; Tübingen: J. C. B. Mohr [Paul Siebeck], 1923),

his panegyric of the start of Gaius's rule.[22] The expression of these ideas in the Greek East would help to support the conclusion of Jewett's chapter: "Compared with believing that the Roman gods had already ushered in the golden age through a victorious Caesar, Paul's hope could lead to a far more realistic form of collective responsibility for the creation." The importance of provincial or civic imperial cults is also relevant, as Heen persuasively argues, to understanding a passage in Paul's Letter to the Philippians. These local cults were, as Elliott demonstrates, relevant more broadly to an understanding of how Paul sought to situate his christological theology in contradistinction to the ideology of the ruling power. This analysis of the importance of "the imperial cult" might be extended to include not only cults with an explicit focus on Rome, but the whole apparatus of civic cults that supported the local and the Roman status quo.[23]

Another context is that of patron-client relationships, which were so important in the Roman Empire.[24] Did Paul engage in subversive interpretations of Roman imperial practices of power with regard to patronage and commendation, as Agosto suggests? There is obviously an enormous difference between letters of Cicero or Pliny that commend people for particular positions or specific favors, and letters of Paul that commend people in much more general terms and to communities not governed by bureaucratic rules of procedure and definition. There is a gap between the high level of society represented by Cicero and Pliny and the lower and more peripheral world of Paul, but again, that gap can be bridged by use of documentary evidence (epigraphic and papyrological), which would support the general contrast drawn by Agosto (if not necessarily the claim about subversiveness).[25]

Paul's critique of Gentile depravity does in strict logic imply criticism of part of the ideological basis of imperial rule (emperors are acceptable

---

in English as *Light from the Ancient East* (trans. Lionel R. M. Strachan; London: Hodder & Stoughton, 1910; repr., Peabody, Mass.: Hendrickson, 1995), exploited texts of this sort.

22. *Legatio ad Gaium* 8–13.

23. This broader context is the focus of Beard, North, and Price, *Religions of Rome;* and Price, *Religions of the Ancient Greeks.*

24. The important monograph by R. P. Saller, *Personal Patronage under the Early Empire* (Cambridge: Cambridge University Press, 1981), needs to be read with along with H. M. Cotton, "The Role of Cicero's Letters of Recommendation: *iustitia versus gratia,*" *Hermes* 114 (1986): 443–60; A. F. Wallace-Hadrill, ed., *Patronage in Ancient Society* (London and New York: Routledge, 1989); R. P. Saller, in CAH 11 (2000): 838–51.

25. H. M. Cotton, *Documentary Letters of Recommendation in Latin from the Roman Empire* (Beiträge zur klassischen Philologie 132; Königstein: Hain, 1981).

because they are virtuous), but this entailment was not necessarily intended by the author or perceived by the audience. The right context in which to set this argument of Paul's is the ongoing Greek and Roman polemic against the sexual passions (as is elegantly argued in the second half of Knust's paper). Paul's cultural critique is political, but not narrowly so.

Paul certainly needs to be set in part in relationship to the contemporary Gentile world, and certainly has "political" points to make. As this volume shows, Paul's "political" points are not focused on Rome itself, but on the local structures of power (at whose apex was the reception of Rome), and his critiques were not narrowly political, but encompassed broader aspects of local social and religious values.

CONTRIBUTORS

EFRAIN AGOSTO is Professor of New Testament and Director of the Programa de Ministerios Hispanos at Hartford Seminary in Connecticut. He is the author of the forthcoming book, *Leadership in the New Testament.*

NEIL ELLIOTT is a Chaplain at the University of Minnesota Episcopal Center and teaches at the United Theological Seminary and Metro State University. He is author of *Liberating Paul: The Justice of God and the Politics of the Apostle,* as well as many articles on Paul.

ERIK M. HEEN is Associate Professor of New Testament and Greek at The Lutheran Theological Seminary at Philadelphia. He is currently working on The Letter to the Hebrews volume in the Ancient Christian Commentary on Scripture series.

RICHARD A. HORSLEY is Distinguished Professor of Liberal Arts and the Study of Religion at the University of Massachusetts Boston, author of many books, and editor of *Paul and Empire* and *Paul and Politics* (both Trinity Press).

ROBERT JEWETT is Henry R. Kendall Professor Emeritus at Garrett-Evngelical Theological Seminary and Visiting Professor at the University of Heidelberg. Among his many books are *Paul the Apostle to America* and the forthcoming commentary on Romans in the Hermeneia Series.

JENNIFER WRIGHT KNUST is Assistant Professor of Religious Studies at the College of the Holy Cross and author of the forthcoming book *Abandoned to Lust: Sexual Slander and Ancient Christianity*. She has recently received fellowships in support of a project on the New Testament *pericopae adulterae*.

SIMON R. F. PRICE is Fellow and Tutor in Ancient History at Lady Margaret Hall, Oxford. His books include *Rituals and Power: The Roman Imperial Cult in Asia Minor; Religions of Rome,* with Mary Beard and John North; *Religions of the Ancient Greeks;* and *The Oxford Dictionary of Classical Myth and Religion,* with Emily Kearns.

ROLLIN A. RAMSARAN is Professor of New Testament at Emmanuel School of Religion (A Graduate Seminary) in Johnson City, Tennessee, and author of *Liberating Words: Paul's Use of Rhetorical Maxims in 1 Corinthians 1–10.*

ABRAHAM SMITH is Associate Professor of New Testament at Perkins School of Theology and author of *Comfort One Another* (on 1 Thessalonians) and the commentary on First and Second Thessalonians in the *New Interpreters Bible.*

INDEX